TOM WRIGHT was taken to his first game at Easter Road aged nine, a friendly against Leicester City at Easter Road in February 1957. Little did he realise that football, and Hibs in particular, would become such a major influence in his life from that day on. Wright has now been a Hibs supporter for over 50 years, and has the scars to prove it. He is following in a family tradition of Hibs fans, which can be traced back to at least World War 1. Now retired after many years running a picture framing shop in the city, he is now the official club historian and a member of the Hibernian Historical Trust, a supporters-led initiative whose aims are to protect, preserve and promote the proud history of the club. He is also the author of *The Golden Years: Hibernian in the Days of the Famous Five*, *Hibernian: From Joe Baker to Turnbull's Tornadoes*, *Leith: A Glimpse of Times Past*, *Hibernian: The Life and Times of a Famous Football Club*, *The History of the Hibs Quiz Book* and co-author of *Crops: The Alex Cropley Story* and *Hibs Through and Through: The Eric Stevenson Story*.

The Rise and Eventual Fall of Turnbull's Tornadoes

TOM WRIGHT

Luath Press Limited
EDINBURGH
www.luath.co.uk

First published 2023
Reprinted 2024, 2026

ISBN: 978-1-80425-110-2

The author's right to be identified as author of this book under the Copyright, Designs and Patents Act 1988 has been asserted.

The paper used in this book is recyclable. It is made from low chlorine pulps produced in a low energy, low emission manner from renewable forests.

Printed and bound by Robertson Printers, Forfar

Typeset in 11.5 point Sabon by Lapiz

© Tom Wright 2023

Contents

Acknowledgements	5
Foreword	9
Introduction	11
A New Beginning	13
The Return of Eddie Turnbull	26
Scottish Cup Disappointment (1971–72)	39
The League Cup and Victory at Tynecastle (1972–73)	67
A New Challenge (1973–74)	117
A Traditional Period (1974–75)	145
The Premier League and Nightmare at Montrose (1975–76)	166
A Shock Exit for Pat Stanton (1976–77)	190
Sponsorship and a Battle with the Cameras (1977–78)	213
An International Dispute and Another Cup Final (1978–79)	245
George Best, the End of the Road for Eddie Turnbull and Relegation (1979–80)	269
The Aftermath (1980–81)	290
Eddie Turnbull	301

Acknowledgements

MY THANKS TO former players John Fraser, Jim Herriot, Jim Black, Kenny Davidson, John Brownlie, Willie Murray, Alex Cropley, Pat Stanton and John Blackley for their help in making this a labour of love. Also to the staff at the National Museum of Scotland in Edinburgh. My main sources have been the *Scotsman*, *Evening News*, *Daily Mail* and *Daily Record*, together with Hibs programmes from the time and many other publications far too numerous to mention. Most of the images in this book are from my own personal collection. Where necessary, every effort has been made to locate image copyright holders.

Foreword

LITTLE DID I know when Bob Shankly gave me the chance to join the ground staff at Easter Road at the age of 17 that I was embarking on the adventure of my life and a career in football that has enriched and given me so much.

Like many schoolboy footballers I dreamed of signing for a big club and playing for my country and I have to thank Mr Shankly for giving me the chance to fulfil that dream and become a professional footballer.

But it was Eddie Turnbull who was the making of me as a player and playing under him as part of Turnbull's Tornadoes undoubtedly gave me the best years of my football life and enough great memories and lasting friendships to last a lifetime.

It was a privilege to play alongside so many outstanding players – Pat Stanton, John Brownlie, Jimmy O'Rourke and Alex Cropley to name but a few – and I don't mind admitting that it pains me to this day that we didn't win more trophies to add to the solitary League Cup triumph. In particular, recalling the three Hampden defeats by Celtic when we lost six goals each time still distresses me to this day. I am happy to acknowledge that Celtic had an outstanding team during that era but there is no doubt in my mind that we should have brought more silverware to the Easter Road boardroom.

I have Hibs to thank for so many great memories of European football under the lights at Easter Road and for all my seven Scotland caps which, I don't mind admitting, was an achievement beyond my wildest dreams. Seeing the world while fulfilling your life's ambition was an added bonus and a great source of enjoyment.

I only left Hibs to further my career down south in 1977 because as a boy, I had also dreamed of playing in England's legendary football arenas such as St James' Park, White Hart Lane and Old Trafford.

I hope you all understand that Hibs is in my blood and will be for as long as I live. Accordingly it is my absolute pleasure to write this foreword to Tom Wright's latest offering and I hope you will all enjoy reading it as much as I will.

John Blackley
GGTTH

Introduction

EVEN TODAY THE name 'Turnbull's Tornadoes' brings back magical memories of a defining period in the history of the club and the attacking and entertaining football that thrilled the country for only too short a time. The players' names from that period still roll easily from the tongue, not only by those privileged to have witnessed them in their prime but also the younger fans who have followed in print or hearsay the exploits of a side that had been widely considered in their day as not only one of the best sides in the entire country but much further afield, a legacy that survives to this very day.

The halcyon golden post-war years when Hibs had led the way in European football and beyond were long gone to be followed by a gradual deterioration that would lead to near relegation on the last day of the season in 1964. The following few years however would see a steady improvement in fortune but it was only after the arrival of a somewhat brash but charismatic Eddie Turnbull at the start of the new decade that would bring in an exciting new era for the club and the birth of a legendary side that had thrilled supporters wherever they played.

The 1970s had been a defining period, not just for Hibs but for Scottish football, a time when the country had not only qualified for two World Cup finals but had also witnessed the advent of the Premier League, sponsorship both on and off the field and many other innovations that would help shape the game as we know it today. This book follows the path from the beginning to the eventual descent into relegation, the fantastic players, exciting events, controversies and much more.

A New Beginning

FOLLOWING NEGOTIATIONS THAT had been ongoing for several weeks, in September 1970 the 48-year-old millionaire Edinburgh businessman Tom Hart had acquired the major shareholding in Hibernian Football Club from the previous chairman William Harrower. The owner of a thriving building business, Hart was a lifelong Hibs supporter who rarely missed a game home or away. A regular visitor to the Easter Road boardroom on match days, he had often travelled overseas with the official party and as far as the supporters were concerned they could not have asked for anyone better to take over the running of the club. One of Hart's first tasks had been to elect a new Hibs-minded board of directors that included the former Hibs and Scotland goalkeeper Tommy Younger who was already at the club as PR man and secretary of 'The Hibernian', a social club situated in the car park adjacent to the east terracing. Although initially tremendously successful, poor management and regular trouble both inside and outside the premises – in one instance resulting in a death – would soon result in its closure.

Jimmy Kerr, another former Hibs goalkeeper who had joined the club from Ormiston Primrose in 1936 aged just 17 before going on to give the club many years of sterling service, was now not only a director of the football club but also a partner in Hart's highly successful building business. The long-serving Kenny McIntyre who had spent many years as the club secretary had now been made a director and he would be joined on the board by the lifelong supporter and renowned Queen's surgeon Sir John Bruce who would replace Harrower as chairman. Harrower however would remain on the board as President, Hart himself as managing director, the new set-up completed by Cecil Graham replacing McIntyre as club secretary.

A man of drive, enthusiasm and energy, Tom Hart's personal goal would be to take the club back to the top of Scottish football. The previous decade had been one of mixed fortunes for the Easter Road side. Long gone were the halcyon post-war years when Hibs, led by the illustrious Famous Five forward line had been widely recognised as the most entertaining side in the entire country, winning three league titles inside a five-year period while also becoming the first ever British side to enter the inaugural European Cup in 1955. Since then there had been a gradual decline in fortune. Only narrowly managing to escape relegation on the final day of the 1962–63 season, the situation had improved dramatically with the introduction of the former Dunfermline manager Jock Stein who in just under a year would lead the previously relegation-haunted side to within touching distance of the league and cup double before stunning everyone at Easter Road, both players and supporters alike, with his premature move to take over a similar position at Celtic.

After an earlier approach from the Parkhead side Stein had initially vowed to remain at Easter Road until the end of the season, but concerned that Celtic would not wait, after a Scottish Cup victory against Rangers at Easter Road at the beginning of March, the fans elation at the victory – the first time that Hibs had defeated Rangers three times in the same season – had been brought to an abrupt end later that evening with the announcement that Stein would be leaving, not at the end of the season as originally promised but immediately.

His successor at Easter Road would be his great friend Bob Shankly who was then manager of Dundee. It seems likely that Shankly had already been well aware of Stein's imminent departure as he had watched the game against Rangers from the Easter Road stand instead of his side's 3–0 cup victory over Forfar that same afternoon, and it would be no surprise to learn in midweek that he had now replaced Stein as manager of Hibs and he would spend the next few years at Easter Road. However, just a few games into the 1969–70 season the disillusioned Shankly suddenly announced his resignation after a victory over St Mirren, claiming that there was no fun in the game anymore. Only then was it discovered that he had actually resigned ten months earlier after the sale of Colin Stein to Rangers against his will, but had been persuaded by the directors to change his mind which he now claimed had been a huge mistake on his part. Shankly himself would be succeeded in the Easter Road hot seat by the former Hibs player Willie MacFarlane and with the club ending the season in a more than respectable third in the table, the supporters could perhaps have been excused if anticipating even better in the months ahead.

Just a few months earlier an article in the *Evening News* had suggested that an American consortium had been intending to make a takeover bid for Hibs. It turned out that the wealthy owner of the multimillion-dollar North American soccer club Atlanta Chiefs, an offshoot of the baseball club of the same name, had already been in lengthy negotiations with the English First Division side Aston Villa with a view to purchasing the club. The move however had ultimately come to nothing, and after looking around England for another suitable candidate only then had he seemingly turned his attention in the direction of Easter Road, a move that had possibly been influenced by the clubs successful six-week tour of the states in 1967. At that time literally millions of dollars were being invested into the fairly recently established North American Soccer League but unfortunately this had failed to generate any great interest among the general public with attendances inside a giant stadium capable of holding almost 60,000 often attracting less than 6,000, and it was felt that expanding links into Europe may possibly be the way ahead. Although the Hibs chairman Harrower later acknowledged that he had been aware of the rumours, he confirmed that no actual approach had been made, and no more would be heard regarding takeover bids until 1970.

Just before the start of the new season the Hibs captain Pat Stanton, the inaugural winner of the Hibs Supporters Association Player of the Year award a couple of years earlier, had now received an even greater accolade when he was voted the Scottish Football Writers' Player of the Year for 1969–70, an honour only rarely bestowed on a player outside the Old Firm. Widely respected throughout the game, Stanton would later receive the richly deserved award at a ceremony in Glasgow, the event also attended by some of his teammates.

Perhaps an early sign that even better days lay not too far ahead, Tom Hart's first game in control of the club had been a 2–0 defeat of

Celtic, both goals scored by the former Celtic player Joe McBride, Hibs' first home victory over the Parkhead side for 12 years, a result that would see the Easter Road side sitting top equal in the table.

Behind the scenes however it had been obvious for some time that all was not well between manager MacFarlane and the chairman, the pair sharing what could only be described as an uneasy relationship and in the circumstances there was always only going to be one winner. Both could be brash, forthright personalities accustomed to getting their own way and it was soon obvious that something had to give. MacFarlane, a former miner who had joined the club from Tranent Juniors in 1954 had been a member of the Easter Road side that faced the German Rot Weiss of Essen in the home leg of the inaugural European Cup in 1955 before a move to Raith Rovers in 1958. Later, after just a handful of games for Morton, in 1961 he had been appointed manager of the East of Scotland side Hawick Royal Albert, later moving to Stirling Albion before joining Hibs in 1969. An enthusiastic and charismatic character who enjoyed a laugh, he was popular with the players and had some good ideas, but tried to be both one of the lads and also a strict disciplinarian, a combination that rarely worked for a successful football manager. Although it had been well known to insiders that Hart and MacFarlane did not get on, including rumours of dressing room interference, perhaps the first public display that all was not well between the pair surfaced after a game against Morton at Cappielow played during a thunderstorm, when after just 33 minutes the referee had been left with no other alternative but to abandon the game after what had already been a heavily waterlogged pitch became totally unplayable. After the game MacFarlane had been highly critical of the referee for even allowing the game to start in the first place, but instead of backing his manager, Hart had distanced himself from MacFarlane's comments by stating publicly that 'Hibs wished to abide by the referee's decisions at all times regardless of the circumstances', a statement perhaps understandably that would not have gone down too well with MacFarlane.

Just a few weeks later, and incredibly on the morning of a Fairs Cup game against Liverpool at Easter Road, arguably the club's most important fixture for several years, the situation came to a head. MacFarlane was sacked on the spot after refusing to comply with Hart's earlier instructions that both Joe McBride and Johnny Graham were to be left out of the side that evening, finally bringing to an end the uneasy atmosphere between the pair that had been evident to several insiders for months. The players themselves had been completely unaware of the unfolding situation, they themselves surprised at the exclusion of both players from the line up in the dressing room just before the game. Somewhat curiously McBride had still been listed as one of the substitutes although there would be no place for Graham. The reason behind Hart's directive that both were not to be selected remains unclear to this day, possibly McBride's reluctance to move to Edinburgh, travelling through to Easter Road each day by car. He was also an extremely charismatic character and another reason may well have been that he had too much influence in the dressing room. Regardless, Hart's decision had provoked widespread condemnation, both among the supporters and the media, all united in support of the manager. According to *The Scotsman* the following morning the club had become much smaller because of this decision, a view shared by many of the other newspapers: *The Daily Record* of the opinion that 'Scottish football has seldom witnessed a sadder or more sickening scene than the self-humiliation of the once proud Hibs.' *The Daily Mail* however perhaps summed it up best: 'On the eve of one of the most important games in the history of the club, Hibs have managed to behave as though they were intent on some sort of football suicide.'

A goal scorer of proven ability, Joe McBride had joined Hibs as a replacement for Colin Stein after the latter's record-breaking transfer to Rangers in October 1968 where he scored on his debut in a 6–1 defeat at Ibrox. Just a few days later McBride had scored a hat-trick against Locomotive Leipzig in the Fairs Cup at Easter Road, the first ever Hibs player to score a treble in a European competition. After a nomadic career with spells at Kilmarnock, Wolves, Luton Town, Partick Thistle and Motherwell, in 1965 the prolific McBride had been manager Jock Stein's first signing for Celtic and during the 1966–67 season he had scored 33 goals before Christmas until a cartilage injury had kept him out for the rest of the season including the Parkhead side's historic European

Cup win. Later struggling to regain a regular place in the first team he had decided to resurrect his career at Easter Road. Although he had ended both the 1968–69 and 1969–70 seasons as Hibs' top goal scorer, some observers felt that McBride was a typical street wise, cocky and confident Glasgow lad who could be quite opinionated at times and for some time there had been rumours of unrest in the dressing room. Graham, who also hailed from Glasgow, was a close friend of McBride's and although much quieter, had possibly been tarred with the same brush. Whatever the reason for both players' exclusion against Liverpool, Tom Hart was a direct and outspoken personality who didn't suffer fools gladly and though perhaps it had only been a matter of time before he and MacFarlane had clashed, Hart always going to end the winner.

MacFarlane's time as manager at Easter Road had started well with a 2–0 win at Tynecastle, a victory that had immediately endeared him to the Hibs fans. However, although he had been voted manager of the month for October, since then results had been inconsistent to say the least. Just five wins from the previous 12 may well have played a part, but there seems little doubt that the personality clash between the pair had been the main reason behind his sacking. MacFarlane however had left a legacy that would serve the club well in the coming seasons. The previous November he had returned to his former club Stirling Albion to sign full-back Erich Schaedler for around £8,000 before turning his attention towards the Manchester City target Arthur Duncan from Partick Thistle for what would turn out to be a bargain fee of £35,000. It wouldn't take Schaedler long to demonstrate what was soon to become his legendary ferocious tackling skills and yet another great favourite of the fans. Making his first team debut at half-time in a friendly against the Polish side Gornik at Easter Road just before Christmas, teammate Peter Cormack had been carried off after the pair had clashed going for the same ball. Considering that Gornik were wearing all white jerseys and Hibs their traditional green, it was perhaps an early indication of Schaedler's 100% commitment to the cause.

Following the sale of Peter Marinello to Arsenal a few months later, Duncan would make a scoring debut in a 2–1 defeat by Celtic at Easter Road, the first of a record 594 appearances for the club in all competitions and 111 goals over the following 14 seasons.

Although possibly lacking tactically, MacFarlane had more than made up for it with his incredible enthusiasm and this had clearly been demonstrated by the odd circumstances behind the signing of the 18-year-old Kenny Davidson from Loanhead United in 1970. A reserve fixture between Hibs and Airdrie at Easter Road had been in real danger of being cancelled owing to the heavy fog that had been hanging over the city all day making visibility almost impossible. The manager however had insisted that the game should still go ahead as arranged as he had been keen to assess the performance of trialist Davidson in action for himself before any potential signing could be discussed. During what Davidson would later describe as a 'trial by fog' because visibility had been limited to just a few yards, the outside right had been more than surprised to find manager MacFarlane in his training gear running alongside him trackside for much of the game scrutinising his every move. Signed later that evening, incredibly after just two games for the reserves when he had scored a hat-trick against the then Cowdenbeath and future Hibs goalkeeper Jim McArthur and another against Aberdeen, Davidson had been surprised to learn that he would be accompanying the first team to Sweden in midweek for the return Fairs Cup game against Malmo. The problem was that he still lacked a passport, and it had required a mad dash through to the passport office in Glasgow by Secretary Cecil Graham to rectify matters. Not only did the youngster travel with the squad, but would be making his first team debut in place of the injured Eric Stevenson. Never at any time appearing overawed at his quick promotion, as well as impressing his new teammates, Davidson's terrific acceleration and tremendous ball control had created constant danger in the Malmo penalty area and it appeared that Hibs had unearthed yet another exciting prospect. His first goals for the first team would come just a few days later in an otherwise uninspiring 3–3 draw with St Mirren, although he himself had played well, and already big things were being expected of him. However, as so often happens, after the explosive start to his senior career the youngster appeared to lose his way at Easter Road, the situation not helped by a horrendous leg break received after an accidental clash with the Celtic goalkeeper Dennis Connaghan in a reserve game at Parkhead a few seasons later. Sadly, he would never play for the first team again and would soon be on his way to Dunfermline, finally ending his playing career with Meadowbank Thistle.

Meanwhile, Dave Ewing, a close friend of the Hibs director Tommy Younger, had been a surprise addition to the backroom staff when he had been appointed assistant trainer to Tom McNiven a short time before, an appointment that no doubt would also have come as a complete surprise to MacFarlane. Now, after less than two weeks at Easter Road, Ewing had been installed as caretaker manager for the game against Liverpool later that evening, the position made permanent the following morning.

The game against Liverpool had been goalless at the interval with Hibs more than holding their own, when with just 15 minutes remaining a rare Jim Black blunder – his only mistake of the evening – conceding a Toshack goal, would give Liverpool the lead and eventual victory. Hibs' first home defeat in European competition for nine years and the first time during that same period that they had failed to score at home. Perhaps even more concerning however was the fact that it had been the third consecutive game that the side had failed to find the net.

In the return leg at Anfield, a 2–0 defeat, Hibs had been much improved from the first game, the forwards this time creating several openings in the Liverpool penalty area only to find the future England goalkeeper Ray Clemence at the top of his game. Unfortunately, once again it would be defensive failings that would cost Hibs dear, goalkeeper Roy Baines at fault for both goals, particularly the second when he had allowed a deceiving Boersma lob to drop into the net behind him. Although Joe McBride had been in the starting lineup at centre-forward and Johnny Graham on the substitute's bench it seemed obvious even then that neither would have a long-term future at the club, and the game at Anfield would turn out to be McBride's last in a green and white jersey.

At that time Hibs had been finding goals extremely difficult to come by, with only five in the previous ten games, but somewhat incredibly, Joe McBride, a natural and prolific goal scorer had been allowed to join Dunfermline for the bargain fee of around £4,000, opening his account for his new side by scoring twice on his debut as Hibs were losing 1–0 at Tannadice on Boxing Day, the clubs sixth blank in the previous seven games.

A 0–0 draw at Tynecastle on New Year's Day, the Edinburgh rivals' third consecutive goalless draw in the holiday fixture, had according to the local press been uninspiring to say the least, both sets of fans regularly displaying their displeasure at the lack of entertainment on offer by barracking the players throughout. While Hearts had controlled the majority of the game without really looking like scoring, in the later stages Hibs had scorned a couple of decent chances to take the lead but despite the referee adding an additional few minutes at the end, in truth both sides could probably have played all night and still not scored.

In the then traditional holiday game on the 2 January, Hibs had drawn 2–2 with Cowdenbeath at Easter Road, their first goals under manager Ewing's tenure. In front of a disappointing crowd of just over 7,000, the lucky ones said to have been those who had stayed away, as the supporters were making their way from the ground at the end of what had been another disappointing performance the result had paled into insignificance with the breaking news that several people had lost their lives during the Rangers–Celtic game at Ibrox that afternoon after a barrier at stairway 13 collapsed at the end of the game. During the evening the casualty figures kept rising eventually reaching 66 and making it then the worst ever accident at a football game in the entire country. A disaster fund had immediately been set up, the Hibs Supporters Club like most other sporting organisations on both sides of the border making a sizeable donation, the club itself donating part of that afternoon's gate receipts. The following Saturday at Parkhead both Celtic and Hibs took the field wearing black armbands in respect of those that had lost their lives, a minute's silence meticulously observed by everyone inside the ground with similar tributes taking place throughout the country. Considering the tragic circumstances the home side's eventual 2–1 victory had meant little to the players or either set of fans, a reminder that football was just a game. A game between a Celtic/Rangers select and an International XI that included Hibs' Pat Stanton, would later take place at

Hampden, the proceeds donated to the disaster fund in aid of the dependants of the victims of the tragic accident.

Back at Easter Road, although the new manager had been born in Perth, Dave Ewing had spent his professional playing career in England with Manchester City, lining up alongside Bobby Johnstone in both the 1955 and 1956 FA Cup finals before joining Crewe Alexandria and finally non-league Ashton United. After a short spell managing Crewe he had returned to Maine Road and had been part of the backroom staff during Manchester City's great run in the 1960s that had seen the club win the League Championship, FA Cup and Cup Winners' Cup in successive seasons. Seeking pastures new, he had left City only at the beginning of the season to take up a coaching role at Sheffield Wednesday when he learned of Hibs' interest and had no hesitation in moving back to Scotland. The experienced Ewing was a respected figure in the game and popular with the players but, according to some, possibly too nice to be a football manager. Yet another with great enthusiasm, Ewing had possibly also lacked the necessary rapport with the directors and according to many of the players at that time would probably have made a better second man. His time at Easter Road however would prove to be less than inspiring with just five wins from his 21 league games and although the club had managed to reach the semi-final of the Scottish Cup, they were to lose to Rangers after a replay. It was after the first game at Hampden that Ewing had famously been overheard by a newspaper reporter telling his players in the dressing room that 'Rangers were rubbish and not a football team at all', only to find his comments plastered over the back pages of the following morning's papers, which obviously didn't go down too well in Glasgow, Rangers however going through to the final after a 2–1 victory in the replay.

With just three goals in his first four games against the six conceded it was obvious that something had to be done and in a surprise move Ewing had made his way to Sunderland to bring the former fan favourite Joe Baker back to Easter Road. At that time Baker had already made it clear to the Sunderland directors that he would definitely be returning to Scotland at the end of the season, an announcement that had immediately drawn the attention of both Hibs and St Mirren. However, upon learning of Hibs' interest there was only ever going to be one destination for the former English international and that was Easter Road.

Although born in the Birkenhead area of Liverpool during the war, Baker had moved with his family to Wishaw in Lanarkshire to escape the bombing of the English port when he was just a few weeks old. Already capped for the Scottish Schoolboys side against England at Goodison in 1954, he had first come to the attention of Hibs when scoring five for Lanarkshire Schools against Edinburgh at Tynecastle the following year and was soon snapped up on provisional terms and farmed out to Armadale Thistle, a common practice among senior sides at that time.

By the start of the 1957–58 season, the legendary centre-forward Lawrie Reilly had been struggling to recover from the cartilage injury that would eventually lead to his premature retirement from the game aged just 29. However, the absence of the Scottish international would be made much easier to bear for the Hibs fans with the emergence of the young Baker who would soon burst onto the scene with dynamic impact as the brightest young talent to light up the Scottish game for many years.

Called up from the Junior ranks only during the summer, after just one game for the reserves at the start of the 1957–58 season when perhaps surprisingly he had failed to score in an 8–1 victory over East Fife, the 17-year-old Baker would make his league debut in a 4–1 defeat by Airdrie at Broomfield the following Saturday to become an almost first team regular, the first of 190 appearances he would make for the Easter Road side in all games while scoring an incredible 167 goals. Just a few weeks later Hibs would be invited to officially open the new Tynecastle floodlights, and although Tommy Preston had taken the goalscoring honours with a hat-trick in the 4–2 victory, it was the lightning-fast Baker that really took the eye when scoring the other, his first goal for the league side. Even this early he looked every inch a star in the making. Scoring twice on his home debut against Queen's Park on the Saturday and a hat-trick against Tottenham in a 5–2 floodlight friendly on the Monday, it would be just the start of a true Roy of the Rovers fairy tale and the birth of yet another Hibs legend.

For Baker it had been goals all the way, scoring over 100 before he had turned 21 including all four in Hibs' famous 4–3 defeat of red-hot favourites Hearts in a Scottish Cup tie at Tynecastle in 1958, his 42 league goals during the 1959–60 season still a club record to this day. In November 1959, he made football history when becoming the first ever player from outside the Football League to be capped at full international level for England, making a goalscoring debut in the 2–1 defeat of Ireland at Wembley, the first of eight appearances for the full side including a 1–1 draw with Scotland at Hampden in 1960. Although born in England, Baker was as Scottish as the next man and would later confess that being booed by the home support that afternoon and a stranger to his teammates that he would much rather have been wearing the blue of Scotland. With a number of clubs chasing his signature, during the summer of 1961 he had signed for Torino. His short stay in Italy however would be an unhappy one, including a serious late night car crash that almost cost him his life, and he would soon become new manager Billy Wright's first signing for Arsenal. Later, after spells with Nottingham Forest and Sunderland he would rejoin his first love Hibs where he still retained legendary status among the Easter Road support.

Resplendent in white boots, quite an innovation at that time, captain for the day Baker would make a goal scoring debut second time around against Eddie Turnbull's Aberdeen. Shattering goalkeeper Bobby Clark's then Scottish record of over 12 games without conceding a goal, Hibs scored twice inside four second-half minutes in a 2–1 victory, Stanton scoring the first with a fierce drive that gave Clark no chance, Baker himself scoring what would turn out to be the winner with a header from close range a few minutes later.

Several weeks later, a goal in the very first minute of the game, one of two Baker would score that afternoon in a 3–1 victory against Airdrie, would help Hibs to their first league win in seven games. Another in a one-sided 5–1 victory against Clyde on the final day would see the former English international end the campaign as Hibs' top marksman with eight goals despite having only joined the club in the January; Hibs eventually finishing 12th in the table, a hugely disappointing nine places below the third-place finish of the previous season.

A planned end of season trip to North America and Bermuda had been cancelled almost at the last minute mainly due to problems with the travel arrangements, and instead as a reward for what had been another difficult campaign, the players had been treated to a two-week close season break in Majorca. Perhaps ominously the manager had not accompanied the players on the trip, and although all the backroom staff were believed to have only recently signed new five-year contracts, in reality the writing was probably already on the wall for Ewing, and only a few weeks before the start of the new season he would tender his resignation. Whether he had indeed resigned or had been pushed remains unclear, but he would give his reasons for leaving as his family failing to settle in Edinburgh and also a desire to return to coaching in England, and thus he would soon join First Division Crystal Palace.

Perhaps tellingly, after replacing MacFarlane as manager, Ewing's previous position as assistant trainer had remained unfilled and it would now seem more than likely that he had only been brought to the club in the first place to eventually replace MacFarlane although probably not so soon, only circumstances finally dictating events. There is no doubt however that Ewing had been under extreme pressure to achieve results. With only seven wins from his 26 games in charge and seven drawn, even after his appointment it had seemed likely that Tom Hart had already set his mind on bringing Eddie Turnbull back to his former stomping ground. Ewing's last action at Easter Road was to pay a £50 fine after mistakenly entering Kenny Davidson's name on the team sheet before the recent cup tie against Rangers instead of Eric Stevenson's.

The Return of Eddie Turnbull

THE NEWS OF Ewing's sudden resignation had immediately led to the expected newspaper speculation regarding his possible replacement, including somewhat predictably the former Hibs player Willie Ormond who was then manager at St Johnstone. Other potential candidates had included the former Dunfermline manager Willie Cunningham who was then with Falkirk, the former Easter Road players George Farm, Pat Quinn, Bertie Auld and even Jimmy Bonthrone who was then assistant to Eddie Turnbull at Aberdeen. There had even been the fanciful rumour doing the rounds that Tommy Docherty who had only recently resigned as manager of Porto had been spotted in the vicinity of Easter Road in the preceding days. Although Turnbull's name had also been mentioned, it was thought highly unlikely that he would leave an Aberdeen side that he had built into potential league champions. As far as the Hibs Managing Director Tom Hart was concerned however there was only one man in the frame to lead his new Easter Road revolution and that was Eddie Turnbull.

A major stumbling block had been that the pair had fallen out several years earlier, but on learning that Turnbull's wife Carol had failed to settle in the Grampian area, initial contact had been made by the astute Hart through the well-known *Edinburgh Evening News* reporter and lifelong Hibs fan Stewart Brown. An arrangement was made to set up what was intended to have been a clandestine meeting between the parties at a hotel in St Andrews, only for Turnbull to be recognised by a waitress who had once worked in the Hibs Supporters Club. Regardless, he had eventually agreed to return to Edinburgh but only after he had contacted the Aberdeen chairman Dick Donald personally with the news that although he would be leaving Pittodrie it would be with the deepest regret, and only then could any official announcement be made. Now after what had been 24 hours of hectic negotiations, after a further meeting with Tom Hart and director Tommy

Younger later that evening at the Gleneagles Hotel, Turnbull duly signed a five-year contract and was now manager of Hibs, a move according to him that was 'just like coming home'. Interviewed sometime later Turnbull would admit that only a move to Easter Road would have persuaded him to leave Pittodrie.

After leaving Easter Road so abruptly in March 1963, he had spent a brief spell as trainer at Queen's Park helping the amateurs to fourth place in the table, their highest position for many years, before taking over as manager of Aberdeen in March 1965. It was while at Queen's Park that he had been contacted by a journalist friend who advised him that if he were to apply for the then vacant manager's position at Aberdeen after the recent sacking of Tommy Pearson, then he would be well in the running. At the subsequent interview Turnbull had been surprised at the apparent lack of ambition that appeared to be running through a club that had won the League and League Cup not all that long before, an enquiry as to the level of success that would be expected were his application to be successful met with a mystified silence. On learning that he would be notified once the other interviews had been completed, in true Turnbull style he had immediately informed the Aberdeen directors that the last train back to Glasgow left at six o'clock: if he had not heard anything by then he would be off. Shortly after he had been called back to be receive the news that his application had been successful and that he was now the manager of Aberdeen.

At Pittodrie he had inherited a team that had been drifting aimlessly in the lower reaches of the league for several years but in a short time he had assembled an extremely talented and well organised side that would soon gain a deserved reputation as robust, skilful and disciplined opponents, and there was widespread disbelief throughout the entire country that he would even have considered leaving Pittodrie to join a mid-table side that had ended the previous season ten places and 24 points below them in the table. As well as leading the 'Dons' to the Scottish Cup final in 1967 where they would lose to Celtic, in 1970 the side had gone one step further by actually winning the competition and had finished the season just ended second in the table only two points behind champions Celtic. It seemed certain to everyone at the club that even better days lay not too far ahead. A strict disciplinarian, during his time at Aberdeen Turnbull had introduced the ruling that no longer would players be allowed to be picked up or dropped off on the way to, or back from games, everyone now required to report to Pittodrie. One example that perhaps demonstrates his almost single-minded determination came after a game against Morton at Cappielow when he was approached by the Danish player Jens Petersen telling him that as several of his fellow countrymen had arranged a party in Glasgow that evening he and his wife, who was already at the function, planned to stay overnight and he would not be returning to Pittodrie on the team coach. Turnbull calmly explained to the player that he clearly knew the rules and that there could be no exceptions, Petersen made to travel all the way back to Aberdeen only to catch a taxi back to Glasgow. This was in the pre-motorway days when the journey between both cities would likely take several hours, but to give him his due when relating the story many years later, Turnbull had confessed that he had probably been far too unbending on that occasion.

His work in transforming what had been an underperforming side into one capable of challenging for honours in such a short period of time had not gone unnoticed, and shortly after Rangers' humiliating Scottish Cup defeat by Second Division Berwick Rangers in 1967, Turnbull had been invited to attend an interview in Glasgow. With the then Rangers manager Scott Symon's position clearly under threat, Turnbull had been seen as a possible readymade replacement. However, after learning that if he were to be offered and ultimately accept the position of manager that he would not have had complete control of team affairs and that the directors would also have a say in the team selection he promptly got up and left the room.

Previously, he had spent wartime service in the Royal Navy, including time as a torpedo man aboard the destroyer HMS *Bulldog* that had earlier gained fame for the capture of the secret enigma code machine from the sinking German submarine U-110 in 1941, although this had been before he had joined the ship.

The then 23-year-old Eddie Turnbull had signed for Hibs in 1946 after just one game for the Grangemouth Junior side Forth Rangers against Dunipace in a local cup semi-final at Brockville.

His intelligent and forceful style of play had obviously impressed a watching Hibs scout, and he was invited through to Easter Road the following morning for signing talks. On the advice of an older brother who had accompanied him through to Edinburgh, Turnbull had no intention of signing any contract. However, after the go ahead from the brother – who had in the meantime been fortified by a few stiff whisky's poured by the astute Hibs manager Willie McCartney – the offer of a £20 signing-on fee and the suggestion that he could possibly be included in the party for Hibs' forthcoming tour of Czechoslovakia, Turnbull had duly signed on the dotted line. Only to then find himself left at home as the Hibs players made their way overseas on the club's first continental tour since the 1920s. The rest as they say is history.

As an integral member of the Famous Five forward line, considered by many to have been Scotland's finest ever attack, Turnbull had won three League Championship medals and nine full Scotland caps, taking part in all three games in the 1958 World Cup finals in Sweden. Only the second Hibs player to play in the finals of the competition after Willie Ormond in Switzerland in 1954, when he had laid on the pass for Jimmy Murray of Hearts to score Scotland's first ever goal in a World Cup finals in the 1–1 draw with Yugoslavia. Retiring from the playing side of the game in 1959 to take up the position of trainer at Easter Road, his last ever game in a green and white jersey a 2–1 defeat by Gijon during the club's close season tour of Spain.

Demonstrating even then a great attention to detail that would eventually establish his reputation as one of the finest tacticians in the game along with a determination that Hibs should be the fittest side in the country, Turnbull had immediately foregone a holiday at his in-laws' house in the north of Scotland to enrol on a weight training course. Some of the Hibs players at the time however, including Tommy Preston, would later complain that he often had a tendency to overdo things with the weights and that the players often felt shattered on a Saturday even before the kick-off.

After Hugh Shaw's sudden resignation in 1961 Turnbull had been hotly tipped to replace the long-serving manager, but much to his obvious disappointment the position had gone instead to the relatively unknown former Queen's Park and Clyde player Walter Galbraith. It was well known however that the two men would have a somewhat strained relationship, Turnbull sceptical of Galbraith's managerial capabilities and tactical know-how. Even then it had come as a complete surprise when one morning after training, and without the prospects of another position on the horizon, the often impetuous Turnbull had unexpectedly tendered his resignation, stunning not only the supporters but everyone at the club.

Back at Pittodrie Turnbull's decision to rejoin Hibs with immediate effect had come as an even bigger shock. Pre-season training had already started when he dropped the bombshell news and he made his farewells to the stunned players the following morning watched by Jimmy Bonthrone who would now be replacing him in the Pittodrie hot seat.

The announcement that he would be returning to Easter Road had been met with widespread elation by the Hibs fans and it would be impossible to overstate the excitement generated in the city by the news, an appointment that had also caught the players completely by surprise. Although they would obviously have heard the rumours, like so many others, few thought that he would be leaving what had been considered to be future league champions at Pittodrie to return to Easter Road. Several of his former teammates however including Lawrie Reilly and Gordon Smith had also been elated at the breaking news, Reilly suggesting that the signing had been the best made by the club in years. The secretary of the Hibs Supporters Association had been even more ecstatic when declaring that the appointment had been a shot in the arm for the fans and a real incentive for the club: 'He has proved himself at Aberdeen and every Hibs supporter will be willing to give him time to improve the team knowing that can bring back the glory days to Easter Road.'

Turnbull had lost no time in outlining his aims for the immediate future:

> I am ambitious and want the Hibs players to be the same. You have got to be ambitious to win anything. I would like us to win all three trophies this coming season, but if we win only one then I will be satisfied.

The new manager's arrival would have an immediate impact both on and off the field. One of the first in the country to recognise the advantage of watching games from an elevated position, one of his first tasks had been to select a seat in the director's box complete with a telephone connection to the dugout where, according to him, he would have a far better view of the proceedings taking place on the field. With an almost obsession to succeed, he had also been well aware of the psychological advantage of the players being smartly turned out. During his days as a player at Easter Road, chairman Harry Swan had always inspected the strips hanging up in the dressing room the day before a game, and taking a leaf out of Swan's book, when handed a shabby tracksuit on his first day, just as he had done when taking over at Aberdeen, he immediately ordered all the substandard training gear to be thrown on the boiler-room fire and replaced with brand-new kit. Previously, those arriving first for training in the morning would get the choice of the best gear from the drying room, leaving the latecomers to fight for what was left. Now each player would receive his own personalised training kit and track suit, each item bearing the individual's squad number.

Training had also changed completely, now far more organised and disciplined. According to some of the players, under Dave Ewing it had often become mundane and repetitively boring, but all this was about to change. A rigorous and varied warm up overseen by Tom McNiven would now be followed by the players being put through their paces with a circuit training session that was both inventive and revolutionary for that time, and although demanding, would always be varied and interesting, every exercise with a purpose and usually geared to a game situation. Most of the exercises would now also involve the use of a ball, each session meticulously recorded in a 'Bible' by trainer John Fraser that could be referred to in the future, Fraser himself often watching in awe at just what was taking place on the field in front of him. On the first day's training at nearby Hawkhill, a demanding workout had been followed by a small-scale practice match, the manager watching quietly from a distance, even that early probably assessing who might be in his plans for the future and who would not. That first day Turnbull had taken the opportunity to renew his acquaintance with both Joe Baker and Eric Stevenson, the only players still on the books from his first time at the club, both no doubt already well aware of the new manager's determination to succeed. A great admirer of Eric Stevenson, a player he had tried to sign on several occasions when manager at Aberdeen, that first morning he had taken the player aside to say that he was relying on him. Although nodding in agreement, at that time Stevenson was having personal problems and was aware even then that he was no longer capable of living up to the manager's expectations and that he would not remain long at Easter Road.

One day each week the players would be put through a particularly punishing and demanding routine that in time would go some way in making the club the fittest side in the country. Some of the players would occasionally ask trainer John Fraser as to what day of that particular week the punishing session was due to take place, only for Turnbull to brusquely order Fraser in his own inimitable style to: 'Tell them f*** all.' For weeks the defence would be recalled in the afternoons when they would be put through various tactical permutations, two against three, three against four, often seven against the back four until they all had developed an almost telepathic understanding of each other's play, with the result that when the forwards were introduced into the sessions the defence would rarely concede a goal.

Unlike his early days at Aberdeen, at Easter Road Turnbull had inherited a squad of players with obvious potential, several soon to form the nucleus of a celebrated side and all would benefit greatly under the new managers demanding regime.

Just days after returning from the club's summer trip to Majorca, the supremely talented former Airdrie ball-boy John Brownlie had been surprised to receive a call from the national team manager Bobby Brown informing him that he had been included in the Scotland squad for the forthcoming friendly games against both Denmark and Russia; the announcement later confirmed by telegram – a form of communication that would appear prehistoric nowadays. Expecting only to make up the numbers, Brownlie, who perhaps surprisingly had not yet served the usual apprenticeship in the under-23 side before his call up to the full squad, had sat out the 1–0 defeat by Denmark but had been surprised to be selected in what was a depleted Scotland side for the game against Russia in front of 100,000 mainly partisan fans inside the Lennin Stadium in Moscow. During the game, another 1–0 defeat, the Hibs youngster had been one of the very few to have played well and already looked destined to have a huge international future ahead of him. First coming to the attention of Hibs as a 13-year-old, Brownlie had joined the Easter Road ground staff on leaving school while turning out on a Saturday for Edina Hibs alongside both Willie McEwan and Alex Cropley. Farmed out to Pumpherston Juniors to toughen him up, a common practice among senior clubs at that time, he quickly learned to take care of himself against mostly older players. Ever present in the second team during the 1969–70 season, he made his first team debut for Hibs at right half as an 18-year-old in place of Blackley in the final game of the season, an away game against Dunfermline, and such was his impact that within weeks of the start of the following season he would be a regular in the first team. Originally an extremely average inside-forward or centre-half, it was only when reverting to full-back that he would find his true position, his exciting forays up the right wing soon making him a great favourite with the fans. Now less than a year after his Hibs debut and still only 19, he had won the first of what would eventually be seven full caps, only injury preventing him from collecting many more.

Brownlie was only one of several internationals at the club at that time. Lining up alongside him in Moscow had been teammate Pat Stanton, his ninth appearance for the full side. Making his international debut along with teammate Jim Scott against Holland at Hampden in 1966 although he had never let the side down he would often find himself excluded for the next game, and until recently had experienced great difficulty in claiming a regular place in the side, one of the main reasons according to many: the 'Glasgow' bias of the Scottish selectors.

Back at Easter Road, the strict disciplinarian Turnbull would leave the players in absolutely no doubt as to what would be expected in the future. That first morning, full-back Erich Schaedler had arrived at training sporting a beard, but after a 'quiet word' from the manager he appeared the following morning clean shaven. Sometime later Alan Gordon had turned up for training one morning wearing gloves, bringing an immediate response from the manager: 'F*****g gloves: I was in the Russian convoys during the war and I didn't wear f*****g gloves, get them off!' an instruction that again had been instantly obeyed. Before his first game in charge, a friendly against Middlesbrough at Easter Road, some of the players had arrived at the ground after the allotted time, a mistake they would not make again. In truth it was a discipline that had been sadly lacking at that time. Previously the players had more or less been allowed to do as they pleased, but things would now be different. Pre-season training consisting of morning and afternoon sessions had already started before Turnbull's arrival, and some of the players had regularly wandered along to the nearest pub for a couple of pints before returning for the afternoon session. All that had now been stopped by a manager who knew exactly what was going on.

Although he had always been a gruff and dour personality, as a player Turnbull usually had time to help the younger players with a quiet word of advice, a pat on the back or a 'well done' when needed, but all that now seemed to have changed. Unlike many other managers including Jock Stein, Turnbull didn't always have a great rapport with the players, and although admired as a coach, most found him extremely difficult to get near to. A former associate at the time felt that although he had been a rugged and determined competitor as a player, he had since gained a reputation as a managerial hard man and now often appeared to go out of his way to prove it. For some reason he now found it difficult to give credit. Not for him the comforting arm around the shoulder, and rarely if ever a welcome word of encouragement. To give him his due he called a spade a spade and you always knew exactly where you stood with him. While not a particularly big man he had a presence and could be a frightening figure if the occasion warranted. Perhaps surprisingly though, some former players say that on trips abroad he could occasionally be good company when he would entertain the players with stories of his time as a player or his escapades in the Royal Navy during the war, far different from the normally abrasive personality at training or in the dressing room. These occasions however would be extremely few and far between. Sometimes unconsciously funny with some of his sayings, he had once described an extremely slim player as having legs that would not have lasted a postman a week. On another occasion disparagingly describing a scout as being unable to tell the difference between a half back and a 'f*****g half brick'.

That first morning at training two newcomers would be meeting their new teammates for the first time. Bertie Auld, a European Cup winner with Celtic in 1967 and the winner of six consecutive championship medals with the Parkhead side had been Dave Ewing's last signing for the club. The often-tempestuous Auld had won the first of his three Scotland caps against Holland in 1959 during his first spell at Parkhead before a move to Birmingham City in 1961 but perhaps surprisingly on his return to Celtic would never feature in the international set-up again. Joining the former Lisbon Lion at Easter Road was the Scottish Junior international goalkeeper Eddie Pryce who had been signed from Kirkintilloch Rob Roy during the summer. At that time the 14-year-old Craigroyston schoolboy Gordon Strachan who had been signed on provisional forms just a few weeks earlier had been training with the club during the summer. However, a dispute between the player's father and Turnbull had resulted in the suggestion, although not delivered as diplomatically, that it would perhaps be best if the talented youngster continued his career elsewhere. To be fair to Turnbull he had only been at the club a few weeks and would have known little about the player, Hibs' loss and ultimately of great benefit to several others. On another occasion it is said that a promising young player had been invited to Easter Road for trials. The youngster however, a keen golfer, had already agreed to take part in a golf competition that same day and not wishing to let his colleagues down had sent his apologies. Unhappy at what he considered to have been a rebuff, instead of arranging another trial the often-impulsive Turnbull never again contacted the player, who eventually went on to collect over two dozen Scotland caps and win Championships, League Cups, the European Cup and the FA Cup in the near future with one of the top sides in England.

The new manager would have the opportunity to assess his new charges in competitive action for the first time in a pre-season friendly against Middlesbrough, the first game between the sides at Easter Road since 1959. Then Joe Baker had celebrated his call up for the forthcoming under-23's game against France by scoring yet another hat-trick in a quite incredible 6–6 draw against the English Second Division side in a friendly, bringing Hibs' total to an incredible 32 goals in a little over two weeks. Facing Hibs at Easter Road that evening had been a certain Brian Clough along with goalkeeper Peter Taylor who would later form a prolific managerial partnership with the centre-forward. Already capped twice for the full England side, Clough had been hotly tipped to replace West Bromwich Albion's Derek Kevin permanently in the England side. However, such was Baker's reputation at that time that before the game the England selectors had announced that they would be travelling up to Edinburgh to run the rule over the two prospective centre-forward candidates for the forthcoming game against Ireland. On the night there would be only one winner. Although Clough had managed to score twice in a thrilling, high scoring game, the fast, intelligent and always dangerous Baker had scored a hat-trick to completely overshadow the less mobile Clough and it now appeared that there was no way the selectors could ignore the claims of the Hibs player. Unfortunately, the England selectors had failed to make the game when their plane was fog-bound in London, but according to one newspaper report the following morning: 'on this showing Baker would have walked into the England side'. Their prediction would turn out to be correct and the Hibs player made a goalscoring debut for the full side in a 2–1 victory over Ireland at Wembley. Clough would never play for England again. That evening the current Hibs manager had been a member of the backroom staff, Baker now the only surviving player from the game still at Easter Road.

Both Gordon Marshall and Thomson Allan had been freed at the end of the previous season, leaving only Roy Baines as the first-choice goalkeeper. Baines however had been injured during training and, left with only the untried former Kirkintilloch player Eddie Pryce, Turnbull had been left with no other option but to play the inexperienced youngster against the English Second

Division side. With both Bertie Auld and the England World Cup winner Nobby Stiles making their debuts for their respective sides, the game would soon turn out to be a personal vendetta between the vastly experienced pair which may well have been a throwback to Auld's earlier time in England with Birmingham City. Both seemed to be totally ignorant of the fact that the game was a 'friendly' and after only five minutes Stiles had been the first to be warned by the referee for a heavy challenge on Auld that had left the Hibs player requiring treatment. As he was being attended to on the field by Tom McNiven, it was noticeable that Auld's eyes never left Stiles for a second and it was only too obvious what was coming next. Just a few minutes later it was the Hibs player's turn to be lectured by the referee after a tackle that left Stiles writhing on the ground in some discomfort. With Joe Baker displaying touches reminiscent of the player of old, Hibs had the better of the first half although Middlesbrough came more into it after Auld had been substituted at half-time. With neither side looking likely to break the deadlock, the game suddenly burst into life in the dying minutes when the visitors scored twice inside 30 seconds, leaving the inexperienced Pryce, who had otherwise played well, helpless on both occasions.

Still with no other option available, the young goalkeeper had kept his place in the no-scoring draw with German side Shalke in a friendly at Easter Road a few days later. Before the game the long-serving former player, trainer and groundsman Jimmy McColl had received a presentation to commemorate his 50 years' service at the club from his all-time favourite player Gordon Smith watched by all the other members of Famous Five and former teammate from the 1920s Johnny Halligan.

Pryce would also play in the 4-2 defeat by Middlesbrough in the return friendly at Ayresome Park on the Saturday, but perhaps of the mind that it would have been unfair to throw the inexperienced youngster into the fray, Turnbull moved quickly to sign the former Dunfermline goalkeeper Jim Herriot from the South African side Durban City. A delay in receiving Herriot's clearance had initially prevented the Scottish international goalkeeper from making his official debut, but regardless Turnbull had decided to risk the wrath of the Scottish authorities by playing the still unregistered Herriot under the assumed name of Pryce in a 2–1 defeat by York City in a friendly at Bootham Crescent a few days later. Although the goalkeeper had played in England for several years and had made several appearances for Scotland, incredibly nobody seemed to have noticed the deception.

Although none of the pre-season games had ended in victory, interviewed after the Middlesbrough game Turnbull had reportedly 'not been overly disappointed with the results as the games had been used mainly to get to know the capabilities of the players before the serious work started', although there is no doubt that he would have been extremely concerned at just how easily several of the goals had been conceded.

Scottish Cup Disappointment (1971–72)

THE PREVIOUS SEASON had seen a fall in the average attendance at Easter Road of over 3,000, the lowest by far the 3,310 that had witnessed the 5–1 victory over Clyde on the final day. Now after the appointment of Turnbull, season ticket sales alone had already almost doubled, and the supporters were not to be disappointed. In a League Cup section also comprising of Dundee United, Motherwell and Kilmarnock, four straight wins with two games left to play had already been enough to ensure qualification for the quarter-finals of the competition for the third time in four seasons. As an early sign of the expectancy now surrounding Easter Road the attendance at the game against Dundee United had been more than double that of the league game between the sides the previous season.

With goalkeeper Herriot making his official competitive debut in the opening game against Motherwell at Fir Park, after a no-scoring first half Hibs had eventually coasted to a 3–0 victory with a performance that had apparently pleased the manager. Although somewhat premature, many were already tipping Hibs as favourites to top the section, some even going as far as to predict an all green final against Celtic. So far Herriot had not been overworked but in the final section game against Kilmarnock he had been called upon to demonstrate his quality when making a tremendous save late in the game to earn his side a point, and with 14 goals scored against just three conceded there were already early signs that the hours spent on the training ground were starting to pay dividends. Having missed the start of the campaign through suspension after being sent off against Falkirk the previous season, John Blackley had made his return to the side at Rugby Park and although they were not to know it at the time, the fans that had made their way through from Edinburgh had just witnessed the first ever outing as a unit of a defence that barring injury would soon become the recognised formation: Herriot, Brownlie and Schaedler, Stanton, Black and Blackley.

The no-score draw had prevented Hibs from topping the section with maximum points. A feat not achieved by the club since 1950 during the days of the Famous Five when, already leading Dundee in the final section game at Dens Park, the referee had been forced to abandon the game midway through the second half after the already heavy pitch had become completely waterlogged due to the incessant rain that had been falling all day. Because the section had already been won however, the authorities saw no need to replay the game and the result was allowed to stand.

Although Hibs had gone through the League Cup section unbeaten, the players would have been well aware that they would undoubtedly face a far stiffer test in the first Edinburgh derby of the season at Tynecastle. Hearts themselves had failed to qualify for the latter stages of the League Cup competition ending the section in second place, but would obviously be desperate to put one over their city rivals, particularly at home. However, watched by a crowd of around 28,000, one of the drabbest derbies for many years had provided little entertainment and very few scoring opportunities for either side. The game had seemed destined to end goalless until just four minutes from the end when after collecting a pass from Johnny Hamilton on the edge of the box, Alex Cropley had cleverly turned the Hearts captain Alan Anderson before proceeding to thunder a tremendous 25-yard drive past the despairing dive of Jim Cruickshank and into the roof of the net to bring the house down. It had been a strike deserving to win any game but just to make sure, in the very last minute substitute Johnny Hamilton who had replaced Eric Stevenson midway through the second half, coolly despatched the ball past the advancing Hearts goalkeeper to give the visitors a somewhat flattering 2–0 victory. After the game Cropley had been taken aside by the manager to be told that his strike had been a great goal as all good strikers always knew exactly where the goals were. It had now been eight years since Hearts had managed a victory over their city rivals at Tynecastle and had not even scored in the previous six games between the sides.

SCOTTISH CUP DISAPPOINTMENT (1971–72)

After 11 seasons at Easter Road, it would turn out to be Eric Stevenson's last ever first team start, and although he would be listed as a substitute on several occasions, after 12 seasons at Easter Road he would soon be on his way to Ayr United.

In six of the seven games so far the scores had been level at the interval, but with the exception of the goalless draw against Kilmarnock all the others had eventually ended in victory, a clear indication of the manager's well recognised ability to change things tactically during the break. He was regularly quoted as saying: 'regardless of the work done during the week, a manager only earns his money at half-time during a game'. With just the three goals conceded it had already been a major improvement on the previous season's 'defensive jitters' and even this early it would appear that Turnbull had found a settled defensive set-up. One of the main reasons had been the signing of goalkeeper Jim Herriot who had made an immediate impact. The hard-working Herriot who returned to the ground most afternoons for individual training, had been nicknamed 'Bob' by the rest of the players on account of his 'sleepy looking eyes' similar to that of film star Robert Mitchum. A tremendous organiser inside the penalty area, the vastly experienced goalkeeper had signed for Dunfermline in 1958, collecting a runners-up medal in the 1965 Scottish Cup final against Celtic before joining Second Division Birmingham City for around £18,000 during the summer and winning several Scotland caps during his six seasons with the midlands club. A fall out with the directors however had resulted in the threat of his registration being withheld which could possibly have prevented any future Scotland call up and would eventually lead to loan spells at both Aston Villa and Mansfield Town before ultimately being freed. He could well have joined Celtic. Contacted by Jock Stein through an intermediary with the advice that he was not to sign anything until he had heard from the Celtic manager, Herriot had rejected several offers from clubs on both sides of the border including the player-manager position at non-league Corby Town. After hearing nothing he eventually managed to contact Stein personally only to now be told that he should try to get fixed up elsewhere. Perhaps understandably Herriot had been furious and the two would not speak again for several years.

Now deciding to accept a six-week contract with the South African side Durban City, he had been in the final few days of the short-term agreement and had been considering the offer to extend his stay when he received the call from Hibs. The Morton chairman Hal Stewart had also been keen to sign the experienced goalkeeper as had several English league sides, but on hearing of Hibs' interest there was only going to be one destination for the former international goalkeeper. Although pleased to be returning to Scotland, according to Herriot himself the main attraction had been the opportunity to work under Eddie Turnbull and it would not take him long to prove that he would be an astute signing. It later transpired that Herriot could well have joined Hibs almost ten years earlier when he was understudy to Eddie Connachan at East End Park, only for the then Dunfermline manager Jock Stein to veto the move. Well known for his distinctive habit of spreading mud on both cheekbones during floodlit games, similar to the custom of many American Football players, the goalkeeper had picked up the tip from Stein during his Dunfermline days after complaining that he was losing the flight of the ball due to the glare of the low stand-mounted floodlights during a game against Kilmarnock at Rugby Park.

While at Birmingham he had also achieved fame of a different kind, although one that the goalkeeper would be unaware of for several years. In 1970 Alf Wight, the Sunderland born veterinary surgeon and fanatical 'Black Cats' supporter had decided to adopt the pen name James Herriot for a series of books that he was then writing entitled *All Creatures Great and Small* and *It Shouldn't Happen to a Vet* after watching Herriot starring for Birmingham City in an FA Cup tie against Manchester United on TV. Years later the author would present Herriot with a signed copy of his book in exchange for one of the goalkeeper's Scotland Jerseys.

Meanwhile a surprise defeat by Falkirk over two legs in the quarter-finals of the League Cup had put paid to any notions of winning the trophy for the first time, the Bairns deservedly progressing into the semi-finals where they would meet the eventual if unlikely winners of the competition, Partick Thistle. Regardless, in only six short weeks Turnbull had completely transformed a team that had previously been regarded as a talented but disorganised

SCOTTISH CUP DISAPPOINTMENT (1971-72)

side into one now seemingly capable of challenging for honours, and people were beginning to sit up and take notice.

After five league games Hibs were now second in the table only one point behind leaders Aberdeen, one of the highlights a 4-1 victory at Tannadice. Inspired by man-of-the-match Pat Stanton who scored twice, the impressive all-round performance had left one local journalist possibly somewhat prematurely to suggest that: 'Hibs lean years could soon be over'.

Turnbull refused to be complacent with the results so far, and it was obvious that the next two fixtures, against third-placed Celtic and the league leaders Aberdeen would be far more difficult and possibly determine just how far the side had already come. In the game against Celtic at Easter Road the demand had been so great that the kick-off had to be delayed for several minutes to allow the huge crowd, estimated to have been well over 40,000, time to enter the stadium, testimony if any was still needed that something special was beginning to happen at Easter Road. However, in a game that had been fast and furious throughout, despite having the bulk of the pressure Hibs had lacked sharpness in front of goal, a solitary strike by Macari late in the second-half allowing the visitors to leapfrog Hibs into second place in the table, the Easter Road side dropping to fourth.

Just prior to the kick-off at Pittodrie the following Saturday and in front of the ground's biggest attendance of the season with the exception of the visit of Rangers and Celtic, a great number having made their way from Edinburgh, Eddie Turnbull had been presented with an inscribed cigarette lighter by the Aberdeen players in recognition of his achievements during his time at the club. The gesture had clearly not been appreciated by a large section of the home support, who perhaps understandably had been extremely disappointed at the former manager's decision to rejoin Hibs and had barracked Turnbull throughout the presentation. During the first half of what some had described as a 'grudge match' Hibs had again been the better side in the early stages, an Arthur Duncan strike giving the visitors an interval lead, the first goal that Aberdeen had conceded in the league that season. However, in a tremendous second half fightback a goal by the future Hibs player Joe Harper closely followed by another from the up-and-coming, Edinburgh-born centre-half Willie Young had eventually been enough to secure the points for the home side. Regardless of the consecutive defeats, Hibs' impressive performances against two of the favourites to lift the title had attracted many admirers, one newspaper reporter although again somewhat prematurely even going as far as to compare the current side to the Famous Five. Yet another of the opinion that: 'Hibs are an entertaining side striving to play the game as it was meant to be played.' Turnbull however, always keen to keep his players feet firmly on the ground was quick to point out: 'We are still far from a championship winning side. This is something I personally have never claimed, only others.'

It was around this time that Alex Cropley became the sixth player then at Easter Road to win full international honours when along with teammate Pat Stanton he had been called into the Scotland squad for the forthcoming European Championship game against Portugal at Hampden. After seven games without a victory the then Scotland manager Bobby Brown had recently resigned to be replaced by the former Chelsea and Aston Villa boss Tommy Docherty. Docherty's appointment however had coincided with a new international ruling that a player no longer had to play for the country of his birth but could now represent that of his parent's birthright, and along with the Arsenal goalkeeper Bob Wilson Cropley became the first to take advantage of the new ruling. Born in the English army garrison town of Aldershot where his Edinburgh-born father John was turning out for the local league side he had returned to Scotland with the family when only a few years old and although he had already been watched by representatives of the FA selection committee, Cropley considered himself as Scottish as the next man.

Born in Chesterfield, Bob Wilson had also been included in the Scotland squad for the game against Portugal only because of his family connections, his great uncle Sir John Ure Primrose, a former Lord Provost of Glasgow and chairman of Rangers. Primrose had actually performed the official opening of Hampden Park in 1903, and now his great nephew was about to make his first ever appearance at the national stadium. At that time Scotland had been well out of the running for qualification for the

SCOTTISH CUP DISAPPOINTMENT (1971-72)

Championships and as far as Cropley himself was concerned both he and Wilson had only been included in the squad as a publicity stunt in an attempt by Docherty to increase the attendance for the forthcoming game and he had not expected to play. Not only would he be selected, but along with teammate Pat Stanton had been one of the successes in Scotland's 2-1 victory, the following morning's newspapers all full of praise for the Hibs youngster, one claiming somewhat lyrically that there had been 'class in the heroic raiding of Alex Cropley, a new boy with a glowing future who had performed with a maturity belying his years.' Like Brownlie a few months earlier, but only because of the change in the regulations, he had made his full international debut before serving the accepted apprenticeship in the under-23s.

Meanwhile back at Easter Road the vastly experienced Joe Baker who had been injured in the League Cup game against Motherwell several weeks earlier had made his long-awaited return to action in an emphatic 6-0 defeat of Falkirk at Easter Road, a victory that allowed the home side a modicum of revenge for the earlier elimination from the League Cup. Although failing to score himself, Baker's presence, speed and power had helped set up several openings for his teammates before being forced to retire late in the game. The day however had unquestionably belonged to Arthur Duncan. As his former side Partick Thistle were stunning the football world by unexpectedly defeating Celtic 4-1 in the League Cup final at Hampden, Duncan had taken the honours at Easter Road by scoring four of his side's goals and it could well have been more. The often unpredictable but exciting Duncan had been injured at the beginning of the year missing the end of the previous season. Unable to regain a first team place he had spent several frustrating months at the start of the present campaign in the reserves only recently managing to force himself back into the reckoning and his goals would go some way in re-establishing a regular place in the side. Extremely popular with the supporters, Duncan had earned the nickname 'Nijinsky' after the famous racehorse because of his electric pace. One particular fan had also named him the 'Road Runner' after the cartoon character of the same name that was popular on TV at the time, and often when Arthur was on one of his regular lightning-fast forays down the left wing the sound 'Beep-Beep' could clearly be heard emanating loudly from the enclosure.

Failing to make a first team start since the beginning of the season it was obvious that Johnny Graham did not figure in Eddie Turnbull's long-term plans and he was allowed to join Ayr United. Graham, a £17,000 Willie MacFarlane signing from Falkirk in 1969 had joined the club a few days after the acquisition of Erich Schaedler from Stirling Albion. Just hours after putting pen to paper he had made an immediate impact by scoring twice in a 3–1 home victory against Airdrie, form that would later earn him a Scottish League cap against England. However, although managing to survive Tom Hart's 'mini purge' before the Liverpool game, since then he had struggled to stake a regular place in the side.

Eric Stevenson, at that time the longest serving player at Easter Road, would soon join Graham at Somerset Park. Turnbull had been a long-time admirer of the player. Although not yet turned 30, a time when his best years should still have been ahead of him, Stevenson had been experiencing personal problems, and feeling that a move would perhaps be in the best interest of both parties, he had decided to join his former Easter Road teammate Ally McLeod who was then manager at Ayr. Stevenson had already discussed the situation with the manager, but although he had listened, typically, Turnbull had shown not a lot of sympathy, agreeing that perhaps a move would be in the best interests of both parties. Stevenson however would later recall that he had known almost immediately that he had made the wrong decision in moving to Somerset Park, even before playing a game, and would soon announce his premature retirement from the game to concentrate on his business interests in the Bonnyrigg area.

As Stevenson was making his way to Ayr, after a week of negotiations that very same day Turnbull had signed the mercurial Alex Edwards from Dunfermline for the bargain fee of £13,000, and once again it would turn out to be an inspired signing. In March 1962, just five days after his 16th birthday Edwards had become Scotland's second youngest outfield player to make a league debut when lining up against Hibs at East End Park. Goalkeeper Ronnie Simpson had turned out for Queen's Park in a Glasgow Cup tie when deputising for the future Rangers and Scotland goalkeeper Bobby Brown at the age of 14, and also held the record as the youngest ever to make a competitive debut when he lined up against Hibs in a League Cup tie at Hampden in August 1946 aged just 15. Coincidentally, as well as making their competitive debuts against the Easter Road side both Simpson and Edwards would later go on to play for the club. In yet another coincidence Edwards and Andy Penman who had been the youngest ever Scottish outfield player aged 15, 18 days younger than Edwards when making his competitive debut for Dundee against Hearts in 1959 had both been born in the Scottish coastal town of Rosyth.

Edwards, immensely talented but often petulant had been capped for Scotland at both Amateur and Professional Youth level and also the under-23 side. Quite incredibly, though also a Scottish Cup winner against Hearts with the Fife side in 1968 and a veteran of many European games including the famous 6–2 Fairs Cup victory against Valencia in 1962 when still only 16, he would never win a full cap. At the time of his signing he was still serving a 28-day ban after being ordered off for the fourth time in his senior career and would be unable to make his Hibs debut for several weeks. While it was then against the rules to sign a player while he was under suspension, just as with Jim Herriot a couple of months earlier Turnbull again turned a blind eye to the regulations. Later, after pleading ignorance to the ruling he would be severely censured by the authorities.

While at Dunfermline, Edwards, a huge favourite with the fans, had been 'tapped' by the Leeds United manager Don Revie who is said to have offered the Fife side £70,000 for the talented player, a move that in all likelihood would also have more than doubled his wages. Edwards however was such a valuable commodity for Dunfermline at that time, who having recently sold Roy Barry to Coventry for £40,000 probably had no immediate need of the money and had refused to sanction the move, a decision that obviously didn't go down too well with the player. The often-tempestuous Edwards had also fallen out with manager George Farm after being asked to take what effectively would be a drop in wages after a private agreement between himself and Chairman

Leonard Jack had come to an end after the director's recent death. Now extremely unhappy at Dunfermline, after further offers from Southampton and Crystal Palace had also been turned down, Edwards had walked out of the club to work on a building site. It was only after Alec Wright had replaced Farm as manager at East End Park that Dunfermline had finally agreed to listen to offers for the unsettled player and he had eventually been allowed to join Hibs. The fee was to prove a bargain, Turnbull reportedly saying that if Dunfermline had only held on to the player then in all likelihood he would eventually have been worth £100,000.

According to the player himself Edwards had arrived at Easter Road to find a happy camp, full of confident characters that mingled and socialised together, everyone mixing well with no cliques, and had immediately been welcomed into the fold. At Easter Road he would be renewing acquaintance with his former Dunfermline teammate Jim Herriot and already knew several of the players previously even having gone on holiday with Jimmy O'Rourke and was looking forward to an new exciting challenge.

Meanwhile, both Alex Cropley and Pat Stanton had also been selected for the Scotland side to face Belgium at Pittodrie. Stanton, who had only recently been described by manager Tommy Docherty as: 'the best defensive half back in the country and a better player than Bobby Moore,' would earn rave reviews when forming an impressive defensive partnership with Aberdeen's Martin Buchan in the 1–0 victory. The evening however would not end quite so well for Cropley who had been on the receiving end of some solid tackling throughout, and he limped off early in the second half to be replaced by a certain Kenny Dalglish who would be making his first ever appearance for the full Scotland side. Despite Tommy Docherty stating publicly before his debut against Portugal just a few weeks earlier that the Hibs player should now go out and buy a big display cabinet for all the caps he was sure to get, Cropley would never play for the full side again. At that time, unlike in England the Scotland players would receive an actual cap, one per season, only if they had played against the home countries, England, Wales or Northern Ireland in a Home International Tournament. Over 30 years later the situation would be remedied after a campaign by the son of the

SCOTTISH CUP DISAPPOINTMENT (1971–72)

former 1950s Scotland player Stewart Imlach that anyone who had played for Scotland in a full international should receive the honour, the Hibs players Alex Cropley, Eddie Turnbull and Keith Wright among those who would retrospectively be presented with an actual cap.

As both Stanton and Cropley were facing Belgium at Hampden, that same evening at Easter Road Alex Edwards was to have made his overdue debut in an East of Scotland Shield fixture against Berwick Rangers only to call off just before the start with a throat infection. In his absence the highly rated 18-year-old Derek Spalding had made his debut, the youngster doing his first team prospects no harm with an assured performance in midfield. The former Easter Road goalkeeper Willie Wilson would be facing Hibs that evening, but the popular 'Man in Black' could do little to prevent the home side's 4–1 victory that would see them progress into the final where they would now face Hearts.

With his earlier suspension now completed Edwards would finally make his long-awaited debut just a few days later in a 2–2 draw with Airdrie at Broomfield and it was immediately evident that his six-week lay-off had done little to effect his energy or enthusiasm. An early Arthur Duncan strike had been cancelled out by two goals inside two minutes by the former Easter Road player Derek Whiteford, but despite Hibs monopolising almost the entire second half with Edwards influential in midfield, it would take a long-range Blackley drive into the roof of the net a few minutes from the end to give the Easter Road side a more than merited share of the points. Although at times struggling against a determined home defence, once again there had been clear signs that they were on the right lines, more so now with the added benefit of the intelligent play of Edwards and he would finally make his keenly anticipated home debut the following Saturday against Kilmarnock when it wouldn't take him long to become a huge favourite with the fans. Almost opening his account in the very first minute of the eventual 3–2 victory with a vicious drive that had been brilliantly saved by goalkeeper Hunter and setting up a second for Joe Baker, Edwards brought the house down when scoring the winner himself with a spectacular 30-yard drive that gave the goalkeeper no chance. Even this early the captivating performance of the diminutive midfielder had confirmed that he would be yet another great acquisition. In only a few short months Eddie Turnbull had installed a renewed sense of purpose and self belief into the side and a seven-game unbeaten run before facing Rangers at Easter Road on Christmas Day had now seen a rise to third in the table.

An earlier impressive 2–0 victory over St Johnstone in Perth had merely confirmed Hibs' strength. Despite Edwards still in need of match fitness, O'Rourke clearly still recovering from a recent bout of flu and Cropley, Baker and Auld all unfit to be replaced by McEwan, Hazel and substitute Hamilton, Hibs had still gone on to dominate the game with a display that had not only impressed the Saints manager Ormond, but captain Alex Rennie who would later describe the Easter Road side on this performance as undoubtedly one of the best in the country.

While it was fairly unusual for league games to take place on Christmas Day it was not unknown, already occurring three times since the end of the war, the last occasion in 1965 when goals by Jim Scott, John McNamee and Peter Cormack had given Hibs a comfortable 3–1 win at Pittodrie. Now in a league game against Rangers at Easter Road that unfortunately had been marred throughout by crowd trouble, Alex Edwards had been in irresistible form. Although, against a visiting side that at best had merely been rugged competitors, Hibs dominating almost the entire 90 minutes of a game that should have been won well before the end. Goalless at the interval, as the teams were about to re-enter the field at the start of the second-half, trouble had broken out between rival fans in the covered enclosure behind the goals. In an attempt to escape the chaos dozens of spectators had spilled out onto the pitch as the police tried desperately to prevent the situation from getting completely out of hand and in the circumstances the referee had rightly called the players back into the safety of the dressing rooms until order had been restored. After a delay of several minutes it was felt safe enough for play to resume, and with the home side now causing all kinds of problems in the Rangers penalty area, the best chance of the game fell to Alex Cropley. Midway through the half he somehow managed to blast the ball high over the bar from close range with only the

SCOTTISH CUP DISAPPOINTMENT (1971-72)

goalkeeper to beat. It would prove an expensive miss. With just seconds remaining, Rangers, who had presented very little threat as an attacking force throughout the entire afternoon won a corner on the right. McLean's swinging kick looked Herriot's ball all the way until the goalkeeper appeared to have been deliberately impeded by Willie Johnston allowing Colin Stein to net easily with a header from close range. Despite vigorous appeals by Herriot and several of his teammates to referee Padden the goal was allowed to stand, the thoroughly undeserved victory now allowing Rangers to leapfrog Hibs into third place in the table.

On New Year's Day a scoreless home draw against Hearts, a game more noted for effort than skill would eventually turn out to be just the latest in the recent series of no-scoring draws between the sides and certainly not one to remember. It had now been four years since either had managed a goal in the holiday fixture, Hearts failing to score in any of the previous seven games against their city rivals. Hibs themselves had managed just four during the same period, leaving one scribe to suggest lightheartedly that the next player to score in the fixture should receive a Knighthood.

By this time the astute Turnbull had moved Pat Stanton into midfield where he could make much more of an impact on the proceedings, and despite the defeat by Rangers and the dropped point at Tynecastle, a recent newspaper poll had nominated Hibs as the most improved side in the country. During this time 45 goals had been scored in both the League and League Cup compared to 41 at the same stage the previous season, but the main difference had been in the goals against column with just 19 conceded compared to 36 the previous campaign, even more testimony to all the hard work put in by the defence at the start of the season.

Around this time Alex Cropley, who had improved out of all recognition since the arrival of Turnbull and was now playing the best football of his career, was said to have been attracting the attention of several English First Division sides. It was even rumoured that the Everton manager Harry Catterick had been among the crowd for the game against Hearts to cast an eye over the influential midfield player. Everton had just recently sold Alan Ball to Arsenal for £250,000 and according to unconfirmed reports the 'Gunners' had been about to make a bid for the

Hibs player when they learned of Ball's availability and now with money to spend, Everton were believed to have identified Cropley as their number one target as a replacement for the World Cup winner. Any bid for Cropley however had immediately been denied by Hibs but it would later turn out that Everton had actually tendered a bid in the region of more than £150,000, but for two players one Cropley the other unidentified. Not long before Dave Ewing had rejected an insulting £25,000 bid from the Crystal Palace manager Bert Head for Cropley, an increased offer of £50,000 also immediately turned down out of hand, but it was well known that the player was then being watched by several others including Arsenal, Liverpool and West Bromwich Albion. Cropley himself, though well aware of the interest, had no desire to leave Easter Road... at least for the moment.

It was not all good news however. Despite a promise to manager Turnbull that he had now changed his ways, just a few weeks after making his debut, Alex Edwards had once again found himself in trouble with officialdom when he was sent off during a surprise defeat by relegation-haunted East Fife at Bayview. Just five minutes into an ill-tempered second-half, Edwards had lashed out at John Love after just the latest in a series of crude tackles on the Hibs player by the inside-forward, referee Crawley having no hesitation in brandishing the red card. In truth it would have been extremely difficult to defend the behaviour of a player who had now been sent off five times in his senior career and booked on numerous other occasions, and it would now appear that he was never going to learn. Just a few weeks later in a game against Ayr United at Somerset Park Edwards had received yet another booking for kicking the ball away after disagreeing with the referee's decision, and one can only begin to wonder at the thoughts of Eddie Turnbull who would have been well aware that with the player's previous disciplinary record that he had taken a huge risk in signing the hugely talented but temperamental Fifer.

It was around then that the once traditional annual dinner dance at the North British Hotel in Princes Street had been reintroduced. Discontinued after the death of chairman Harry Swan some years earlier, the event had always proved extremely popular with the players, staff, guests and various other dignitaries

SCOTTISH CUP DISAPPOINTMENT (1971-72)

while also having a significant part in fostering team spirit and camaraderie. It was now also considered an important step in the rebuilding of a side whose exciting, fast, free-flowing football was beginning to bring the crowds back to Easter Road in numbers.

With Eric Stevenson now at Ayr United, Alex Edwards facing another lengthy suspension, and Joe Baker out with what promised to be another long-term injury, the side was now clearly lightweight up front. Rumours at the time had suggested that Hibs were about to make a move for Airdrie's Drew Jarvie, but instead Turnbull had turned his attention to Dundee United to sign the former Hearts forward Alan Gordon, and what a magnificent piece of business it would turn out to be. After less than a dozen reserve games for Hearts, in 1961 the then 17-year-old Heriot's schoolboy Gordon had made his first team debut for the Tynecastle side in a 2-1 victory against Celtic to become an almost immediate regular. A few months later he had also scored twice in a 4-1 victory against Hibs at Easter Road, the legendary Willie Bauld also scoring what would turn out to be his last ever goal against his archrivals. After six years at Tynecastle and now no longer guaranteed a first team place, Gordon had spent just over a year in South Africa with Durban United before returning to Hearts. A fall out with the club however had hastened his end at Tynecastle and in 1969 he had signed for Dundee United in a deal reputed to be worth around £8,000. After almost three seasons at Tannadice, the highly intelligent and eloquent Gordon, a prolific goalscorer with a particularly lethal prowess in the air, would join Hibs for the bargain fee of around £13,000 just two days before the transfer deadline day after a week of prolonged negotiations, a move apparently against the wishes of the recently appointed Dundee United manager Jim McLean who would later declare that he felt he had been 'done'. Turnbull had been a long-time admirer of the player, having tried to sign him while manager of Aberdeen, only for Hearts to reject his advances. It was apparently only then that he had turned his attentions to Morton's Joe Harper. Although we were not to know it at the time, the final piece in the jigsaw of what was soon to become a legendary side was now in place, Gordon along with his strike partner Jimmy O'Rourke, the perfect foil for the pace of Duncan on the left and the pinpoint accurate crosses of Edwards on the right. This, allied to the intelligent midfield probing of both Stanton and Cropley, the attacking flair of right-back Brownlie and the defensive capabilities of Herriot, Black, Blackley and Schaedler were about to make Hibs a side to be reckoned with.

Gordon made his debut in a 2–1 home defeat by Motherwell, a game in which Hibs did everything but score and certainly hadn't deserved to lose. However, despite lacking service, the newcomer who was yet to score on a debut, had done more than enough to suggest that he would be yet another tremendous asset.

In that season's Scottish Cup Hibs had been drawn away against League Cup holders Partick Thistle in the first round. In the week leading up to the game Alec Edwards had appeared before the disciplinary panel in relation to his earlier sending off against East Fife. According to Edwards himself it was widely accepted that if you appeared before the panel in the morning before they had partaken of a 'liquid lunch' then you were far more likely to receive a lighter sentence than if you were called in the afternoon. Unfortunately Edwards case would not be heard until early afternoon when, accompanied by the club lawyer, he had noticed that the chairman appeared to be asleep. Whether the rumour was true or not, he had received what many thought to be a savage eight-week suspension plus a £50 fine. At the same meeting a Clydebank player had been banned for nine weeks while yet another who had been up before the committee for the sixth time had merely received a seven-day suspension, the lack of consistency difficult to understand.

Edwards lengthy ban however would not start until the following week allowing him to play in the cup game against Partick Thistle at Firhill on the Saturday, and if selected it would be his last appearance in the competition until the semi-final stage, were Hibs to make it that far. As it would turn out he would sit out the cup game, his place taken by Johnny Hamilton forming a right-wing partnership with the recalled Jimmy O'Rourke.

The lifelong Hibs supporter O'Rourke who had been in the Scottish Schoolboys side that defeated England Schools at Wembley in the Victory Shield in 1961, could well have signed for Celtic with Manchester United and others also hovering in the background. However, there was only ever going to be one destination for the Hibs-mad youngster and that was Easter Road. At that time working in an electrical warehouse during the day and training at Easter Road in the evenings he had been earning rave reviews in the second team, performances that would ultimately earn him quick promotion. Surprised to be called away from work one afternoon, he arrived at Easter Road only to discover that he had been included in the side that would face Utrecht in the Fairs Cup later that evening. Still only 16, he became at that time not only the youngest player ever to make a first team appearance for the Easter Road side, but also the youngest ever to take part in a competitive European tournament. Despite receiving harsh treatment throughout the entire 90 minutes from his immediate opponent who would be jeered from the field at the end, the youngster had otherwise performed well with a goal disallowed for offside, and only a tremendous save by the goalkeeper in the late stages had prevented him from opening his account when his well struck shot from close range had been turned over the bar. His impressive all-round performance in the eventual 2–1 victory would result in him becoming an almost automatic first team choice.

Unfortunately, during a game against Dundee United at Tannadice the following season he had received a serious injury, later diagnosed as torn ligaments, a setback that would severely curtail his progress at Easter Road. While the physical recovery had taken several months, it would take the player much longer to get over the injury mentally, and although he would figure regularly in the first team during the following few seasons, frequently as a replacement in the case of injury, he had often struggled to hold down a permanent place. Frustrated, at the end of the previous campaign he had asked for a transfer, a move that had prevented him from accompanying the party on the two-week summer break to Majorca. However, with a new manager now in place he had withdrawn his demand, and for the next few seasons would go on to form a prolific goalscoring partnership with Alan Gordon. Although already a huge favourite with the Hibs fans because of his all-action and determined style of play, O'Rourke would later confess that he had Eddie Turnbull to thank for really making him a player.

Both Alan Gordon and Erich Schaedler would score their first goals for the club in a 2–0 Scottish Cup victory against Partick Thistle at Firhill, a result that would eventually see Hibs go all the way to that year's final. Watched by the biggest crowd of the day, the Edinburgh side had never at any time looked in any real danger of losing after Gordon had taken advantage of a misplaced clearance by a defender to thunder the ball past goalkeeper Alan Rough after just eight minutes. Just two minutes after the break the game was already as good as over when Schaedler added a second. A long throw by the full-back had found Gordon lurking at the edge of the penalty area who proceeded to nod the ball back to him. Without hesitation Schaedler then proceeded to blast a tremendous first time drive past the despairing dive of Rough from all of 25 yards and into the roof of the net to put the final result beyond doubt, a goal that not only surprised the Hibs fans inside the ground, but probably the player himself.

For several weeks the team had been playing well without always receiving the rewards their efforts had deserved, but in his post-match interview Turnbull had reportedly been well satisfied at the way things were progressing. Somewhat uncharacteristically however, for a manager that had normally tried to keep the players' feet firmly on the ground, the victory had also drawn the comment: 'We are in the second round draw on merit and with the right kind of luck we won't be far away at the end.'

Before that there would be a quite remarkable game at Brockville where Johnny Hamilton gave Hibs the lead after just ten seconds, even before many of the travelling fans had made their way into the ground. Direct from the kick-off a Gordon pass had found Hamilton at the edge of the opponent's penalty box. Hesitating only briefly, the youngster had then proceeded to crash a powerful drive past the Falkirk goalkeeper Donaldson, the strike just failing to beat the Scottish record of seven seconds by Willie Sharp of Partick Thistle against Queen of the South in 1947.

In a hard-fought encounter the points would not be won without cost. Ten minutes before half-time Cropley had been the victim of a rash tackle by the former Dunfermline and Rangers player Alex Ferguson just outside the home penalty area that left him in a crumpled heap on the ground as play was allowed to

SCOTTISH CUP DISAPPOINTMENT (1971–72)

continue. Eventually managing to make his way to the touchline for treatment he was to be replaced by substitute Joe Baker who was making his first appearance in almost three months after his own earlier injury. To make matters even worse as Cropley was being taken down the tunnel on a stretcher on his way to hospital he had been spat on by a supporter. X-Rays at the hospital would confirm that his left ankle was broken, an injury that would result in a player who at that time was well on top of his game missing the remainder of the season. Late in the game and the scores level at 2–2, Ferguson had been sent off after a clash with Erich Schaedler, Baker scoring what turned out to be the winner with a trademark flying header from a suspiciously offside-looking position in the dying minutes, the linesman initially raising his flag before lowering it again. Despite the understandably furious appeals of the Falkirk players who had hesitated briefly on seeing the linesman raise his flag, the goal had been allowed to stand, the hard-earned victory allowing Hibs to consolidate fourth place in the table. As the side was embarking on a run that would eventually take them all the way to the cup final, like so many before him and since, Cropley would now be starting out on the long soul-destroying road back to full fitness. Apart from the very real concern that your career could possibly be over, the biggest enemy in recovering from a serious long-term injury was boredom. With weeks of inactivity before the plaster is removed, followed by many weeks of gentle exercises gradually increasing in tempo, all the time the player desperate to get back into action. Cropley would later joke that during this time he must have watched every cowboy film ever made on TV.

Sometime later during a coaching course at Largs, the then St Mirren manager Ferguson had asked John Fraser to introduce him to Turnbull, only for Fraser to be told in no uncertain terms by the Hibs manager: 'No f****** chance, he broke Cropley's leg.'

The signing of the 27-year-old Alan Gordon had added a completely new dimension to the side, his ability in the air creating constant danger in the opposition penalty area, and of the next ten games only two would end in defeat. During this time Gordon had scored five goals including a double in a completely one-sided 7–1 home victory against the unfortunate St Johnstone,

Hibs' biggest win of the season and a game that would also see the return of Alex Edwards after his lengthy lay-off.

Included in the impressive run had been victories over both Airdrie and Aberdeen in the Scottish Cup as Hibs progressed to the semi-final stage of the competition. In the home game against Aberdeen this time it would take O'Rourke all of 17 seconds to open the scoring, a goal by Baker in the second half sealing the 2–0 victory, Hibs' first Scottish Cup success over 'the Dons' for 24 years.

In the days leading up to the game the Easter Road season ticket holders had been furious to discover that the precious briefs – with the exception of those held by the debenture holders – would not now be applicable for the game and that they would have to pay at the gate instead. A decision that would ultimately lead to numerous letters both to the newspapers and the club itself all complaining at what had been seen merely as a blatant attempt to exploit the expected huge demand for the game and extract more revenue from loyal supporters. Previously a season ticket had always entitled the holder admission to all domestic games, several supporters reminding the club that they seemed to have forgotten that when things had not been going well in the past it was the loyal season ticket holders that had helped make up the numbers by paying in advance. The chairman of the Supporters Club had also voiced his concern over the recent closure of the Boys' and OAP's gate insisting that young fans in particular, the future lifeblood of the club, should be encouraged not chased away. Whether Hart's plan had influenced the turnout or not, a disappointingly low crowd of just over 25,000 had watched a game that had been expected to have attracted over 40,000.

Completely missing the point a statement later released by the club suggested that the Hibs supporters already more than received value for their season ticket money, pointing out that Aberdeen and Hearts fans were already paying more. However, it would not to be the last time that Hart would fall out with his own supporters.

By now Hibs knew that their semi-final opponents would be Rangers, the fourth meeting of the sides in the competition in as many years. The recent St Johnstone result, but perhaps more

SCOTTISH CUP DISAPPOINTMENT (1971-72)

importantly the performance, would no doubt have given the watching Rangers manager Willie Waddell plenty to think about.

In the semi-final at Hampden, an O'Rourke goal had cancelled out an earlier strike by McDonald as Hibs came storming back in the second half, but despite a much improved performance that at times had left the Ibrox side hanging on and desperate for the final whistle, there was to be no more scoring and for a second consecutive season it would again require a replay to separate the sides. Before the game however the chairman of the Hibs Supporters Association had felt it necessary to advise the Easter Road fans not to flaunt their colours after the earlier trouble between both sets of fans, although the game itself passed without any real problems on either side. In the replay Hibs' eventual 2–0 victory had failed to adequately reflect the Edinburgh side's almost total dominance of the game, and according to one newspaper the following morning: 'only rash finishing had prevented the occasion from developing into Rangers unhappiest experience at Hampden since losing 7–1 to Celtic in the 1957 League Cup Final.' Yet another found it 'almost embarrassing to see one side with such superiority in a cup semi-final'. With both Stanton and Edwards in brilliant form dictating play from midfield, Hibs had started the game in determined mood. Stanton himself opened the scoring after only 12 minutes with a shot that had been deflected past the Rangers goalkeeper McCloy, a lead which on the balance of play, could, and should well have been more. With Rangers at times reeling under the onslaught, the final result was eventually put beyond doubt midway through the second half when Edwards completed a totally one-sided display with a low shot from close range to send Hibs into their first Scottish Cup final for 14 years, the convincing victory already guaranteeing the Edinburgh side a place in the following seasons Cup Winners' Cup.

On the eve of the Cup final a surprise announcement that the immensely popular Joe Baker had been freed had left the Hibs supporters stunned, the decision probably even taking the player himself completely by surprise. Baker had recently found himself on the fringes of the first team either as a substitute or replaced during games, possibly early indications that he would perhaps not be part of Eddie Turnbull's long-term plans. His last ever goal, his 200th in 257 appearances in all games during his two spells with the club, a quite phenomenal record, had been scored in Hibs 3–0 victory against Partick Thistle almost two months earlier. His last ever appearance in a green and white jersey as a substitute in the semi-final replay against Rangers. To give Turnbull his due Baker had missed a large part of the season through injury including a spell in hospital to have a calcium growth removed from a thigh muscle, an injury according to the manager that had resulted in the player losing much of his devastating pace although this was not an opinion shared by all. While several of the players were convinced that Baker had not lost any of his previous sharpness, others felt that although he still had his devastating pace he no longer had his tremendous acceleration from a standing start, others however that Turnbull, who did not appreciate anyone receiving more exposure than him was envious of the fan favourite Baker and that this had merely been an excuse to free him. Although both Baker and Turnbull would meet occasionally over the following years the atmosphere between the pair would remain visibly frosty until the very end.

Incredibly, despite his illustrious playing career the cup final against Celtic could well have been Baker's last chance to collect his first winners medal in senior football, the nearest when Hibs had lost narrowly to Clyde in the 1958 Scottish Cup final. In 1966 he had been included in the initial 40-man England squad for the World Cup finals only to drop out when the pool had later been reduced to its final 22 missing out on a possible opportunity to win a World Cup Winner's medal. At Nottingham Forest the following year he had been a member of the side defeated by Spurs at the semi-final stage of the FA Cup competition, while ending that same season as runners-up to champions Manchester United. Magnanimous despite the obvious disappointment of his free transfer, Baker remained generous in his praise for the current Hibs team under Turnbull, a side he felt that would have been more than capable of holding its own against any of the teams he had played with during his long career. A goalscorer in both legs of the famous Fairs Cup victory over Barcelona in the early 1960s, it is not widely known that Barcelona had earlier tried to

SCOTTISH CUP DISAPPOINTMENT (1971–72)

sign the player after a game between the sides during the club's close season tour of Spain in 1959 when an approach said to have been worth around £40,000 had been rejected.

Just days after the semi-final Hibs continued their recent dominance over Rangers with a 2–1 victory in Glasgow, a result that had now lifted the Easter Road side into third place in the table. At that time Rangers had just recently qualified for the final of the Cup Winners' Cup that was soon to take place in Barcelona against Moscow Dynamo. Bearing in mind that the game at Ibrox had been between both the current Scottish Cup and Cup Winners' Cup finalists, it would be a major understatement to describe the attendance estimated to have been just over 10,000 as disappointing. That afternoon Hibs had taken the opportunity to rest both Alex Edwards and Arthur Duncan for the final, the 16-year-old former Edinburgh Thistle player Alex McGhee making his first team debut while there had also been a return for Bertie Auld who so far had only managed fleeting appearances from the substitute bench during the previous few months. After a fairly dull goalless first half, the game had suddenly burst into life after the interval when Jimmy O'Rourke opened the scoring from the penalty spot after Alan Gordon had been brought down inside the box by goalkeeper McCloy. Although Rangers managed to pull one back through Derek Johnstone just two minutes later, Bertie Auld scored what was to prove be the winner from a 20-yard free kick, a goal that undoubtedly would have given the former Celtic player even greater satisfaction by scoring what would turn out to be his last ever goal in professional football at the home of the Parkhead side's greatest rivals. In truth the end result had once again greatly flattered Rangers and many of the meagre crowd had already started to make their way to the exits long before the end. The victory however should have been the perfect tonic for Hibs before the forthcoming Scottish Cup final a few days later.

As expected their opponents in the final would be champions Celtic, the Glasgow side's fifth appearance at the ultimate stage of the competition over the previous eight seasons, and the first Scottish Cup final between the sides for almost 50 years. In Edinburgh the demand for tickets had been incredible, one newly engaged couple said to have spent over 18 hours camped outside

Easter Road to ensure receiving the coveted briefs and would later be joined by many others. In the morning the headmaster of the adjacent Norton Park School where Alex Cropley had been a former pupil, would take pity on some with a welcoming cup of tea, a marvellous gesture that had been greatly appreciated by all. However, after both clubs had received their usual allocation for the game, the remaining tickets had gone on public sale, but unbelievably only in Glasgow. Although it had been possible to pay at the gate on the day, it was a fact that didn't go down too well in Edinburgh and was perhaps yet another example of what was commonly felt to have been the west coast bias of the Scottish football authorities. On the football front, although Hibs had more than demonstrated recently that they could compete against Glasgow's 'big two', being a final there had possibly been a slight lack of self belief, the players fully aware that they would be facing one of the best sides in Europe at that time. On the day a convoy of almost a 100 coaches and a couple of football specials leaving from Waverley Station had been joined by hundreds of cars, all making their way through to Hampden in the hope that at last this was to be Hibs' year. Unfortunately, according to one player years later 'we would have been far better staying at home.' As Leeds United were defeating Arsenal in the Centenary Cup Final at Wembley, well over 105,000 supporters had packed inside Hampden, including an estimated 30,000 that had made their way from Edinburgh, one an 83-year-old who had actually witnessed Hibs' last win the cup in 1902. As to the game itself, after just two minutes John Hazel had been harshly penalised for a tackle on Johnstone in midfield. From the resulting free kick deep into the Hibs penalty area, Alan Gordon who had been delegated the task of marking the dangerous Billy McNeil at free kicks and corners had been caught ball watching allowing the Celtic captain to open the scoring from close range to leave the Easter Road side even this early with a mountain to climb. Gordon would make up for his earlier mistake ten minutes later when taking advantage of a low Duncan cross from the left to lash the ball high into the net to equalise despite the close attentions of centre-half McNeil and goalkeeper Williams. Another

SCOTTISH CUP DISAPPOINTMENT (1971–72)

goal shortly before half-time by the former Motherwell player Dixie Deans, the first of three he was to score that afternoon, the first hat-trick in a Scottish Cup final for almost 70 years, had given his side an interval lead. Ten minutes into the second half Deans scored again after taking advantage of a terrible mix-up in the Hibs penalty area when Brownlie had been short with a passback to goalkeeper Herriot and this time there would be no way back. With Hibs now forced to push men forward in an attempt to save the game Celtic took full advantage of the extra space at the back to score another three in the final quarter of an hour, the eventual 6–1 scoreline the heaviest in a Scottish Cup final since Renton had defeated Cambuslang by the same score 84 years before. Midway through the second half Arthur Duncan, one of the few Hibs players to have performed to anything like their true potential that afternoon had been carried off after receiving a head knock to be replaced by Bertie Auld and would spend a few days in hospital suffering from concussion. After a tremendous career spanning almost 18 seasons, it would turn out to be Auld's last ever game and he would soon be offered a coaching role at Easter Road.

Hibs had undoubtedly missed the balance that the injured Cropley would have provided but even the absence of the inspirational midfielder could not be used as an excuse for the humiliating defeat. Although Hibs had missed another couple of opportunities to score again, in reality quite simply many of the players didn't turn up.

Hibs: Herriot, Brownlie and Schaedler, Stanton, Black and Blackley, Edwards, Hazel Gordon, Cropley and Duncan (sub) Auld
Celtic: Williams, Craig and Brogan, Murdoch, McNeil and Connolly, Johnstone, Deans, Macari, Dalglish and Callaghan (sub) Lennox
Referee: A McKenzie (Larbert)

As the bitterly disappointed Hibs fans made their weary way back to Edinburgh after what had been a hugely embarrassing defeat, in the Hampden dressing room the mood had understandably been subdued, manager Eddie Turnbull who had almost missed the game because of illness, telling his obviously bitterly disappointed players to lift their heads that they would soon be back. After the game Jock Stein, magnanimous in victory and no doubt recognising the quality of his opponents, would say that 'he hoped for the sake of Eddie Turnbull that Hibs would win something with this team next season.' Both managers would ultimately be proved right.

After the game John Blackley had met up with his mum and dad in the Hampden car park. When his dad asked to see his medal the clearly still desperately disappointed Blackley threw the medal the length of the car park, his dad running to retrieve it. The humiliating cup final defeat apart, a game according to Turnbull that had possibly come too soon for his side, there had been more than enough evidence during the previous nine months to suggest that the club was on the right lines. The inspired signings of Herriot, Edwards and Gordon had helped develop the latent talent already at the club, and optimism was high that things could only get better, and according to Turnbull the results and performances had already been well ahead of his expectations at that stage. During the season 21 players had been used, seven only sparingly including the youngsters Dennis Nelson and Alex McGhee who had featured just once and Alex Pringle twice. 62 league goals had been scored compared to the 47 the previous season, but again the biggest difference had been in the goals against column with just 34 conceded compared to 53 the previous campaign. Jimmy O'Rourke, now the longest serving player at the club had ended the season as top goalscorer with 15 in all games as Hibs eventually finished fourth in the table behind Celtic, Rangers and Aberdeen as opposed to twelfth the previous season. As runners-up in the cup final Hibs had automatically qualified for the Cup Winners' Cup for the first time, the 62 goals scored throughout the season also enough for them to qualify for the following seasons Drybrough Cup, a recently inaugurated sponsored pre-season competition that would be competed by the four top scoring sides in each division.

Figures released by the Scottish League around that time had also revealed that while attendances at the majority of the Scottish

SCOTTISH CUP DISAPPOINTMENT (1971–72)

sides had been dropping alarmingly during the season, as much as 20,000 for Edinburgh rivals Hearts, at Easter Road they had risen by more than 53,000. Despite the otherwise disappointing end to the season there had been enough highlights throughout the entire campaign to indicate that the club was heading in the right direction.

At the end of the season John Brownlie had won his fourth full cap in a 1–0 defeat by England at Hampden. Displaying his by now well recognised attacking flair he almost opened the scoring inside the first few minutes after his lob caught out goalkeeper Banks before a ball that many claimed to have already crossed the line was eventually cleared to safety. In a foul-filled encounter that would later be described as an absolute disgrace and perhaps the nastiest ever meeting between the sides, a first half goal by Alan Ball eventually gave England victory and the Home Championship title. Regardless, in a game that would not be remembered long for its good football and sportsmanship, Brownlie's assured performance would have done his growing reputation no harm.

In the end of the season clear-out goalkeeper Roy Baines, Alex Pringle and Dennis Nelson had been among the dozen players freed. Pringle would soon join Dundee and Baines his former Easter Road colleague Chris Shevlane at Morton. The highly rated Nelson who had joined the club from Broxburn in 1969 and had made just one appearance for the first team would soon join Dunfermline. After his pre-season in the starting 11, goalkeeper Eddie Pryce had managed only around half a dozen games for the third team, and now surplus to requirements, like Shevlane had been released midway through the season to return to the Junior ranks.

A proposed three-game close season tour of Canada had been cancelled almost at the last minute, and instead the players had all enjoyed a 13-day trip to San Marino only a short distance from the millionaire's playground at Cannes on the French Riviera, an area that had been a popular destination for the former Hibs player Gordon Smith during the 1950s. Although not yet back to full fitness, Alex Cropley whose absence in the cup final had been a huge miss, had also been included in the party along with the 16-year-old Alex McGhee. Cropley would later relate that as the team resplendent in their new club blazers were exiting the coach on arriving at their hotel in San Marino, a couple of elderly American tourists were overheard saying: 'Oh look, that must be the band arriving.' There would be no games on the trip, purely rest and relaxation in anticipation of what would turn out to be a truly momentous season.

The League Cup and Victory at Tynecastle (1972–73)

THE PREVIOUS SEASON's cup final humiliation apart, Eddie Turnbull's second season at Easter Road would be one of high expectation. During the summer, Hibs, or more precisely Pat Stanton, had become embroiled in a bitter war of words with the Scotland manager Tommy Docherty. Several months earlier the club had been asked to release both John Brownlie and Stanton for Scotland's forthcoming mini-World Cup tournament in Brazil. Hibs however had agreed to release one or the other but not both. Docherty had then opted for the experienced Stanton but as the player's wife had just recently given birth to their second child, on the advice of a doctor that she was badly in need of a holiday Stanton had understandably pulled out of the squad. The news of the player's withdrawal had been relayed to the SFA by letter accompanied by a doctor's certificate and that was thought to be the end of the matter. Docherty however, clearly infuriated that he had not been contacted personally by the player, had now asked Hibs to release John Brownlie for the trip in his place but for whatever reason Turnbull had been reluctant to do so. Scotland had initially agreed to travel to Brazil only if a first-class pool of players had been available and perhaps understandably Docherty had been frustrated at a number of withdrawals and had not been slow in letting his feelings known. An official statement released by Hibs regarding the Brownlie situation had also made it clear that the club were surprised that no outcry had been made when only one of the four proposed Celtic players had agreed to travel to Brazil and that the Rangers player Sandy Jardine whose wife was then expecting a baby had also been allowed to withdraw without complaint. Docherty now stated that although he was a huge fan of a player that he had only recently described as better than England's Bobby Moore, neither Stanton nor for that matter the Chelsea player Charlie Cooke, would ever play for Scotland again while he was the manager. The issue would eventually be resolved but not for several months, Docherty eventually apologising for any 'misunderstanding', adding that Stanton would now be recalled for the forthcoming World Cup match against Denmark at Hampden in November. The player's recall to the side would appear to have been a major 'coincidence', occurring immediately after a meeting of the International Selection Committee, and it now seems pretty obvious that Docherty had been ordered to reinstate the Hibs captain.

In preparation for what would turn out to be another demanding but ultimately rewarding season the club had embarked on a three-game tour of Ireland. In a 2–0 victory against Home Farm in the opening match, Alan Gordon had the misfortune to fracture his cheekbone after a collision with an opponent in the first few minutes to be replaced by O'Rourke, an injury fortunately that would not prevent him from being ready for the start of the new season. In a 2–0 win against Waterford a few days later the 17-year-old former grounds staff youngster Willie Murray had made a goalscoring debut only two minutes after replacing Alex Cropley at half-time. At the start of the previous season Tom Hart had resurrected Hibs' third team that, although proving highly successful, had been discontinued as a cost cutting measure in the early 1950s. As well as several appearances for the reserves, Murray, just one of several promising youngsters on Hibs' books at that time had ended the previous season as the top goalscorer in the third team and was yet another predicted to have a bright future ahead of him at Easter Road.

The former Hibs goalkeeper Roy Baines, then a registered player with Morton, was to have faced his former teammates as a guest signing in the final tour game against Cork Hibs that had eventually ended goalless, but had been unable to make the journey to Ireland in time for the kick-off. A surprise visitor in the Hibs party however had been the former Motherwell and Scotland player Wilson Humphries who had been invited to accompany the team on the trip by Tom Hart and immediately after the return to Scotland his appointment as first team coach would be confirmed. A member of the Motherwell side that defeated Hibs

THE LEAGUE CUP AND VICTORY AT TYNECASTLE (1972–73)

in the 1950 League Cup Final and also a Scottish Cup winner against Celtic in 1952, after 10 years at Fir Park Humphries would later have spells at St Mirren, Dundee United and Hamilton before taking over as manager at Love Street. His time in Paisley however would be brief when resigning the previous January. Disillusioned, he had turned his back on the game to return to teaching, and would later confess that only the opportunity to work with Eddie Turnbull would have tempted him back into football. The gregarious Humphries had a fairly unusual but otherwise humorous party piece. Lying on a bench in the dressing room he would lift his legs high into the air take a cigarette lighter from his pocket and proceed to light his flatulence, the sheet of flame shooting across the dressing room leaving everyone in hysterics. Extremely popular with the rest of the players, the former English teacher was perhaps the ideal person to lift the mood in the dressing room and a perfect foil for the customary dourness of the manager. Humphries would now join Stan Vincent, physiotherapist Tom McNiven and former player John Fraser as part of the backroom staff, all having a significant part to play in the development of the club during the following few years.

A product of the Edinburgh Thistle side that had supplied Hibs with several players over the years including Lawrie Reilly and Archie Buchanan, the versatile John Fraser had joined the club in 1954 as yet another potential replacement for the great Gordon Smith, making his first team debut in Hibs' 5–1 away victory against East Fife in the November. Comfortable on wing, centre-forward or full-back, he had been a member of the Hibs side that lost only narrowly to Clyde in the 1958 Scottish Cup final, and after 12 seasons and almost 300 appearances wearing the green and white he had spent a short spell as player-coach with Stenhousemuir. Before leaving Easter Road he had been assured by the then manager Bob Shankly that if possible he would be brought back in some capacity in the future. Initially returning to coach the youngsters in the evenings, the position had eventually been made full-time and during the following decade he would go on to serve under four different managers, Shankly, MacFarlane, Ewing and now Eddie Turnbull.

Tom McNiven had been the youngest trainer and physiotherapist in the game when joining Third Lanark five years before, aged just 24, at one stage effectively taking charge of the side for a short time after the resignation of a manager before a replacement could be found. Joining Hibs in 1963 as a direct replacement for Eddie Turnbull after the latter's surprise resignation, McNiven had already agreed to sign for Morton when he became aware of Hibs' interest, and fortunately for a generation of Hibs and later Scotland players, Morton did not stand in the way of his joining the Easter Road side, coincidently on the very same day as Pat Stanton. A former Stonehouse Violet player and runner of some repute, McNiven was another who was extremely popular with the players. As well as his medical expertise, particularly an unsurpassed talent for strapping an injury and the patience required to help a player recover mentally from an injury – something that was often overlooked in those days – perhaps more importantly he could be trusted not to pass on any of the gossip or rumours that are usually to be associated with a treatment room. Generally considered to have been well before his time, he was probably only truly appreciated by the players when they had experienced what was on offer after they had moved elsewhere.

The former Hibs player Stan Vincent completed the backroom staff looking after the East of Scotland side playing out of City Park. Signed from Cowdenbeath during the 1963–64 season Vincent had made his debut in a 0–0 draw against Dunfermline, scoring his first goal for the club in a 3–2 victory in the two team Festival of Sport Competition in Cannes of all places just three days later. Although he would also collect a Summer Cup Winner's medal the following season he would struggle to hold down a regular first team place at Easter Road before a move to Falkirk. Later, he would move on to St Johnstone and East Fife, before being released by the Irish side Ballymena the previous season to look after the Easter Road youngsters.

With Herriot now the only goalkeeper on the books, Turnbull had moved to sign the 19-year-old former Scottish Junior international Bobby Robertson from Whitburn Juniors. Previously with Rangers, the highly rated youngster had failed to make the first team at Ibrox but now with full-time training under his belt he

THE LEAGUE CUP AND VICTORY AT TYNECASTLE (1972-73)

looked forward to another opportunity to make the breakthrough into the topflight at Easter Road. Unfortunately it would be asking a lot of any youngster to replace the experienced Herriot and although he would make several first team appearances including a couple in Europe, he would join Bonnyrigg Rose at the end of the following season.

Once again the new campaign would kick off with the sponsored Drybrough Cup competition featuring the top four scoring sides from each division the previous season. The inaugural tournament had been won by Jimmy Bonthrone's Aberdeen when defeating Celtic 2–1 at Pittodrie, but perhaps predictably, despite Rangers and Celtic's initial reluctance to take part, particularly the latter, the final of a competition that had proved immediately popular with the fans had now been moved to Glasgow.

At a time when sponsorship in the game was still very much a sensitive subject, in 1970 the Watney Cup had been the very first football competition in the entire country to be backed financially by a commercial interest, Derby County defeating Manchester United 4–1 in that year's final and would soon be followed by the Texaco Cup and later in 1975 the Anglo Scottish Cup. The Drybrough Cup however had been the first ever sponsored football tournament exclusively for Scottish sides and would give Hibs an early opportunity to avenge the hugely embarrassing defeat in the previous season's cup final.

Designed to create more goals and entertainment, the tournament had been played under experimental rules that you could now only be offside if inside a line drawn from touchline to touchline 18 yards from goal. Arthur Duncan immediately took to the system and would sometimes casually walk along the entire 18-yard line and back again taking a couple of defenders who were all well aware of his devastating pace along with him, allowing his teammates to take advantage of the space that had been left.

By now the green and white hooped collar had been replaced by the more distinctive all white crew-neck, the previous all white socks reverting back to the traditional green topped by a broad white band.

After a 4–0 home win over Second Division Montrose in the opening round Hibs had been drawn to face Rangers in the semi-final at Easter Road. In a midfield that had been almost totally dominated by Edwards, Stanton, and Cropley once again in terms of football ability alone there had been only one team in it. Any attempt by the visitors to nullify the fast skilful football of the home side with their usual physical and aggressive play proving ineffectual, the eventual 3–0 scoreline failed to adequately to reflect the huge gulf between the sides. Yet again the game had been marred by violence both on and off the field. In a nasty foul-filled first half, Stanton put Hibs ahead just before break and within seconds trouble had broken out in the covered enclosure behind the goals. The area soon resembling a war zone as the air was filled with a hail of bottles, cans and coins, several supporters were injured as they made a desperate attempt to escape the turmoil taking place all around them and it would be ten minutes before the police could finally manage to restore order. As well as several dozen arrests, several fans had required hospital treatment including a police officer with a suspected fractured skull. While the Hibs fans had been in no way blameless, the majority of the trouble appeared to have been caused by the visiting support, the traditional covered enclosure at the home end of the ground that had earlier been identified by the police as a potential trouble spot, seen to be liberally bedecked with blue and white scarves. After the eventual restart Rangers had created a couple of chances, only for two goals by Alan Gordon to finally confirm Hibs' superiority and they would now face Celtic in the final at Hampden on the Saturday.

After the final whistle the visiting supporters had reportedly left a trail of destruction from the stadium all the way into the centre of the town, a football special from Waverley containing over 200 fans allegedly taking over three hours to reach Glasgow, forced to stop over a dozen times before reaching its final destination and on several occasions before it had even left Edinburgh. It appeared that not a single carriage had escaped major damage with toilet doors torn off, bulbs smashed, windows broken, fire extinguishers damaged, and several of the carriage ceilings wrecked. With the final damage estimated to have been in the region of £5,000, the incidents seriously called into question the future use of football specials for fans of the Ibrox club. Glasgow's senior magistrate

THE LEAGUE CUP AND VICTORY AT TYNECASTLE (1972–73)

Baillie Stewart Stevenson had gone even further by suggesting that in future cattle trucks should be used for the hooligan fans instead. The Rangers General Manager Willie Waddell had also been forthright in his condemnation of the wanton vandalism while also making reference to the club's recent embarrassing night of shame in Barcelona after the Cup Winners' Cup Final against Moscow Dynamo when because of the significant rioting that was then taking place on the pitch the cup had to be presented to the victorious Rangers players in the safety of the dressing room. The rioting that continued into the city centre later that evening would eventually result in Rangers being banned from European competition for two years, later reduced to one on appeal.

The final at Hampden against Celtic had now presented Hibs with an early opportunity, even if only in some small measure, to atone for the humiliating Scottish Cup final defeat just a few months earlier but already many were wondering just how the Easter Road players would react to the situation mentally after the highly embarrassing result. Before the kick-off the Hibs fans among the near 50,000 crowd had been surprised to discover that Alex Edwards had been left out of the starting line up and had not even been on the bench. Any enquiry to the manager as to why the influential midfielder had been left out would merely result in the curt reply 'He's just not, that's all.' The 'mystery' however would be cleared up after the game when it was revealed that Edwards had been attending hospital as a day patient regarding a minor complaint and had been unable to make the game. Meanwhile, showing little sign of an inferiority complex Hibs started the game well and after just four minutes Alan Gordon was on hand to take advantage of a mistake by Williams after the goalkeeper had failed to hold a long-range shot from Stanton. Although they had then been forced to survive an early spell of Celtic pressure Gordon added a second midway through the half. After the interval an own goal by the Celtic captain Billy McNeil now meant that with just under 30 minutes remaining Hibs now held what was felt to be a commanding 3–0 lead. Immediately after the goal, trouble had broken out on the terracing at the Celtic end of the ground, a number of fans spilling out on to the pitch in an attempt to escape the flying missiles. With several requiring treatment on the field, the game was held up for several minutes before the police could finally take control of the situation. The delay appeared to have unsettled Hibs, and quickly taking the initiative Celtic came storming back to level things, Jimmy Johnstone scoring the equaliser in the very last minute to force extra time.

The interval however gave the astute Turnbull time to reorganise the side and the goal rush that had now been anticipated by the Celtic fans failed to materialise. With Hibs now starting to dominate the extra-time period, a tremendous 25-yard drive by substitute Jimmy O'Rourke who had replaced Hamilton at the end of the 90 minutes; and another in the very last seconds of the game by Arthur Duncan from what appeared to be an almost impossible angle near the bye-line, would give the Edinburgh side what in the end was a thoroughly deserved 5–3 victory, the players each standing to share the promised £1,000 bonus for the winners. Interviewed immediately after the game, a visibly elated Eddie Turnbull had been delighted for his players: 'They came to Hampden with last season's 6–1 Scottish Cup defeat by Celtic still fresh in their minds, but overcame this and fought back after the five-minute crowd stoppage had shattered their rhythm.'

While there's no way the Drybrough Cup could be considered a major competition, make no mistake, particularly after the previous embarrassing cup final defeat it had been heralded as a great victory by everyone at Easter Road, particularly as both sides of the 'Old Firm' had been overcome to win the trophy. Turnbull however had remained cautious in reminding not only his players, but the now ecstatic supporters, that the season had not yet started, adding that while he was happy for them, 'until they do it during the season in the League Cup, League or Scottish Cup then they will have proved nothing'.

Hibs: Herriot, Brownlie and Schaedler, Stanton, Black and Blackley, Hamilton, Hazel, Gordon, Cropley and Duncan (subs) O'Rourke and Robertson
Celtic: Williams, McGrain and Brogan, Murdoch, McNeil and Connolly, Johnstone, Deans, Dalglish, Macari and Callaghan (sub) Wilson and Connaghan
Referee: Bill Mullan (Dalkeith)

THE LEAGUE CUP AND VICTORY AT TYNECASTLE (1972-73)

For the second time in just a few days a game involving the Easter Road side had been disrupted by crowd trouble and although most of the disorder had appeared to have been caused mainly by the opposition fans on both occasions, Hibs would later be required by the SFA to forward a report of the incidents. The BBC had also come in for some heavy criticism by failing to show the crowd disruptions, both during the earlier game against Rangers and also in the recorded highlights of the cup final that were shown on TV later that evening. Denying censorship, the television company now claimed that the cameras had been shut down during the interval as normal, seemingly oblivious to the fact that the unsavoury incident at Hampden had taken place midway through the second half while the game was still in progress. According to a company spokesman later, the commentator had been unsure as to whether he should mention the incident that evening and had decided not to, the excuse doing little to allay the fears of the supporters from the east side of the country that this was yet another example of the 'Glasgow bias' at work.

In the final preparations for the forthcoming season the English First Division side West Bromwich Albion had agreed to play a friendly at Easter Road. At half-time the Drybrough Cup had been paraded around the ground in front of the delighted supporters, and although the spelling of the sponsor's name on the banner had been misspelt, few in the ground were caring. The game itself however had failed to live up to expectations after the excitement of just a few days earlier, and despite Hibs' almost total domination throughout the entire 90 minutes, the visitors had capitalised on a couple of uncharacteristic errors by goalkeeper Jim Herriot to record a 2-0 victory. While the defeat would obviously not have been to the liking of the manager, Turnbull would no doubt have been delighted with the overall performance. Several English managers had been at the game, including Everton's Harry Catterick who was said to have been watching Alex Cropley. Later rumours that Manchester United had already made an approach for John Brownlie were described by Turnbull as 'absolute rubbish.'

At that time talks had been taking place between the police and Glasgow's 'Big Two' regarding the hooligan problem, but only that morning Hibs had revealed their own plans to help solve the issue. The announcement that the covered enclosure behind the goals at the north end of the ground that had been a magnet for troublemakers almost since the beginning, was now to be fenced off and seated, would no doubt have delighted the Lothian and Borders constabulary. Violence at football matches in this country was nothing new, stretching back to the late 1880s including a riot between rival Rangers and Celtic fans after the 1909 cup final replay at Hampden when the turnstiles had been set alight on learning that there was to be no extra time, only another replay. More recently there had been trouble between the sides at Parkhead on New Year's Day 1952, but regrettably the incidents in the game had been steadily increasing since the mid-1960s.

The season proper would now kick off with a new look League Cup format that for the first time would feature teams from the lower league in the same section as the First Division sides. Also, now the top two from each section would go forward into the later stages of the competition as opposed to just one in previous years. The new format however would fail to prove universally popular with the fans, particularly during the early stages when just 3,876 had attended Hibs game against Queen of the South at Palmerston, and only 1,693 against Queen's Park at Hampden, attendance figures only slightly better than the 1,029 that had bothered turning up for Queen's Park's home game against Aberdeen a few days later.

After home and away victories over both Queen of the South and Queen's Park, a 4–1 away defeat by Aberdeen had left Hibs having to win the return game in Edinburgh by several goals if they were to have any hope of topping the section. After almost totally dominating the opening period at Pittodrie, Hibs had found themselves three behind, all scored inside a 13-minute spell in the first half leaving them with it all to do in the second period. An Edwards strike after the interval gave Hibs the chance to get back into the game when with just 20 minutes remaining, Joe Harper put a game that was anything but as one-sided as the final scoreline would suggest beyond all doubt. The strike however would be shrouded in controversy. After chasing a long through ball, Harper had immediately drawn up, realising he was several

THE LEAGUE CUP AND VICTORY AT TYNECASTLE (1972–73)

yards offside and allowing the ball to run back to Herriot. The goalkeeper left his goal to side foot the ball up field for the free kick to be taken, only for Harper to now realise that the referee had not blown his whistle and he proceeded to lob the ball over the stranded Herriot and into the net to finally secure victory for the home side. Despite the furious protests of the Hibs players that had led to the game being held up for several minutes, the goal was allowed to stand. That evening the 18-year-old Tony Higgins had made his first team debut in place of the injured Alan Gordon, but perhaps understandably the inexperienced youngster could do little to affect the final result. Like Murray, Higgins was yet another of a number of promising youngsters on Hibs' books at that time. A provisional signing from Kilsyth St Pats, he had joined the full-time staff during the previous season, but after only a few games for the reserves Turnbull had had absolutely no hesitation in throwing the tall, heavily built youngster into the fray. The intelligent Higgins had earlier been faced with the dilemma of either continuing his education at university or becoming a full-time footballer, and it was only after being persuaded by Turnbull that he had the ability to make it in the game that he had decided to turn his back on a degree in engineering.

In the return leg against Aberdeen at Easter Road on the Wednesday, unfortunately goals by Duncan and O'Rourke in the eventual 2–1 victory would not be enough for Hibs to top the table. Although both sides had finished the section level on the same number of points, the 'Dons' goal difference had proved superior. With the top two teams now going forward to the later stages of the competition Hibs were through to the second round where they would face Dundee United. Although the Hibs fans could not possibly have known it at the time, that evening at Easter Road they had just witnessed the first ever outing as a complete unit in a competitive fixture of an 11 that were destined to become part of Scottish football folklore. Herriot, Brownlie and Schaedler, Stanton, Black and Blackley, Edwards, O'Rourke, Gordon, Cropley and Duncan – the Turnbull's Tornadoes.

After the Drybrough Cup success against champions Celtic, the expectations amongst the Hibs support were now even greater than before. But, on the opening day of the new league campaign, a goal by Joe Harper at Pittodrie had been the difference between the sides before Hibs faced Hearts in the first Edinburgh derby of the season at Easter Road.

To the surprise of the supporters, Hibs had taken the field wearing a changed strip of all dark green jerseys with white collars and cuffs in a move that was said to have been specifically designed to combat Hearts' then 'Ajax' style jerseys that featured more white than usual. With the covered enclosure behind the goals now completely fenced off, a disappointingly poor crowd of just over 21,000, far less than had been expected, turned out to be the lowest home gate against their great rivals at the same stage of the season for eight years.

Displaying far more imagination and football ability than their opponents, Hibs took immediate control of the midfield straight from the start, Alex Cropley opening the scoring midway through the half. Although still well on top after the break it would take the Easter Road side some time to score a second, thanks mainly to the outstanding performance by the Hearts goalkeeper Garland, in particular, two magnificent saves from O'Rourke. Until, just a few minutes from the end when Stanton cemented a result that had never been in any real doubt. It had now been four years since Hearts had even scored a goal against Hibs in a league game, the victory over their city rival's an ideal boost before facing the Portuguese side Sporting Lisbon in the Cup Winners' Cup in midweek.

Then managed by the former West Bromwich Albion and England centre-forward Ronnie Allan, Sporting had lost only narrowly to Benfica in the previous season's national cup final to qualify for the competition and were expected to provide a tough challenge. Like Hibs, the Lisbon side had also taken part in the inaugural European Cup competition in 1955 only to exit at the first-round stage after defeat by Partizan Belgrade but had gone on to win the Cup Winners' Cup in 1964. This would be the fourth time that Hibs had faced Portuguese opposition in a competitive European fixture, the previous games against Belenenses, Porto and Guimarães all eventually won on aggregate although only the game against Belenenses had been successful away from home.

THE LEAGUE CUP AND VICTORY AT TYNECASTLE (1972–73)

For the trip to Portugal the club had decided for the first time to charter its own aircraft, the flight departing from what was then Abbotsinch Airport. To help defray the expense, a number of supporters including the former players Gordon Smith, Willie Clark and Tommy Preston had been given the opportunity to accompany the official party on the trip at a much reduced rate. The inexperienced youngsters Tony Higgins, Willie McEwan, Kenny Davidson, John Hazel, and the as yet untested John Saltoun and John Minford had all been included in the party. Although all 17 would be available to strip for action if required, it would be no surprise to discover what was now the accepted first 11 taking its place at the kick-off.

Before the game at the Estádio José Alvalade stadium in Lisbon the players had been surprised to say the least when taking the field to the unlikely strains of the Hector Nicol record 'Glory Glory to the Hibees' that the Portuguese officials had somehow managed to obtain, a gesture also greatly appreciated by the travelling fans at one end of the ground.

Adopting what would become Turnbull's habit in European games, to the surprise of the home side and their supporters who would probably have been expecting the visitors to adopt the now well accepted custom by away sides in Europe to sit back in defence, Hibs went into the attack right from the first whistle. Now wearing new look all purple jerseys with white shorts, Sporting had been left chasing 'purple shadows'. Alex Cropley struck the post with a tremendous drive as early as the first minute and although creating another couple of decent chances – the best an O'Rourke effort that went narrowly past the post with the goalkeeper beaten – the first half ended goalless. Fifteen minutes after the restart Herriot had quite clearly been punched full in the face by an opponent, and although the goalkeeper had required treatment from Tom McNiven the incident had been completely ignored by the referee. Possibly still feeling the effects of the blow, a couple of mistakes by the goalkeeper immediately after the incident had allowed Sporting to score twice within a minute to take the lead, the first when he had been caught off his line, the second when he slipped coming out to collect a harmless looking cross ball. Although Sporting could have scored again soon after, to their great credit Hibs fought their way back into the game and were well on top when Arthur Duncan scored the away goal that might possibly prove vital in the return leg in Edinburgh. According to captain Pat Stanton, that evening in Portugal Hibs could have taken on anyone, a view shared by Eddie Turnbull who had described the performance as possibly the club's best ever in Europe. For some time now there had been signs that something big was starting to happen at Easter Road, but that evening in Lisbon had perhaps been the first real tangible indication of something really special.

Not everyone had been happy with the team's performance however. Turnbull would later be less than enamoured by comments made by chairman John Bruce who for some reason had been highly critical of the performance. But it was in the dressing room after the game that the now well-known and amusing incident took place when a tray of watches that were being carried into room as gifts for the party had been inadvertently knocked high into the air by Eddie Turnbull. The comment from the impish Johnny Hamilton: 'Time flys eh boss' leaving everyone in hysterics. Apparently Turnbull had then ordered the players to pick up the watches, several of which appeared to have stopped working, with the instructions that any of the broken ones were to be left for the directors.

In the second round of the League Cup at Tannadice against a Dundee United side unbeaten in the previous ten games, Hibs found themselves a goal behind at half-time and two down within a minute of the restart. But, in a tremendous second half fightback that demonstrated the fighting spirit and confidence that was running through the side at that time, a hat-trick by Jimmy O'Rourke followed by a brace from Alex Cropley would eventually secure an emphatic and thoroughly deserved 5–2 victory, a result that did not flatter the visitors in any way. Disappointingly, a crowd of just over 6,000 had bothered to turn up for what had undoubtedly been the tie of the round, prompting an extremely frustrated United manager Jim McLean to comment later that: 'Perhaps on this showing Dundee didn't deserve one team never mind two.' The emphatic victory however now meant that even with the second leg in Edinburgh yet to come a Hibs side that was then sitting top of the table already had one foot firmly in the quarter-finals, and if not before people were now really starting to sit up and take notice.

THE LEAGUE CUP AND VICTORY AT TYNECASTLE (1972–73)

As Hibs were defeating United 3–1 in a league game at home a few days later, that same afternoon at Starks Park the former Hibs player Joe Baker was proving that he still had plenty to offer the game when scoring five in Raith Rovers 8–1 defeat of Berwick Rangers.

In the return leg against Sporting Lisbon in Edinburgh, Hibs really turned on the style in front of well over 26,000 mostly partisan fans although the exciting football to be found at Easter Road at that time was attracting many neutrals particularly for the European games. Alan Gordon opened the scoring midway through the first half with a tremendous trademark header to level the aggregate scores. Despite conceding an equaliser just before half-time that gave their opponents an overall lead on the night, no side could have lived with Hibs in a devastating 45 minutes of second-half magic when another five had been scored to leave their opponents reeling, a display described by one newspaper reporter as 'one that will go down in the history books'. Exaggerated or not, what is certain is that the eventual 6–1 victory, Sporting Lisbon's heaviest ever defeat in a European competition, would have sent a message throughout the continent that Hibs were now a side to be reckoned with. Kicking down the famous slope in the second half, it had taken Jimmy O'Rourke all of three minutes to score the first of his three goals that evening, his second hat-trick in just over a week. Gordon added another as Sporting crumbled under the nonstop onslaught, Duncan finally ending the rout with a drive that came off a defender to complete a fantastic 90 minutes for the home side. It could well have been even more after a tremendous 30-yard drive from John Brownlie late in the game had come crashing back off the post with the goalkeeper beaten. O'Rourke may have taken the goalscoring honours, but on what had been a tremendous evening for Scottish football there had been no failures, each man playing his part. Later, a still shell-shocked Sporting manager Ronnie Allen had been generous in his praise, tipping the Easter Road side to not only to go all the way to the final but actually win the trophy. Sporting Lisbon had won the tournament when defeating HTK Budapest in the 1964 final but since then every British side that had beaten them in the competition Arsenal, Newcastle United and Rangers, had all gone on to actually win the trophy.

As a measure of just how far the club had come under Turnbull in such a short space of time the Hibs fans were now that much harder to please. Despite a 2–1 home win against St Johnstone on the Saturday, the overall display had failed to satisfy, the players leaving the field at the end in no doubt as to their dissatisfaction.

In the return League Cup game against United at Easter Road in midweek, the Hibs fans who were possibly anticipating yet another high scoring game were again to be disappointed. The no-score draw however had been more than enough to qualify for the quarter-finals where they would now meet Airdrie and what would turn out to be yet another memorable evening in what was already proving a quite incredible season.

It was around then that John Brownlie had been voted the Hibernian Supporters Association's Player of the Year, the fifth winner of an award that had previously been won by Jimmy O'Rourke, Chris Shevlane and twice by the inspirational captain Pat Stanton. However, there would be an even bigger accolade to come for the classy full-back when a recent poll of several prominent sports journalists had chosen both him and teammate Pat Stanton in the top Scottish League XI for that season's Rothmans Football Yearbook. Although there was no actual award to go with the honour, the prestige itself would be reward enough, and yet another sign that Hibs were heading in the right direction.

In the cup game against Airdrie at Broomfield, a travelling support that had been rapidly increasing in numbers each week as the side went from strength to strength, were to witness yet another tremendous second half performance that completely blasted Airdrie out of the competition. A Drew Busby penalty shortly after half-time had given the home side a 2–1 lead, but another five second-half goals, four in a scintillating 14-minute spell when Airdrie just could not live with Hibs, already meant that barring a total upset in the return leg at Easter Road that the tie was already as good as over. This time Arthur Duncan had been the hat-trick hero but the real star of the hour had been the former Airdrie ballboy John Brownlie. At that time without doubt the best attacking full-back in the entire country, he scored twice with spectacular drives from well outside the box that gave the future Hibs goalkeeper Roddy McKenzie no chance, Jimmy O'Rourke scoring the

THE LEAGUE CUP AND VICTORY AT TYNECASTLE (1972-73)

other from the penalty spot. Although Brownlie would receive the majority of the praise in the following morning's newspapers, mention must also be made of his full-back partner Erich Schaedler, at that time possibly the most improved player in the country. Although not nearly as flamboyant as Brownlie, Schaedler was no less effective. Hugely underrated by some, but certainly not by his teammates who all appreciated just what he brought to the side, he had improved out of all recognition since signing from Stirling Albion in 1969, more so under the influence of Eddie Turnbull. Perhaps the former Melbourne Thistle and Peebles Rovers player, son of a German prisoner-of-war, had lacked the subtle skills of some of his more skilful teammates but he more than made up for it with his stamina, defensive capabilities, fierce tackling and total commitment to the cause. A tremendous competitor who never let the side down, perhaps rather unkindly Turnbull would often tell the player that his job was to win the ball then pass it to others who could use it. If that was indeed the case then he more than held his end of the bargain and would later be described by one of his colleagues as someone that you would wish to have alongside you in the trenches, qualities that would soon see him called into the Scotland squad.

A fairly quiet individual off the field, at that time Hibs could not have done without what he brought to the side. Rarely beaten he would have been a nightmare to play against, and even in training the other players would often try to keep out of his way. In one game against Hearts one of his tackles had left Kenny Aird in amongst the crowd. Despite everyone expecting him to be booked or even sent off he had merely received a ticking-off from the referee. Later at a corner an enquiry by goalkeeper Jim McArthur as to why he had gone in so hard had been met with the answer, 'Well he kicked me three years ago.' Once described by a teammate as excitable and sometimes appearing as though he was wired to the moon, you would go far to meet a nicer guy. A great car enthusiast, he would often pick Pat Stanton up at the Bonnyrigg Road end in his convertible on the way to training. Pat recalls the bitterly cold winters morning when Erich dutifully arrived to collect him with the car hood down and wearing sunglasses declaring that he was cool, hardly an opinion shared by the freezing cold Stanton or the passersby who could only shake their head in bewilderment. On another occasion Erich had parked the car outside Easter Road before training, again with the hood down. The players had been going through their paces at nearby Hawkhill when the clouds suddenly opened and the rain started to cascade down in buckets when someone reminded Erich that he had left the roof open. Plucking up the courage to ask Turnbull if he could leave in the middle of the exercise, Erich had arrived back at Easter Road to find the car totally drenched throughout, Stanton later saying: 'That's the Nazi's for you,' a lighthearted reference to Erich's dad who had been born in Germany.

Continuing where they had left off at Broomfield in midweek, in a league game at Easter Road a few days later Airdrie had once again been swept away with another spectacular performance, and yet again most of the fireworks had been reserved for the second half. Already one ahead at the interval, now using the slope to their advantage another four would be scored in 12 scintillating second-half minutes to give the home side a comprehensive 5–2 victory. The recent sparkling second-half performances had left many wondering just what was said to the players during the interval, but contrary to popular belief, there would rarely be any screaming or shouting. After allowing time for a refreshing cup of tea, the manager would calmly explain tactically just how, in his own words, they were going to 'beat this lot', and invariably he would be proved right. As far as Turnbull was concerned second best was not nearly good enough and there was now a tremendous confidence running through the entire side allied to a thoroughly professional approach and an almost overpowering desire to be the best in the country.

By now news of Hibs' exploits had spread further afield, and Manchester City were said to have tabled a bid of around £170,000 for captain Pat Stanton, a then Scottish record, only for Eddie Turnbull to state categorically that 'Stanton will finish his career at Easter Road,' a view shared by the player himself who had absolutely no desire to leave Edinburgh.

In the Cup Winners' Cup Hibs had now been drawn against the 'unknown' KS Besa from Albania. The situation however had become confused after the Danish team Fremad Amager, Besa's

THE LEAGUE CUP AND VICTORY AT TYNECASTLE (1972–73)

opponents in the previous round who had lost only on the away goals ruling, had sent an official letter of complaint to the European authorities regarding their treatment while in Albania. As a result, for a time Hibs would be unsure as to just who they would be facing. Amager's protest would eventually be rejected but Hibs would soon discover to their cost that the Danish side's alleged treatment in the Albanian capital would merely be a sign of what was to come.

In the first leg against the Albanian 'dark horses' at Easter Road, Hibs had produced yet another stunning display of attacking football to leave their opponents reeling and it was soon obvious that the visitors had been completely out of their depth at this level. 2–0 ahead at the interval once again most of the fireworks had been reserved for the second half with five goals scored in a devastating 12-minute spell that had simply swept poor Besa away. For Jimmy O'Rourke there would be yet another hat-trick, his fourth of the season so far and a personal best, the others scored by Duncan with two, Cropley, and even full-back Brownlie getting in on the act. Taking the field in shabby kit that looked as though it had faded in the wash, in reality Besa had been a poor side in every sense of the word and in the end it had all been too easy. Although managing to score late on, in truth a stray dog that had wandered on to the field near the end had probably caused the home side more anxiety than their opponents throughout the entire 90 minutes.

At that time Hibs were generally accepted as the most entertaining side in the entire country, and with 21 goals scored in their previous four games it was clear that they were giving the fans just what was wanted.

Meanwhile, with only the inexperienced Bobby Robertson as back-up to Jim Herriot, Turnbull had signed the highly rated 20-year-old goalkeeper Jim McArthur from Cowdenbeath for around £8,500. McArthur was another that the manager had been keeping an eye on for some time after coming across him while at a game watching another player. At that time, in his final year of a physical education course at Dundee University, McArthur would remain part-time, but in a move that would undoubtedly be of tremendous benefit to his game he would turn full-time in the summer. Originally an outfield player, McArthur had been spotted by Cowdenbeath when deputising for an injured goalkeeper and had already attracted the attention of several clubs on both sides of the border. These included Everton and Celtic who some time before had tabled a £1,000 bid for the then 15-year-old that had been rejected by manager Andy Matthews. According to Turnbull McArthur was already a better goalkeeper than Bobby Clark had been at the same age and a Scotland cap in the making, a tremendous compliment considering just how highly the manager rated the then Aberdeen and Scotland goalkeeper. According to McArthur he had arrived at Easter Road to find a dressing room that was anything but quiet, one packed full of personalities but with everyone mixing well with no cliques, a camaraderie that would usually continue after games when most of the players would socialise at several different hostelries around the town including the popular White Cockade in Rose Street, Jinglin' Geordie on the Waverley Steps, or Ken Buchanan's hotel in Ferry Road.

Though obviously signed as one for the future, just a few days after putting pen to paper he had made an earlier than expected first team debut against Dumbarton. Initially listed in the reserve side for the corresponding fixture at Easter Road that same afternoon, McArthur had been drafted into the first team squad almost at the last minute after Herriot had failed a late fitness test. At the aptly named Boghead Hibs had taken the lead inside the first few minutes with a strike by Arthur Duncan but it had required an Alan Gordon goal two minutes from time to save their blushes against the recently promoted side that would only escape relegation by a solitary point at the end of the season. The real hero of the hour however had been the young McArthur. Although possibly at fault for the opening goal in the 2–2 draw when failing to collect a pass-back from Jim Black, the youngster had pulled off several outstanding saves and had already done more than enough to justify Turnbull's confidence in him.

With their commanding lead from the first leg, as could be expected Hibs had strolled into the next round of the League Cup with a 4–1 victory against Airdrie at Easter Road. This would then set them up for yet another meeting at the semi-final stage against

THE LEAGUE CUP AND VICTORY AT TYNECASTLE (1972–73)

old adversaries Rangers at Hampden, but before that there would be the return leg in darkest Albania.

Very rarely is the venue for a game of football mentioned more than the actual game itself, but this was exactly the state of affairs facing Hibs before the away fixture against KS Besa. With a 7–1 lead from the first leg, at that time the most goals scored by Hibs in a competitive European game, the return had been considered to be merely a holiday for the players but it would turn out to be anything but, rather what could only be described as a journey into the land that time forgot. One of the players had a friend who owned an Italian restaurant in the city who had visited Albania some time before and had warned him that he would not be remotely prepared for what lay ahead.

What would eventually turn out to be an unbelievable experience had started with a delay of several hours at Turnhouse on account of the airport in Tirana being closed due to fog, and things were to go rapidly downhill from there. The party arrived in Albania to find a runway surrounded by armed guards, anti-aircraft guns, tanks and jet fighters, a situation even that early in the journey starting to appear even more ominous when the authorities were seen siphoning the fuel from the aircraft to prevent it taking off again without permission. At the airport terminal that in reality had just been a few shanty shacks, the club had initially been prevented from unloading the food that had been brought from Edinburgh, consent eventually granted only after a lengthy argument. The nightmare however was only just beginning. On the journey to the hotel nothing could have prepared the players for the sights facing them on the way, no one having experienced anything quite like it before. Except for the occasional limousine driven by officials in the Chinese influenced communist country, the wide roads had been completely empty except for the occasional donkey and the even rarer ill-clad pedestrian; scenes that would later be described sarcastically by some of the players as 'rush hour in Teblisi,' almost like being back in the dark ages. The vast majority of the extremely poor population had been dressed in scruffy clothes only one step removed from rags and living in housing that could only be described as slums, the sight of shabbily dressed kids begging in the streets truly heartbreaking. Believing that they had thought of everything, the club had even 'borrowed' their own chef from the North British Hotel on Princes Street, but arrived at the hotel to discover that they were now refused permission to use their own food. Some of the players had offered the ill-clad but curious youngsters some sweets only to receive an abrupt 'NO' from an official who curtly pointed out that they were 'too proud to take them'. The local cuisine was found to be almost impossible to digest, some after ordering scrambled eggs from the menu finding it unrecognisable from anything they had ever experienced or tasted before, and it was only after yet another lengthy argument that they had eventually been granted permission to use their own food. The strict instructions that no one was allowed to leave the hotel without an official 'guide' had proved totally unnecessary as there was nowhere to go and absolutely nothing of interest to see, but luckily the club had had the foresight to bring along a selection of games to help pass the time. It was now obvious that a deliberate effort was being made to make Hibs stay as uncomfortable as possible. The situation only relaxed slightly after Tom McNiven had assisted a member of the hotel staff who had taken ill, and director Jimmy Kerr, a trained plumber, helping with some of the sanitary problems but always with someone hovering in the background watching their every move.

The obvious deliberate obstruction continued in the morning when transport to take the players to training had been refused, and again it was only after yet another lengthy dispute that a coach had eventually been laid on although the journalists travelling with the party, one from a London-based newspaper, had all been refused permission to accompany the players. Initially to have taken place at the national stadium in Tirana, at almost the last minute the game had been switched to Duress more than 25 miles away, the players arriving at the ground to find a substandard, badly rutted, uneven pitch with goalposts of dubious dimensions that would have disgraced a Junior side back in Scotland. A complaint that one of the crossbars appeared to be a few inches below regulation height was quickly remedied to the bemusement of everyone including the UEFA officials that

THE LEAGUE CUP AND VICTORY AT TYNECASTLE (1972–73)

had accompanied the Hibs party, by a labourer digging a shallow trench along the length of the goal line.

By now everyone just wanted the game to be over with. In a scrappy game played in front of almost 17,000 highly excitable partisan fans, after a no-scoring first 45 minutes Besa had somewhat surprisingly taken the lead against the run of play midway through the second half only for Alan Gordon to equalise six minutes later. Herriot, who had been an injury doubt before the game had been replaced midway through the second half by Bobby Robertson who was making his European debut. The young goalkeeper was called into action to make a couple of decent saves near the end but there would was to be no more scoring, the eventual 8–2 aggregate victory safely easing Hibs into the quarter-finals.

Although Besa had been keen enough and had competed reasonably well it was obvious that they had been fighting a losing battle from the start. One of their players who had been wearing better quality kit than the others and could actually play a bit even appeared to have been a 'ringer' brought in especially for the occasion.

At the post-match reception the attitude of the Albanians had thawed somewhat, but by then everyone just wanted to go home. Even then what had truly been a trip to hell and back was not quite over when the flight carrying the party back to Edinburgh the following morning had to be diverted to Glasgow because of the exceptionally high winds, the final leg of the journey to the capital completed by coach.

Psychological mind games had always been a part of playing in Europe, but the behaviour of the Albanians had been well and truly over and above anything that could, and should, have been expected. After the game Turnbull had been fulsome in his praise for the players' patience in putting up with the constant provocation, aggravation and disruption they had been forced to endure over the previous few days, and Hibs would later make an official complaint to UEFA. Whatever the reason, there would be no Albanian sides in any of the European competitions the following season.

In a final humorous footnote to what had been a truly remarkable affair, because of the initial restrictions, the team had arrived back in Edinburgh with a great amount of unused food. Several of the players had been about to help themselves rather than let it go to waste when Tom McNiven stepped forward to let them know in no uncertain terms that the food belonged to the football club and was to be left alone. A short while later some of the players were still sitting in a car outside the ground discussing the trip, when to their surprise they spotted Tom popping his head around the stadium door and look both ways, before emerging with a huge box of the groceries.

In contrast to the alarming drop in attendances elsewhere in the country, for some months the crowds at Easter Road had been steadily increasing, up over 100,000 from the same stage the previous season although much of this could obviously be down to the Drybrough Cup, Europe and the extended run in the League Cup. At that time many in the game held serious concerns that football was being seriously overexposed on the small screen and that this could possibly be discouraging people from attending live games, but while others dithered the Hibs chairman took decisive action. Hart, a forthright personality who was no stranger to controversy and never afraid to speak his mind whether it be against the football authorities or the television companies, had banned the TV cameras from covering a home game against Rangers that was to have been shown as highlights later that evening. He had probably been vindicated when a crowd of over 38,000 turned up at the gate, almost 13,000 more than the corresponding fixture the previous season. Regardless of the criticism he would later receive in some quarters, there could be no mistaking Hart's overwhelming desire, endeavour and genuine commitment to make Hibs the best side in the country. As far as he personally was concerned, the decision had been taken not only in the long-term interest of the club but the game in general.

With Hibs due to meet the Ibrox side twice inside a few days including the League Cup semi-final at Hampden, in the league game at Easter Road on the Saturday they had only been denied the victory their performance had deserved thanks mainly to a tremendous display by the Ranger's goalkeeper Peter McCloy. Undeserved or not however the 2–1 defeat, Rangers first victory against Hibs in five attempts and the Edinburgh side's first

THE LEAGUE CUP AND VICTORY AT TYNECASTLE (1972–73)

home defeat of the season would have done little to inspire confidence for the forthcoming cup semi-final between the sides in midweek. Unfortunately, in what was now becoming an almost regular occurrence the game had once again been interrupted by a pitch invasion after fighting had broken out on the terracing at the 'Dunbar' end of the ground.

In the semi-final at Hampden in midweek, a game that had started brightly soon developed into a scrappy untidy affair packed with stoppages and little football or inspiration from either side. With precious little in the way of goalmouth action, a fixture that had seemed likely to end goalless suddenly burst into life when with just over 15 minutes remaining Brownlie collected a loose ball just inside the Rangers half. There appeared little danger as the defender started to make a run deep into the opponent's territory, somehow managing to shrug off several attempts to dispossess him, not all of them legal. Now finding himself just outside the Rangers penalty area he proceeded to send a tremendous 20-yard drive past the despairing dive of McCloy and into the corner of the net for the only goal. Forced to survive a near thing in the dying seconds of the game when a Matheson effort had come crashing back off the underside of the crossbar with Herriot stranded, a goal then would have been hard on Hibs and in the end Brownlie's strike would be enough to send his side into only its third ever League Cup final. On the downside a booking received by Alex Edwards would now mean him facing yet another lengthy suspension although it would not prevent him from taking part in the cup final.

Although it had not been remotely funny at the time, at the next training session the joker Jimmy O'Rourke would have his teammates in stitches by repeatedly bouncing the ball off the crossbar, saying over and over again; 'hard lines Willie... hard lines Willie...' a reference to Matheson's near miss in the semi-final.

In his column in the *Daily Mail* the morning after the game Alec Young had been generous in his praise of the Easter Road side: 'In the space of just 16 months Eddie Turnbull has transformed Hibs into one of Scotland's most exciting sides. When the ball runs for them they are devastating, and when it doesn't they remain entertaining.'

A few days after the semi-final, the former Musselburgh Windsor player Bobby Smith, yet another of the promising youngsters on Hibs' books at that time, would make his first team debut against the recently promoted Arbroath at Gayfield. Replacing Jimmy O'Rourke during the second half of the 3–2 victory, it would be the first of several appearances the wholehearted, versatile player would make that season. One of Eddie Turnbull's first signings, the spirited Smith who was comfortable either in midfield or full-back, would eventually go on to make well over 300 appearances during his three spells with the club, one a short-term loan from Leicester City in 1982. But with the talent available to the manager at that particular time, it would have been an extremely difficult task for any inexperienced youngster to force themselves into a first team that almost picked itself, each knowing the other's strengths and weaknesses. In the corresponding reserve game at Easter Road that same afternoon, the former Highland League player Des Bremner who had been signed only the previous day after three weeks on trial at Easter Road had made a goalscoring start to his Hibs career in a 3–1 victory. His would soon turn out to have been a most fortuitous signing.

Meanwhile, it would be absolutely no surprise to learn that yet again Celtic would be Hibs' opponents in the final, the third meeting of the sides at the ultimate stage of a competition in just under a year. This time however there would be no controversy. The players had all been aware that they had not only let themselves down in the Scottish Cup final but also the fans and had been determined to repay their loyalty. Watched by a crowd of over 70,000 on a dreary, overcast winter afternoon at Hampden the now accepted 11 had taken their place at the kick-off, Stanton, Blackley and O'Rourke the only survivors from Hibs' last appearance in a League Cup final three years before. Inspired by captain Stanton who many felt had his best ever game in a green and white jersey that afternoon, Hibs never at any time looked in any real danger of losing the match. In the opening period there had been very few genuine opportunities for either side. The best came in the closing minutes of the half when the Celtic captain McNeil almost put the ball into his own net while attempting a pass-back to his goalkeeper, Evans doing well to save Stanton's

THE LEAGUE CUP AND VICTORY AT TYNECASTLE (1972–73)

powerful header from the resulting corner. At half-time Hibs had left the field to resounding applause from the fans who had mostly congregated at the west end of the ground, encouragement according to Jimmy O'Rourke that had convinced him that it would turn out to be Hibs' day. At half-time the astute Turnbull had made a tactical change by moving Pat Stanton into a more attacking midfield role and it worked to perfection. Stein had also made a change in moving Jimmy Johnstone, who had been having little success on the right wing against Schaedler, over to the left only for the highly talented but occasionally temperamental winger to find the outstanding Brownlie also in uncompromising mood, and he would eventually be replaced by Callaghan midway through the half.

With Hibs now much the better side, two goals inside six minutes midway through the second half by Stanton and O'Rourke had given the Easter Road side a deserved lead, the first after the captain had capitalised on an intelligent chip from an Edwards free kick over the Celtic wall to open the scoring from close range. Stanton would later recall that the ball had seemed to take an age in coming down, and it appeared to everyone in the ground that he had missed his chance when forced to take an extra step to evade a tackle before proceeding to smash the ball past Williams in the Celtic goal. Just minutes later the captain this time had turned provider when his tremendous inch perfect cross from out wide on the right was met by the inrushing O'Rourke who wasted no time in sending a tremendous header high into the net. Hibs were now well on top and there were several near misses in the Celtic penalty area that should have resulted in goals, Stanton hitting the post with a long-range drive soon after a Gordon effort had struck a defender standing on the goal line when it had appeared far easier to score. With 13 minutes remaining Dalglish pulled one back leaving the Hibs fans on the terracing biting their nails, but in reality there had never been any real danger of the Easter Road side losing the match, the final 2–1 victory far more convincing than the scoreline would suggest. Incredibly, two pupils that had played together in the same school side and were now professionals at the same club had both scored the winning goals in a major cup final, an incredibly rare if not unique event. Goal scorers invariably receive most of the credit after a victory, but that afternoon at Hampden the entire defence had also been in tremendous form particularly during the later stages of the game, none more so than the unassuming Jim Black. Strong, quick and good in the air, the signing of Black had brought solidity to the defence and he had been immense in repulsing the by then infrequent Celtic attacks late in the game.

Before receiving the cup from Glasgow Lord Provost Sir William Gray they were all well aware that the side had let the supporters down in the earlier Scottish Cup final. Despite a recent SFA directive that the winning side was not to approach their supporters after receiving the cup, on the final whistle Stanton had encouraged the overjoyed Hibs players to make their way to the west end of the ground. There, the huge majority of the by now delirious Hibs support had congregated to receive a rapturous reception, finally proving not only to the fans but probably also themselves that they could do it.

Before going up to receive their medals every player had been personally congratulated by Jock Stein, a tremendous gesture by an obviously disappointed Celtic manager. Not only had Hibs gained sweet revenge for the humiliating cup final defeat only seven months earlier by winning the clubs first major cup in living memory, but it had been a victory for skill as well as determination. The players returned to the dressing room after the game as a result of the tremendous energy expelled in defeating a side that rated at the time as one of the very best in Europe. Only then had it been revealed that in the run up to the final it had been a closely guarded secret that full-back John Brownlie had been receiving daily intensive treatment for an injury received the previous Saturday right up to the kick-off, but fortunately the inspirational defender had been able to take his place at the start, allowing Turnbull to field an unchanged side from the 11 that had defeated Rangers in the semi-final, a side now and forever after known as the 'Turnbull's Tornadoes'. Pat Stanton's dad, a fervent Hibs supporter had not attended the game thinking that after attending so many losing cup finals in the past that it might be him that had brought the side bad luck.

THE LEAGUE CUP AND VICTORY AT TYNECASTLE (1972-73)

Back in Edinburgh later that evening, as could be expected, the streets had been packed with jubilant supporters. As the open-top bus, so often superfluous to requirements after cup finals involving the Easter Road side, made its way through the city, the players each took turns to display the cup to the ecstatic masses. All the way through Corstorphine, Haymarket, Princes Street and on to the foot of Leith Walk before returning to the North British Hotel in Princes Street, the bus had been surrounded by thousands of delirious fans including Pat Stanton's dad, the traffic brought to a complete standstill at the junction of the North Bridge and Princes Street. Later the players and staff including both the second and third teams that had also been in action that afternoon, as well as the many guests, would all join in the celebrations that would go on well into the night. The fans too making their own way to pubs throughout the city where they would carry on with their own particular celebrations, everyone aware of just how momentous an occasion it had been for the city, providing memories that would last forever. During the celebrations at the North British Hotel a telegram had been received from city rivals Hearts congratulating Hibs on their success, a tremendous gesture that had been truly appreciated.

The former Hibs player Eric Stevenson, then with Ayr United, would later recall that although his then current side had also been in action that same afternoon, he had been at Hampden for the League Cup Final. The fine he later received from his manager and former Easter Road teammate Ally MacLeod was, according to Stevenson, well worth it to see his boyhood heroes winning the cup.

Hibs: Herriot, Brownlie and Schaedler, Stanton, Black and Blackley, Edwards, O'Rourke, Gordon, Cropley and Duncan. (sub) Hamilton
Celtic: Williams, McGrain and Brogan, McCluskey, McNeil and Hay, Johnstone, Connolly, Dalglish, Hood and Macari (sub) Callaghan
Referee: A McKenzie (Larbert)

By now it was even more obvious than before that something special was beginning to stir at Easter Road. But, in the home game against Ayr United seven days later a disappointingly poor crowd of just over 12,000 had been inside the ground at the start, an attendance later described by Tom Hart as an absolute disgrace for a side that had just won a major trophy. Both the Drybrough and League Cups had been paraded around the ground at half-time and according to the chairman, those that had stayed away were the losers. In the 8–1 victory that had perhaps been Hibs' best, although obviously not most important performance of the season so far, Alex Cropley had opened the scoring after just 11 seconds. Hibs' fourth and Alan Gordon's own third goal after just 35 minutes the sides 100th in all competitions so far that season and it was still only December. Gordon's hat-trick, his first for the club and his first in any competitive game since scoring three for Hearts in a 6–3 victory over Aberdeen eight years earlier, had taken his overall total to 25 and already three more than his previous best in an entire season at either Tynecastle or Tannadice. According to the Ayr goalkeeper Jim Stewart 'it had been just like a nightmare with shots raining in from everywhere', the most goals he had ever conceded in a single game beating the seven scored by Aberdeen the previous season. Never one to mince his words, the vastly experienced Ayr manager Ally McLeod would later claim the Hibs display to have been one of the finest performances he had ever seen: 'out of this world'. Former player Eric Stevenson had again watched from the sidelines probably with mixed emotions, one half keen that his Ayr teammates do well, the other half no doubt wishing that he was still wearing the green and white jersey.

Still to come however were three games that could potentially define Hibs' season as far as the championship was concerned, Celtic, Aberdeen and the New Year's Day game against city rivals Hearts at Tynecastle. At that time Alex Edwards was such an influential player for the side and just days before facing Celtic in Glasgow, Hibs had received a huge boost with the news that the booking he had received in the semi-final against Rangers that could well have resulted in yet another lengthy suspension had been rescinded and that he was now free to take part in all three games.

At that time league leaders Celtic had been four points ahead of second placed Hibs both with the same number of games played, only for the titanic battle at Parkhead between a Celtic

THE LEAGUE CUP AND VICTORY AT TYNECASTLE (1972–73)

side desperate for revenge after the cup final defeat and their nearest challengers in the league to eventually end in a 1–1 draw. A goal behind at half-time after Alan Gordon had opened the scoring with a header, Dalglish had equalised during a tremendous second-half fightback by Celtic. But, with the confidence and possibly more importantly the desire running through the Easter Road side at that time Hibs would undoubtedly have been extremely disappointed to be leaving Parkhead, always a difficult venue at any time, with just the single point.

In the corresponding reserve fixture at Easter Road that same afternoon the talented young forward Kenny Davidson who had only just recovered from a previous injury had broken his leg in an accidental clash with the Celtic goalkeeper Dennis Connaghan. Davidson had been on the bench against Ayr United a few days earlier and had been attempting to re-establish himself in the first team when the latest incident occurred. Operated on later that evening, the following day he had received a surprise visitor in the shape of chairman Tom Hart, a gesture that perhaps demonstrated the tremendous spirit running through Easter Road at that time. Unfortunately, the injury was to ultimately seriously hinder the youngster's progress at Easter Road and he would never play for the first team again.

The home game against Aberdeen on the penultimate day of the year had once again found Hibs at their brilliant best, Stanton opening the scoring in the first half only for a battling Aberdeen to draw level through Jarvie. An O'Rourke goal just after half-time had restored Hibs' lead before Alan Gordon, then considered to be playing the best football of his career, put the side further ahead with according to one journalist: 'perhaps the greatest goal scored at Easter Road for years with a spectacular diving header'. Although Aberdeen managed to pull one back, Hibs managed to hold out quite comfortably and were now just two points behind leaders Celtic in the championship race although the Parkhead side now had the advantage of a game in hand.

It was now on to Tynecastle to face city rivals Hearts on New Year's Day. At that time both Edinburgh sides were doing well although Hibs had now been installed as firm favourites by the bookies. Hearts who were then fourth in the table would obviously have been desperate to end their recent dismal record against their great rivals, their last home victory in the holiday fixture dating as far back as 1961. After a light pre-match training session at Easter Road the Hibs players made their way to Tynecastle with a sing song on the coach and apparently had still been singing on their way into the ground.

On 1 January 1973, Britain's first day as official members of the European Union or what would generally become known simply as the Common Market, just under 36,000 fans had packed into Tynecastle for the traditional New Year's Day derby. Inside the opening few minutes Hearts had scorned a couple of decent chances to take the lead, the best when Parke shot wide from inside the penalty area with just the keeper to beat, but that would be almost the last we would see of the home side as an attacking force. At that time Hearts were said to have been playing their best football for several seasons and in the previous 13 and a half hours had conceded just three goals, a figure that it would take a rampaging Hibs side just 26 minutes to equal. O'Rourke opened the scoring early in the first half when blasting past Garland from close range after a long throw-in by Schaedler, further goals by Gordon, a double from Duncan and another by Cropley giving the visitors an already unassailable 5–0 half-time lead.

After the restart Hearts had enjoyed a brief spell of pressure without really troubling the Hibs defence although Donald Ford who was yet to score against Hibs at any level after 300 games for the Tynecastle side had the ball in the net only to be ruled offside. Playing 'brilliant football at a breathtaking pace' Hearts just had no answer to this supremely confident and talented 'green machine' and more goals just had to come. Midway through the second half O'Rourke scored number six from almost on the goal line after taking advantage of great leading up work by Pat Stanton who had carried the ball from inside his own half beating several men on the way, Alan Gordon ending the rout 15 minutes from the end with a header from an Erich Schaedler cross on the left for number seven. For long periods only goalkeeper Kenny Garland had stood between his side and double figures, the historic 7–0 victory, Hibs' best ever in an official game against their closest rivals. It was a victory that also lifted them to the top of the table on goal difference although nearest challengers Celtic, who did not play that afternoon, now had two games in hand, one against Rangers at Ibrox.

Coach John Fraser who had been sent to watch Hearts in their recent game against Dundee had noticed that the Tynecastle side had played without a recognised outside-left that afternoon and had been more than surprised to see that Hearts had adopted the same tactics against Hibs, the extra space allowing the cavalier John Brownlie the freedom to create constant danger with his exciting forays up the right wing. Just before half-time Alex Cropley had been fouled by the Hearts captain Alan Anderson, Cropley somewhat uncharacteristically telling Anderson to 'f*** off', while also enquiring as to the score. A few minutes later as the teams were leaving the field at half-time, Cropley noticed Anderson, who was a giant of a man, making a beeline straight for him, only the intervention of Turnbull preventing the situation from escalating any further. To his credit, during his half-time team talk Eddie Turnbull had instructed his players not to ease up: 'Don't embarrass fellow professionals by taking it easy,' as well as some other unprintable instructions. Turnbull had been friendly with Bobby Seith for many years and would later relate just how difficult it had been to visit the Hearts manager immediately after the game to offer his commiserations.

Later, Turnbull, rarely a man to display any public exuberance or emotion would claim that his side were now playing 'the best football seen in Scotland for 25 years'. A viewpoint mirrored by Hugh Taylor of the *Daily Record* the following morning: 'Hibs are now playing with the flair, polish and venom of a top team – and by that I mean one of the top teams in the world'. Another: 'Invincible Hibs now look outstanding odds on favourites to add to the two trophies already won.' Yet another saying: 'not only are Hibs the team of the moment but the team of the future', but perhaps Alec Young of the *Daily Record* had summed it up best: 'With magic touches reminiscent of the great Real Madrid, Hibs now have a team to take on the world.'

In the dressing room after the game the Hibs players had understandably been ecstatic, none more so than the lifelong Hibs supporters Pat Stanton and Jimmy O'Rourke. However, for Alex Edwards the afternoon would end on a sour note when he left the stadium to discover that his dark green Rover parked nearby had been deliberately scratched from end to end.

Hearts: Garland, Clunie and Jeffries, Thomson, Anderson and Wood, Park, Brown, Ford, Carrutthers and Murray (sub) Lynch
Hibs: Herriot, Brownlie and Schaedler, Stanton, Black and Blackley, Edwards, O'Rourke, Gordon, Cropley and Duncan (sub) Hamilton
Referee: J Gordon (Newport)

Although it was still only the opening day of the year, Hibs had already played 34 games in all competitions, winning 25 and drawing four while scoring a phenomenal total of 115 goals against just 40 conceded, O'Rourke, Gordon and Duncan claiming 71 between them including six hat-tricks.

The past few months had been by far the most exciting experienced by the Hibs fans for a great many years and the overjoyed supporters leaving Tynecastle at the end of the game could well have been forgiven if dreaming of better days ahead. Sadly, although there was still much to come from this hugely talented side, things would never be quite the same again.

While Hearts, in common with most other sides in the country had been given the following day off to recover from the holiday fixtures, at Easter Road it had been business as usual in Turnbull's almost obsession to make Hibs the top side in country. Although explaining to the players that 'everyone will now be out to beat you and that it is important to keep things going,' many were of the opinion that with the players already at peak fitness that the manager was possibly in danger of overdoing things.

Just days after the Hibs game there had been rowdy scenes, both during and after a reserve game between Hearts and Aberdeen at Tynecastle. Well over a hundred home fans, unhappy at the recent heavy defeat at the hands of their great rivals, had demonstrated both inside and outside the ground demanding not

THE LEAGUE CUP AND VICTORY AT TYNECASTLE (1972–73)

only manager Bobby Seith's head but the resignation of the entire board. Although the club was still in a reasonably healthy position in the top half of the table and had lost only once at home that season before the defeat by Hibs, the demonstrations had been clear indications that results against your nearest rivals often meant far more to the supporters who would no doubt have had to endure the taunts of their workmates for some time to come.

In the home game against East Fife on the Saturday the recently appointed Scotland manager Willie Ormond had been in the stand to cast an eye over both Pat Stanton and John Brownlie in view of the forthcoming friendly against England at Hampden. Then managed by the former Motherwell and Hibs player Pat Quinn, the Methil side had clearly set its stall out early in its intentions to leave Easter Road with at least a point with a display of ultra negative football. In what had been seen as a continuation of a personal feud that had carried on from the previous game between the sides, after just two minutes the Fife inside-forward Love had been booked for a foul on Edwards and would soon be followed into the book by Borthwick after just the latest in a series of cynical fouls on the Hibs player. In a dour and negative display, the visitors, including the former Easter Road player Bobby Duncan, had tried everything possible to prevent a Hibs victory, packing their goalmouth while conceding countless fouls as they tried everything but attempt to win the game themselves. Just before half-time John Brownlie, at that time without doubt the best attacking full-back in the entire country, had been carried from the field with a leg broken in two places after a tackle by left-back Ian Printy; an injury that was to prove a huge blow not only for Hibs but also Scotland. The second half had carried on as the first, Willie McEwan replacing the injured Brownlie, with East Fife doing everything, both legal and illegal, to prevent Hibs from taking the lead. Midway through the half Alex Edwards, who again had been the victim of harsh treatment throughout, had been booked for throwing the ball, away, according to some, and *at* an opponent according to others, after just the latest cynical foul. A booking that with his previous disciplinary record seemed certain to earn the highly talented Fifer yet another lengthy ban.

Just minutes from the end and East Fife looking as though they had succeeded in their aims of leaving with at least a point, a late goal by Gordon had allowed Hibs to retain their place at the top of the table. Brownlie's injury and Edwards booking however had cast a giant shadow over Easter Road, both ultimately to have a major bearing on the eventual outcome of Hibs' season.

At the final whistle a mid-table Fife side that had been in no real danger of relegation were booed from the field by a Hibs support less than enamoured at their defensive play and constant time-wasting tactics throughout the entire 90 minutes. Ian Printy would later visit Brownlie in hospital, the Hibs full-back quick to point out that the tackle that had resulted in his broken leg had been a complete accident and attached absolutely no blame to the player.

Around that time Tom Hart had called an informal meeting in Glasgow of the so-called top seven sides to discuss what he described as a crisis in the game, particularly the then alarming drop in attendances elsewhere in the country. According to a recent survey, with only half the season gone the number of supporters passing through the gates had already shown a drop of almost half a million from the previous season, Hearts estimated to be down almost 45,000, Rangers 60,000 and somewhat surprisingly despite being well on the way to an eighth consecutive League Championship success Celtic were said to have lost over 70,000. Because of the style of football then being played at Easter Road attendances had increased but even then not nearly enough to break even. At that year's AGM a loss of more than £27,000 had been declared from the previous financial year and while a welcome improvement from the £40,000 deficit announced at the previous AGM, the figures would obviously still be of major concern. As well as Hibs the meeting had been attended by representatives from Hearts, Dundee, Dundee United, Aberdeen and Celtic, but although invited, Rangers had declined to attend. In what would later be described as a full and meaningful discussion, the subject of league reconstruction had again been raised but although some had been in favour of a change to the three-league system suggested by Hart, the majority had voted for the status quo. The ruling regarding the visiting sides guarantee had

THE LEAGUE CUP AND VICTORY AT TYNECASTLE (1972–73)

also been on the agenda. All had agreed that in this case a review was necessary, possibly that the present guarantee should either be reduced to 20% of the receipts or better still that the home side should now be allowed to keep all the gate money. The latter would obviously be of far greater benefit to the better supported sides, one example that over 17,000 had attended Hibs' recent home game against East Fife opposed to the under 6,000 at the corresponding fixture at Bayview. Other items on the agenda had again included suggested amendments to the existing radio and TV contracts and also that the payments from the football pools companies be increased. One item that had been agreed however was that at 17 weeks the League Cup competition had dragged on far too long and that not only should there be a return to the previous format, but that similar to the Drybrough Cup the League Cup should now also be sponsored, an arrangement that could if necessary eventually extend to the championship. Although they had declined to attend, at a meeting called by Rangers at Ibrox few weeks later the Govan side would go even further with the radical suggestion that in future no points should be awarded in the case of a no-score draw. Several of the items raised would eventually come to fruition but not at that time.

This was not the first time that the subject of league reconstruction had been raised. A decade earlier the game had been facing a similar alarming shortfall at the gates, the then Hibs chairman Harry Swan proposing that the league should be reduced to 16 teams with extra competitions introduced to compensate for any loss of revenue. However just a few months later during a general meeting of the Scottish League management committee Swan was now advocating that the number of teams should be increased to its pre-war 22 with no relegation and four sides promoted from the lower league. At that particular time Hibs had been struggling near the foot of the table and in danger of possible relegation and as expected there would be the obvious accusations of self-interest, a suggestion immediately rejected by the Hibs chairman who was now claiming that clearly more teams would mean more games and consequently far more income!

On the football front there was still much to play for although Hibs' title hopes suffered a severe setback with a 1–0 loss at

Tannadice. Their first defeat in ten games, the winning goal was hotly disputed by the Hibs players claiming that the ball had not crossed the line. Lacking the sparkle of previous weeks against a fast-moving united side, the 19-year-old Des Bremner had made his first team debut at right-back in place of the injured Brownlie, an extremely difficult task for any inexperienced youngster. A member of the Banks o' Dee side that was then a nursery club for Aberdeen, the young Bremner is said to have first come to the notice of manager Turnbull while training at Pittodrie during the school holidays. Unfortunately, a serious car crash at the beginning of the previous season had kept the promising youngster out of the game for over eight months, but now fully recovered he had been signed by Hibs just a few weeks earlier. Turnbull however had seen enough to have had absolutely no hesitation in giving a youngster who had made just a handful of appearances for a highly talented reserve side that at that time could have stood its own in the top league, his debut in place of the Scottish international full-back Brownlie. It would be foolish to claim that Hibs would not have missed the experienced Brownlie, but on the day Bremner had looked a more than capable deputy. Though it was perhaps the youngster's misfortune to be making his first start on an afternoon when the side had played well below its now well accepted high standards. Despite being immediately welcomed into the fold by the rest of the players, many would later joke that they couldn't understand a word he said on account of his rich North of Scotland brogue, but while obviously still lacking experience, on football ability alone Bremner would prove to be yet another valuable asset to the side.

Just days after the disappointment at Tannadice, the players, including the injured John Brownlie, had spent several hours at the Craighall recording studios in Edinburgh under the watchful eye of the Edinburgh-born composer and well-known Hibs supporter Johnny Keating recording a double 'A' side 45 inch single entitled 'Give us a goal/The Hibs Song', the words written by chairman Tom Hart's wife Sheila. On the flip side was the Keating/McPherson inspired 'Turnbull's Tornadoes'. Born into a Hibs-supporting family in the Bingham area of the city Keating

THE LEAGUE CUP AND VICTORY AT TYNECASTLE (1972–73)

is credited as the arranger of the famous 'Z Cars' theme, a programme that was then popular on television and had worked with all the greats including Frank Sinatra and Ella Fitzgerald. He was said to have been impressed with the 'slick' recording that would sell well throughout the Edinburgh area. It was even reputedly considered by the staff at the EMI Studios in London as the best football record they had ever heard including efforts by Chelsea, Manchester City and Leeds United. Jimmy O'Rourke also impressed enough to suggest, hopefully tongue in cheek, that if the record was a success then maybe they could release an album.

It was all happening at that time, both on and off the field. As well as a large full colour poster by artist and avid Hibs fan Harry Gilzean that had been released by the *Evening News* to celebrate the League Cup victory over Celtic, all the players and back room staff had attended a Civic Reception in the City Chambers when Lord Provost Jack Kane had paid tribute to the prestige that the club had brought to the city. Addressing the invited guests the Lord Provost had been generous in his praise:

> Hibs have brought honour for themselves and credit to Scottish football by the high standard of their play. The club has produced some great teams in the past but the present side bids to outshine even the Famous Five. They are a credit to their management, a great team that are destined to get even greater.

Back at Easter Road, and already without the services of the injured John Brownlie, both Pat Stanton and Alex Edwards had been summoned to appear before a disciplinary hearing, Stanton after picking up four bookings. Edwards who was appealing against the caution received against East Fife, had been granted a temporary reprieve when his hearing was postponed to a later date, the club avoiding the possibility of losing the services of both highly influential players at the same time. At the hearing Stanton had received a 14-day suspension, a punishment that even the players' union had considered extremely harsh. Despite the fact that Stanton had been a model professional for almost ten years and had appeared before the panel just once before, several others had only received seven-day bans for a similar offence. He would now sit out a 1–1 draw with Dundee in the league and a 2–0 victory over Morton in the first round of that season's Scottish Cup, a game that would see Tony Higgins score his first goal for the club.

For Edwards however things were about to get even worse. At the next disciplinary hearing his appeal against the booking received against East Fife had been rejected and once again he had received yet another lengthy eight-week suspension. At the same, Alex McDonald of Rangers had been banned for only 14 days for a similar offence. Although, it has to be said that with Edwards' previous disciplinary record, allied to the fact that he had already been well warned regarding his future conduct and both factors would likely have been taken into consideration, the sentence had still been considered extremely harsh.

He would now miss the vital run in as Hibs attempted to secure not only the championship for the first time since 1952, but to go one better than the previous season and actually win the Scottish Cup for the first time since 1902. His last appearance in a green and white jersey for some time would be the high scoring game against Airdrie at Broomfield, when with the diminutive Fifer pulling the strings from midfield, Alan Gordon had taken the opportunity to score all the goals in an extremely one-sided 4–0 victory. Hibs' fourth of the season against a Broomfield side that would end the campaign anchored firmly at the foot of the table and relegation.

For several years the popular sports magazine *France Football* had sponsored a 'Golden Boot' competition for the top league goal scorer in European football. Gordon's four against Airdrie, a personal best, had now not only made him the top goal scorer in Scotland with 24 but equal with Benfica's Eusabio in the battle for the celebrated award. Already beginning to draw admirers from throughout the country and further afield, there would be even further prestige for the Easter Road side when they were rated by the same sports magazine as the best side in Britain at that time; the third best in Europe behind Ajax and Bayern Munich; and just ahead of Liverpool and Benfica. Praise indeed!

In the Scottish Cup, a 2–0 victory over Morton in the first round had set up yet another meeting with old adversaries Rangers, the fifth consecutive season that the sides had met in the competition.

THE LEAGUE CUP AND VICTORY AT TYNECASTLE (1972–73)

Before that however, a 3–1 victory over St Johnstone. Alan Gordon almost predictably managing to get on the score sheet would give Hibs confidence for the forthcoming cup tie at Ibrox, his strike now putting Gordon one ahead of both Eusabio and Bayern Munich's Gerd Muller in the race for the Golden Boot. However, and it would probably come as no surprise considering the then seemingly negative attitude of the Scottish football authorities, that Gordon had already been informed that were he to land the prestigious award then he would not be allowed to receive the trophy as SFA rules did not allow commercial enterprises to profit from football if they did not contribute financially to the game.

By now Hibs had been drawn against the Yugoslavian side Hajduk Split in the quarter-finals of the Cup Winners' Cup. Delighted at having escaped facing the favourites Leeds United, AC Milan or Sparta Prague, manager Turnbull had reportedly been satisfied at the draw: 'At this stage it makes no difference who you are drawn against, but I am convinced that the game against Hajduk Split offers Hibs the best chance of a place in the semi-final.'

There had been a surprise visitor in the team coach that made its way to Glasgow for the cup tie against Rangers in the shape of the Hajduk Split manager Branco Zebec who had travelled to Scotland to observe his future opponents in action. In the opening 45 minutes he would witness a Hibs side that appeared hesitant and perhaps guilty of paying their opponents far too much respect. It was only after Alan Gordon had equalised an earlier strike by Derek Johnstone 30 minutes from the end that they had started to come into the game, passing up several late opportunities to prevent a replay. Hibs had been extremely fortunate to have survived an early scare when apparently everyone inside the ground, with the exception of referee Bobby Davidson and his linesman, had seen Tommy McLean blatantly bundled off the ball by goalkeeper Herriot well inside the Hibs penalty area; the official waving play on, an extremely rare occurrence at Ibrox. Just two minutes later Hibs were level when Gordon scored with a header, his marker later claiming that he had left the ball after hearing a shout to 'leave it'. Regardless, there would be no more scoring and it was now on to the replay at Easter Road in midweek.

At that time both clubs were doing well and such was the interest in the game that both the stand and enclosure had been completely sold out almost an hour before the start. The gates to the ground were closed just after the kick-off with an estimated 49,000, Edinburgh's biggest crowd for several years, packed inside. Dozens of spectators would later claim to have been unable to see any of the action taking place on the field and had made their way to the exits only to find the gates locked, some only managing to leave the ground with the assistance of the police. As to the game itself, Rangers took the lead after only six minutes after a strike by McLean, but for most of the remainder of the game had been forced back on the defensive. In what would later be described as a punishing 90 minutes, the over robust Ibrox side, unable to match Hibs in ability, had instead adopted spoiling tactics, conceding free kick after free kick in an attempt to knock the home side off their stride. Midway through the second half Duncan had drawn Hibs level, only for McLean to score his second of the evening from the penalty spot just minutes later. The game finally ending 2–1, Hibs' first home defeat in the competition for 11 years.

It would not take long to recover from their cup hangover however. Just a few days before facing Hajduk Split in the Cup Winners' Cup, a comprehensive 5–0 home victory against a Dumbarton side that had won only one of their previous 17 games had lifted Hibs into third place in the table, four points behind the then leaders Rangers. With still two games in hand, ideal preparation for the game against Split on the Wednesday, confidence had been boosted even further with the news that their Croatian opponents had lost heavily at home the previous weekend.

Despite the manager's earlier optimism, Hajduk who had only managed to defeat third division Wrexham on the away goals ruling in the previous round, had qualified for the Cup Winners' Cup by defeating Dinamo Zagreb in the national cup final the previous season, and would undoubtedly prove dangerous adversaries that should not be taken lightly.

In the first game at Easter Road both Des Bremner and Tony Higgins had been experiencing their first taste of European football, the young John Salton added to the pool although not listed

THE LEAGUE CUP AND VICTORY AT TYNECASTLE (1972–73)

in the line up. By far the biggest surprise of the evening had been the inclusion of the experienced European campaigner Alex Edwards, who although still suspended from domestic football and had not kicked a ball for almost a month, had been eligible to play in Europe.

Inspired by the big crowd and again wearing the all dark green jerseys, Hibs soon raced into a two-goal lead. The fans, many anticipating yet another six-goal victory had been stunned when the visitors pulled one back just before half-time. Duncan increased Hibs' lead just after the restart and although Hajduk had missed a couple of easy chances Alan Gordon scored his own third to give his side what appeared to be a comfortable three goal cushion. With just 14 minutes remaining Hibs now held a seemingly unassailable lead to take into the return leg in Split when Hajduk scored what would eventually prove to be a vitally important second goal after taking advantage of some shambolic defending in the home penalty area. At 4–1 the tie had probably already been as good as over. With the away goal's ruling now counting double in the event of a draw, Split's second goal, the first time since a 3–3 draw with Belenenses in 1962 that Hibs had conceded twice in a home European game, had now put an entirely different complexion on the tie. The four goals scored that evening however had brought Hibs' total to 19, at that time the highest in the competition, the next nearest the eventual winners AC Milan with 11.

In the return leg in Split the teams had taken the field to a deafening crescendo of firecrackers and rockets from a fiercely partisan crowd, all helping to create an intimidating atmosphere inside the extremely tight stadium. With the still suspended Edwards again taking his place in the line up, Hibs started the game well and were in the ascendancy. Hajduk were creating little danger when two uncharacteristic mistakes by the normally reliable Jim Herriot, after he failed to cut out crosses that seemed the goalkeepers ball all the way, had allowed the home side to take the overall lead courtesy of the away goals ruling.

There was a third goal for Hajduk shortly after the interval, Herriot again failing to collect an easy ball driven across the face of the box forcing the inrushing Blackley to deflect the ball into his own net. Proving academic, the players were all fully aware that the real damage had been done back in Edinburgh. Just minutes from the end Hibs had been dealt yet another blow when fullback Schaedler was carried off with a suspected dislocated shoulder to be replaced by Bobby Smith who was making his European debut. Looking back, although Hajduk had been a marvellous side it was a game that Hibs could well have won had it not been for the stupid defensive mistakes. With the exception of centre-half Jim Black who had been solid throughout, few had played to their true capabilities.

Signed by Bob Shankly from Airdrie in 1969 for £30,000, Black had already made more than 200 appearances for the Broomfield side, and it would not take the experienced player long to become a mainstay in the side. A loss of confidence at the end of the 1970–71 season had resulted in him temporarily losing his place to Pat Stanton, a move that had immediately resulted in a transfer request. A demand that, similar to O'Rourke, had also meant him missing the clubs summer trip to Majorca, only the arrival of Turnbull had seen the player withdraw the request. Though often underrated by the Hibs fans, this was not an opinion shared by either the manager or his teammates who were all well aware of what he brought to the side. Good in the air and strong in the tackle while forming a successful partnership with John Blackley at the heart of the defence, he would just go about his game in a quiet but effective manner. Sometimes appearing rather ungainly and possibly lacking in pace, he more than made up for this with his reading of the game. Goalkeeper Jim Herriot would often say that as far as he personally was concerned Black was not nearly dirty enough for a centre-half, an opinion however that was not always shared by his immediate opponents.

Interviewed after the game, a clearly disappointed Turnbull claimed that he had fully expected his side to go all the way to the final in Salonika, perhaps even win the tournament. The manner of the defeat however leading him to contemplate his future in the game, and for him personally things would never be quite the same again.

While still in Yugoslavia Hibs had been notified that the impressive form shown during the season had already brought its reward

THE LEAGUE CUP AND VICTORY AT TYNECASTLE (1972–73)

when five players, Stanton, Gordon, Schaedler, Blackley and Duncan had all been selected in the Scottish League squad for the forthcoming game against the Football League at Hampden, and undoubtedly this would have been six had it not been for the earlier injury to Brownlie. Somewhat incredibly, once again there had been no place for the fan favourite Alex Edwards who at that time was probably one of the top players in the league. The injury in Split would rule Schaedler out of the running as would a calf sprain later picked up by Gordon, and in the end only Stanton and Duncan would take part in the eventual 2–2 draw.

The result in Yugoslavia would obviously have done little to inspire confidence for the forthcoming crucial league game at Ibrox on the Saturday, but for goalkeeper Herriot the poor display in Split was to prove even more expensive and he would never play for the first team again. With Jim McArthur now replacing Herriot and Bobby Smith making his first ever start, a controversial goal by Tommy McLean late in the second half at Ibrox would severely dent any lingering championship aspirations still held by the Easter Road side. Referee Bobby Davidson, himself no stranger to controversy, had appeared badly at fault. Allowing McLean who looked several yards offside to go through to score what would turn out to be the only goal of the game, John Blackley who had already been booked was sent off after contesting the decision too strongly. To give Davidson his due he had seemed unsure, relying on his linesman who appeared to be in a far better position to judge the situation, but unfortunately for Hibs and to the disbelief of a great many inside the stadium the official had kept his flag down, a quite incredible but not entirely unknown decision in Glasgow.

Although Hibs still remained in third place, five points behind leaders Rangers and still with a game in hand, the defeat at Ibrox had surely all but finally ended any hopes of the title. Any lingering doubts disappearing completely the following Saturday after a scoreless draw against lowly Arbroath at Easter Road, in what had generally been regarded as Hibs' worst performance of the season, the players booed as they left the field at the end by a small section of the support.

A season that had started so promisingly would eventually limp out almost without a whimper when only two of the final eight games would end in a draw, all the others defeats. It would be something of a major understatement to say that the final few months had turned out to be a quite unbelievable anti-climax and disappointment for everyone connected with the club after the events earlier in the campaign.

At Easter Road on the final day of the season, a game surprisingly not covered by the cameras for the TV highlights later that evening, a crowd of over 45,000 taking Hibs' home attendances to over half a million during the entire campaign, had witnessed Celtic winning an eighth successive championship after a hard-fought 3–0 victory. The first time that season Hibs had conceded more than two goals in the same game at home.

Although two cups had been won and a third-place finish in the league achieved, an improvement from the previous season's fourth, the eventual 11-point gap between themselves and champions Celtic was far wider than it should have been for a team with genuine title aspirations. There is no doubt however that the horrendous injury to Brownlie who was then in international form; the savage eight-week suspension handed out to Edwards; along with the injury to Schaedler against Hajduk Split, who incredibly had missed just two games before his return to action; combined with the later suspensions of both Stanton and Blackley would all have contributed to the hugely disappointing end to the season. The consistency of what had become the recognised 11 earlier in the campaign had probably prevented some of the promising youngsters from gaining more game time and it was perhaps this lack of experienced cover that had played such a major part in the disappointing finish.

Reports of Alan Gordon's goalscoring prowess however had attracted admirers from further afield and sometime earlier he had been invited to take part in the testimonial game for the long-serving Hamburg and German international defender Willi Schulz. Because of Hibs' European commitments at that time the club had refused to release the player, but now after the defeat by Hajduk Split, Gordon made his way to Germany where he would line up alongside such luminaries as Denis Law, Bobby Charlton, Bobby Moore, Franz Beckenbauer and Gerd Muller. Coming on as a second-half substitute, Gordon had created a favourable

THE LEAGUE CUP AND VICTORY AT TYNECASTLE (1972–73)

impression and although failing to get on the score sheet himself in the eventual 5–2 defeat, he had managed to lay on both his sides' goals before hitting the crossbar with a tremendous header late in the game. What for him personally had been a tremendously successful season would end in him being nominated as runner-up to Celtic's John Connolly as Scotland's Player of the Year, earning even further acclaim when voted the Hibernian Supporters Association Player of the Year.

While obviously disappointed at the unsatisfactory end to a campaign that had promised so much, the Hibs supporters would have been well aware that during the season just ended they had witnessed football not seen at Easter Road for many years; entertainment that had perhaps been worthy of championship success. Several promising youngsters including McArthur, Bremner, Smith, Higgins, Spalding and Stevens had all made a first team debut, but except for goalkeeper McArthur who had now replaced Herriot permanently, Bremner, and to a lesser extent Higgins, few would be ready to claim a regular first team place in the season ahead.

Perhaps a sign that there is often very little loyalty in the game, after his tremendous contribution during the previous couple of seasons, Jim Herriot's time at Easter Road had ended in acrimony. On his way to a reserve game against Partick Thistle at Firhill just a few weeks from the end of the season the goalkeeper had happened to notice a newspaper billboard announcing that he had been handed a free transfer, news that had come as something of a surprise to the player. A heated meeting with Eddie Turnbull the following morning would change nothing and he was soon to sign for St Mirren. Interviewed later Herriot would confess that although he had wished to end his playing career at Easter Road, his relationship with a manager that some of the players had nicknamed 'Mutley' after the bad-tempered dog in a children's cartoon that was popular on TV around then, had been 'feisty' for some time, Turnbull was rarely seen in a good mood in the dressing room, even after a good victory, his demeanour in direct contrast to the rest of the backroom staff. Although there had sometimes been a pat on the back there had never been a well done or a welcome arm around the shoulder. While it appears that Herriot's poor display against Hajduk Split could well have been a contributing factor, the fact that McArthur's university course that was due to end in the summer would now allow him to turn full-time, the younger player had obviously been considered a long-term replacement. However, in the circumstances Herriot's release could well have been handled far better, if only out of respect for what he had already achieved in the game.

During the season just ended, the trio of Jimmy O'Rourke, Alan Gordon and Arthur Duncan had scored 99 goals between them in all games. Gordon had scored 42 (27 in the league), and although he would not have been permitted to have collected the prestigious trophy had he been successful, he had remained well in the running for the Golden Boot award that would eventually be won by Bayern Munich's Gerd Muller, until the final few weeks of the season finally ending in a more than respectable seventh place.

Surprisingly, mainly because of Brownlie's injury and Herriot's free transfer, what had become known as the 'celebrated 11' – Herriot, Brownlie and Schaedler, Stanton, Black and Blackley, Edwards, O'Rourke, Gordon, Cropley and Duncan, otherwise generally known collectively as Turnbull's Tornadoes – had made just 22 appearances as a complete unit in competitive games, including the occasion when Robertson had replaced goalkeeper Herriot midway through the away game against Besa. Of the 22, 18 had been won, two drawn and just two defeats. A total of 71 league goals had been scored during this time as opposed to just 22 conceded and the impact of the Tornadoes, not only on the club itself but the Scottish game, would go down in football folklore.

At the end of the season both Stanton and Schaedler had been called into the Scotland squad for the home internationals, Stanton captaining the side against Wales and Northern Ireland; only a recurring ankle injury received against Celtic in the final game of the season denying him the honour of leading the side out at Wembley. Schaedler however would again have to be content to watch all three games from the sidelines.

Previously manager of St Johnstone, the former Famous Five legend Willie Ormond had only recently replaced Tommy Docherty as manager of Scotland. His tenure would fail to get off to an auspicious start after a disastrous 5–0 defeat by England at Hampden

THE LEAGUE CUP AND VICTORY AT TYNECASTLE (1972–73)

in a match to celebrate the SFA's centenary, but it was not to be the last we would hear of him at Easter Road.

Along with Herriot, Willie McEwan, Johnny Hamilton and Bertie Auld had also been freed. Auld, who had not made an appearance for the first team since the Scottish Cup final at the end of the previous season, was retained as part of the coaching staff. Hamilton, one of the real characters of the side had made around 20 appearances for the first team during the season including several as a substitute and could perhaps have been considered a surprise 'free'. A talented player with a good football brain, Hamilton had performed well when needed, but perhaps his lifestyle had held him back and he possibly lacked the necessary desire for the topflight game. An ardent Rangers fan he would soon achieve his life's ambition by signing for his boyhood heroes. There are many stories concerning the mischievous Hamilton, including the time when he had accidentally struck the manager on the back of the head with the ball during a training session only to infuriate Turnbull even further with his 'sorry wee man' apology. On another occasion during a shooting session at Easter Road he had blasted the ball high into the back of the covered enclosure before instructing the manager to 'Go get that ball Ned', the rest of the players barely managing to conceal their laughter.

McEwan was yet another who had failed to live up to his early potential. Something of a first team regular before the arrival of Turnbull, there had been early indications that he did not fit into the present manager's plans. Usually finding himself on the fringes of the first team, after 69 appearances in all games during his five seasons at Easter Road he would soon join Second Division Blackpool and eventually go on to have a lengthy career in England both as a player and manager. Turnbull had first come across John Hazel when as manager of Aberdeen he had stopped off in Edinburgh on his way to England on a scouting trip to watch a minor game at Tynecastle and had been impressed with the then Dunipace Juniors player and no doubt would have been disappointed that things hadn't worked out for the youngster at Easter Road.

For Hibs however, after what had been an arduous but ultimately rewarding season, a projected lucrative five game tour of

Australia had been cancelled almost at the last minute by the Australian authorities. It would later emerge that Stoke City had now been invited in Hibs' place, leading to an official protest being lodged with the SFA, Tom Hart claiming that the Easter Road side had turned down an earlier invitation to tour New Zealand in favour of the Australian trip. However, nothing could be done and instead, as some compensation, the entire squad including the 18-year-old David McMillan who was yet to feature in the first team, had embarked on a two-week trip to Benidorm.

To cap what for him personally had been a satisfying season, soon after arriving home from Spain Alan Gordon would learn that he had also been voted the Scottish Player of the Year by the sports magazine *Inside Football*.

A New Challenge (1973–74)

AS WELL AS both the Drybrough and League Cup victories, the tremendous football on offer at Easter Road at that time had now created an even greater expectation among the supporters. While most clubs were still announcing a drop in attendances, Hibs had seen an increase at the gates of around 160,000, an average of more than 17,500 a game, statistics that had not been seen at Easter Road since the 1959–60 season and would not be surpassed until 2017–18.

At the end of the previous campaign the Edinburgh-born defender Gerry Adair had been signed on a free transfer from West Bromwich Albion and would soon be joined at Easter Road by Alex McGregor, an inside-forward who perhaps surprisingly had been released by Ayr United during the summer. Adair had joined West Bromwich straight from school but had experienced great difficulty in breaking into the first team at the Hawthorns. Unfortunately for Adair he would find the competition for first team places at Easter Road just as challenging and after only a handful of appearances would eventually join Dunfermline before a move to Meadowbank Thistle, finally ending his career with the Junior side Armadale Thistle after a spell at Cowdenbeath. During the 1971–72 season McGregor had been something of a regular at Somerset Park but had since struggled to hold down a first team place. Turnbull had been a long-time admirer of a player who although blessed with great skill and tremendous pace had possibly lacked the heart for topflight football. Almost ever present in the reserve side, except for a couple of unused appearances as a substitute, McGregor would also fail to make the breakthrough into the first team at Easter Road and would join the recently relegated Shrewsbury Town in the English Fourth Division midway through the season.

Both players however had joined their teammates on the first day of training as the squad was put through its paces for the forthcoming season at the Jack Kane Centre. The group was also joined by leg break victims John Brownlie and Kenny Davidson, both now seemingly well on the way to full fitness. Unfortunately, on a routine visit to a specialist that same afternoon Brownlie's hopes of forcing himself back into the international set-up in time for the forthcoming World Cup qualifier against Czechoslovakia at Hampden, a game that would ensure Scotland's qualification for the World Cup finals in Germany, would be shattered. He would require another, although this time relatively minor, operation on his injured leg, circumstances however that would obviously also delay his return to the Hibs first team.

With his university course now completed, during the summer Jim McArthur had turned full-time, a move that was certain to greatly benefit his game. Although thought to possibly have been a bit on the short side for a goalkeeper, McArthur's tremendous shot-stopping abilities, allied to his intelligent and accurate distribution and enthusiasm would have more than made up for any lack of inches.

In preparation for the forthcoming season, Hibs had embarked on a three-game tour of Scandinavia with games against the mainly amateur sides Hvidovre in Copenhagen, Swedish Second Division side Klarade and the Norwegian Rosenberg in Trondheim. Before the game the hampers containing the kit had been mislaid at the airport. Tom McNiven and Secretary Cecil Graham were delegated to remain behind to await the return of the missing items and both would later be forced to endure the treacherous hair raising 150-mile journey through the snowcapped mountains in a hired car. The tour however had ended without a win, with defeats by both Hvidovre and Rosenborg, and finally a 2–2 draw with Klarade, the results against amateur opposition perhaps understandably not all that well received by the fans back in Edinburgh. Turnbull on the other hand had been far more positive when stating that the games had been simply practice matches to bring the players up to match fitness, give some of the younger players more game experience, and that the results should not be taken all that seriously. Privately though he would undoubtedly have been extremely concerned at the fact that none of the previous 11 games, a run stretching back to the final few weeks of the previous season, had ended in victory.

A NEW CHALLENGE (1973-74)

The manager meanwhile had been highly optimistic regarding the forthcoming campaign: 'While it was good for the club to win both the Drybrough and League Cups during the previous season that had only been the beginning. The players now have a further years' experience under their belts and we must now look for an all-round improvement and better things to come.'

Before that however would be the defence of the Drybrough Cup and a home game against St Mirren when they would come up against their former teammate Jim Herriot for the first time. During the summer Herriot had joined the Paisley side on a free transfer but his time at Love Street was also to end acrimoniously. Financial promises made by his former Dunfermline teammate Willie Cunningham who had just recently taken over as manager at Love Street had failed to materialise, including him receiving just half the agreed signing-on fee. An appeal to the chairman had fallen on deaf ears when it was discovered that there had been nothing in writing. After just over a season in Paisley, Herriot would join Partick Thistle as back-up to goalkeeper to Alan Rough after an injury to reserve keeper John Arrol. Finally ending what had been an illustrious playing career with a few appearances for Morton before taking up employment on a building site. Although he had only been at Easter Road for 17 months, during which time he had made 98 first team starts in all games, his value to the side should not be understated. His calm and controlling demeanour had helped settle the defence, Alex Edwards, a former teammate at Dunfermline, later claiming that Herriot, who incidentally had never lost a goal against Hearts during his time at Easter Road, had been the best goalkeeper he had played alongside. The former youth international Iain Munro, who had joined the club from St Mirren only at the beginning of the season in a £20,000 deal, would also be making a debut against his former side that afternoon. Probably because of its quick conclusion, the Drybrough Cup competition had grown steadily in popularity and more than 13,000 had attended the St Mirren game, almost 4,000 more than the corresponding fixture against Montrose at the same stage the previous season. Although Hibs had made extremely hard work of the eventual 2–1 victory it would be enough to see them safely through to the semi-final. Munro was an almost immediate hit with the home fans when opening the scoring just after the start of the second half with his first goal for the club. The lead however would be held for all of two minutes, and only a late goal by Arthur Duncan had saved his side's blushes against an extremely determined Second Division outfit.

Earlier, the authorities had decided that now two substitutes could be used in the competition, both O'Rourke and Higgins taking their place on the bench.

It would be no surprise to learn that their opponents in the semi-final were yet again to be Rangers at Easter Road, and in anticipation of another huge crowd the kick-off time had been put back 15 minutes to allow the away fans time to make their way through from Glasgow. A tough battle that had again required extra time to settle the issue had once again been marred by trouble, both on and off the field. Almost from the start weak refereeing had allowed several highly illegal challenges to go unpunished, the majority it has to be said committed by the visiting side who once again had struggled to cope with the superior skill and determination of Hibs. The incidents on the field possibly going some way in creating a highly charged atmosphere between the rival fans on the terracing who already had a history of disorder in the fixture, in the second half the proceedings had been held up for several minutes after supporters had spilled on to the pitch to escape the mayhem taking place all around them. In the end however, victory had gone to the side that had attempted to play the football, a Tony Higgins goal in extra time giving Hibs a deserved 2–1 win and Rangers their first defeat in 27 games.

In the final at Hampden Hibs would be facing a Celtic side that had recently claimed its eighth consecutive league title. In a gruelling encounter that had again required extra time to separate the sides, Celtic had the first real chance of the game when a tremendous Dalglish effort struck the crossbar with McArthur beaten. In blustery conditions that made good football extremely difficult, both sides had missed chances. With Hibs inspired by man-of-the-match John Blackley holding the upper hand, as normal time came to a close with the game still goalless, once again it was on to extra time. During the extra 30 minutes there had again been several chances at both ends with neither side

A NEW CHALLENGE (1973–74)

managing to make the vital breakthrough until the dying seconds. With penalty kicks looming, Alan Gordon ended a good move involving Bremner, Higgins and Cropley by stroking the ball past the advancing Hunter and into the net from just inside the penalty area, a goal that allowed Hibs to retain its hold on the trophy. According to one newspaper the following morning: 'On this performance Hibs will take some stopping, and already look an even better side from that of the previous season.'

In view of the forthcoming Fairs Cup tie against Keflavik, the secretary of the Icelandic FA had been a guest of the club for the games against both Rangers and Celtic and was certain to have been impressed by the performance of the Easter Road side and would no doubt have had plenty to report back in Keflavik.

Hibs: McArthur, Bremner and Schaedler, Stanton, Black and Blackley, Edwards, Higgins, Gordon, Munro and Duncan (subs) Cropley and Smith
Celtic: Hunter, McGrain and Hay, Murray, McNeil, Connolly, McLaughlin, Dalglish, Lennox, Callaghan and Lynch (subs) Hood and Brogan
Referee: A McKenzie (Larbert)

With the Drybrough Cup safely back at Easter Road, the club could now set its sights on retaining its hold on the League Cup. For the one season only the authorities had decided that the League Cup would now also adopt the experimental offside ruling used in the Drybrough Cup and also that two substitutes would now be allowed.

In a section comprising of Morton, Ayr United and Dumbarton, a comprehensive 4–1 victory at Cappielow had got the new season off to a positive start. In what had been a somewhat disappointing first half Morton had opened the scoring, but Turnbull's now well recognised ability to use his substitutes effectively had again been demonstrated when at the start of the second half he had replaced Alex Edwards with Alex Cropley and Alan Gordon with the young Bobby Smith; changes that had paid almost immediate dividends. Turnbull often stated that regardless of the work done during the week, a manager really earned his money at half-time with his changes, either tactical or in personnel to suit a particular situation and usually got it right. The introduction of Smith been particularly effective, the youngster setting up goals for Higgins who scored twice, Duncan during a spirited fightback, Cropley himself scoring a fourth against his former colleague Roy Baines. At that time Baines had been only one of several former Hibs goalkeepers plying their trade in the Scottish League. As well as Herriot at St Mirren, Gordon Marshall was then at Arbroath, Thomson Allan at Dundee and Willie Wilson with Berwick Rangers.

The Morton chairman Hal Stewart had been greatly impressed by the performance of the Easter Road side particularly during the second half and in his post-match interview had described Hibs as 'an absolutely brilliant side, without a single weakness', an opinion shared by one journalist the following morning: 'Going on this performance Hibs hold on the trophy will be difficult to release'. Despite the disappointing end to what had otherwise been a tremendous previous season many of the journalists were now tipping Hibs as potential champions.

Five of the section games would be won comfortably as Hibs qualified for a place in the quarter-finals of the competition for the fifth time in six years. A 1–0 home victory against Dumbarton would be Captain Pat Stanton's 500th appearance for the club. His was a talent that could well have been missed. Training at Easter Road in the evenings since the age of 14, Stanton had fully expected to have been offered a provisional contract after leaving school and both the player and his family, lifelong Hibs supporters, had been more that disappointed when this had failed to materialise. The then Dunfermline manager Jock Stein had been a big admirer of the player and he had already played a trial game at East End Park with a view to signing, moves apparently that had eventually encouraged an approach from Hibs. This belated contact however had infuriated the player's dad who felt that the club had 'mucked' the youngster about. There had also been interest from Hearts, only for Stanton's mother using her logic to advise her son that he would be far better off signing for Hibs as Easter Road was nearer to Niddrie than Tynecastle and cheaper to get to on the bus. Stanton would eventually be offered a full

A NEW CHALLENGE (1973-74)

professional contract by Walter Galbraith but the whole sorry episode had unnecessarily left a bad taste in the mouth.

The final section game would turn out to be a somewhat unexpected heavy defeat by foot of the section Dumbarton at the aptly named Boghead. In the 2-0 victory over Ayr United a few days earlier goalkeeper McArthur had injured his hand when making a save, the proceedings held up for several minutes as he received treatment from Tom McNiven. Although managing to finish the game, an X-Ray later revealed his thumb was broken and would now require surgery and he was expected to be out of action for several weeks. At the pre-match meal at the North British Hotel before making their way to Dumbarton the manager had been conspicuous in his absence, any enquiry from the players met with the curt reply that he would be joining them in Glasgow. With only Bobby Robertson as back-up, the youngster had fully expected to play, but Turnbull had already moved to sign the experienced Irish international Roddie McKenzie from Airdrie for a fee said to be in the region of £8,000. Signed just hours before the game, unfortunately the 27-year-old McKenzie who had been in dispute with his former club for some time over a benefit payment and had not played for several months would have a debut to forget. Conceding a penalty in the first few minutes he would later be badly at fault after accidentally rolling the ball out to the feet of an opponent who had wasted no time in doubling his side's lead. Although he settled as the game went on, Dumbarton had been the better side throughout, against it has to be said an extremely disappointing Hibs side, the home team fully deserving their eventual, albeit surprise 4-1 victory to give Hibs their first defeat in eight games. The final whistle had come as a huge relief, not only for the players but the large travelling support that had made its way through from Edinburgh with great expectations. On this performance it had probably been fortunate that qualification for the next round where they now would meet Raith Rovers and the former Easter Road favourite Joe Baker had already been secured.

In the opening league game against Partick Thistle in Edinburgh the visitors had opened the scoring midway through the first-half only to be forced onto the back foot as Hibs proceeded to bombard the Partick penalty area for the remainder of the game. Only the future Scotland goalkeeper Alan Rough at his very best, allied to some bad luck and poor finishing preventing a far more convincing victory than the final 2–1 scoreline would suggest. The victory however a perfect tonic before facing city rivals Hearts at Tynecastle.

After the recent 7–0 rout over their near neighbours on New Year's Day, the Hibs supporters making their way to the game could possibly have been excused if expecting yet another pleasant afternoon in Gorgie, the Hearts fans no doubt approaching the game with some trepidation. However, it would turn out to be Hearts' day, and at the end of the 90 minutes their fans had fully deserved to celebrate in the summer sunshine after their favourites had ended a ten year wait for a 'derby' victory at Tynecastle, five without even scoring a goal. An early own goal by Schaedler had given Hearts a half-time lead and just after the restart two goals inside a few minutes by Kenny Aird and Donald Ford, the latter's first ever against Hibs after more than 300 appearances in a maroon jersey, had all but already sealed the victory. Sandwiched between both goals had been a strike by Cropley that even the player admitted would probably not have been allowed today when he had clearly kicked the ball from goalkeeper Garland's hands. It was a game that Hibs never looked like winning, against a hard-working Hearts side that straight from start had never allowed them to settle, a Drew Busby goal near the end merely confirming an outcome that had never at any time been in doubt. As the shattered Hibs supporters made their weary way from the ground and the players their way to the dressing room after the final whistle, the Hearts captain Alan Anderson was overheard asking Alex Cropley 'What's the score now?' a reference presumably to the Hibs player's taunt during the earlier New Year's Day game. While acknowledging that Hearts had fully deserved the victory, Turnbull later admitted that he had been extremely concerned at the way several of his players had approached the game. Absolving any of the youngsters from blame, his criticism had been aimed solely towards some of the more experienced players. As far as he was concerned they had not worked nearly hard enough or shown the expected attitude and that several would be

A NEW CHALLENGE (1973–74)

missing from the starting line up for the home League Cup game against Raith Rovers in midweek, a draw incidentally that was said to have delighted the former Hibs and Scotland goalkeeper George Farm who was then the manager at Stark's Park.

At Easter Road in midweek the former fan favourite Joe Baker who was making his first appearance back at the ground since his free transfer almost 17 months earlier had as expected received a rapturous welcome from the Hibs fans among what has to be said was a disappointingly poor crowd of less than 6,000. Despite the manager's pre-match comments, only Alan Gordon had been missing from the starting line up to be replaced by O'Rourke. Perhaps surprisingly, despite ending the previous season as Hibs' second top goal scorer with 34 goals in all competitions including six hat-tricks, this would be O'Rourke's first appearance of the season, spending the majority of this time either in the reserves or on the substitutes' bench. Some felt that the manager had never really rated a player who would have run through broken glass for him all that highly, but others thought differently; his all-action style making him a great favourite with the fans. In what would turn out to be yet another hard-fought encounter, the scores had been level at one goal each when Baker had earned the applause of both sets of fans by giving his side the lead, only for Stanton to equalise for a second time. A goal in the dying minutes by substitute Tony Higgins earning Hibs a hard-fought victory to leave the tie finely balanced with the return leg in Fife still to come.

It was also around that time that a new Tom Hart-inspired club crest was starting to appear in the match programme and also on the club's official stationery. Featuring a ball surrounded by laurel leaves capped by a crown and including the words Hibernian FC and Edinburgh in large letters, it would eventually appear on the jerseys.

In the first round of the UEFA Cup against the Icelandic side Keflavik at Easter Road the visiting side had been backed vocally by almost 200 supporters who had made their way to Edinburgh by special charter plane for the game. Perhaps surprisingly however, it would appear that the lack of hotel space in Scotland's capital city and also the country's main tourist attraction had required a number of them to spend their evenings in Glasgow.

Although Keflavik had joined the Icelandic League as recently as 1956, this would be their fifth appearance in a European competition. So far they had failed to make it past the first round although there had been no disgrace in losing 4–0 on aggregate to Real Madrid in the European Cup the previous season.

At Easter Road Keflavik had made their intentions clear straight from the start with nine men behind the ball at all times, at no point during the 90 minutes threatening Robertson in the home goal. Centre-half Jim Black had opened the scoring midway through the first half during one of his regular forays into the Keflavik penalty area with what would turn out to be only his second goal for the first team. Tony Higgins added a second, his first in European competition, but there was to be no more scoring. While they had dominated almost the entire 90 minutes, both the players and supporters would have been somewhat disappointed considering the side's overall performance to be taking just a two-goal lead into the return leg in Iceland. Although, based on an otherwise impressive display it had generally been felt that the two goals would be more than enough to secure qualification to the next round.

On the Saturday three goals inside four first-half minutes in an eventual 4–1 victory against Ayr United at Easter Road had completely knocked the heart out of their opponents and lifted Hibs into third place in the table. But although they were still winning games with just three defeats from the last 15, so far they had failed to recapture the sparkling form of the previous season. The display against Ayr had offered some encouragement with Cropley in particular in top form, the entire side also showing distinct signs of a return to something resembling their very best. Chairman Hart however had elected to give the second half a miss to watch John Brownlie making his first tentative steps back to full fitness with 45 minutes for the third team against Spartans at Canal Field; heartening news for everyone connected with the club and not least Scotland.

In the return leg at Stark's Park, goals by Duncan and Gordon had been more than enough to see Hibs safely into to the semi-finals and again it would come as no surprise to learn that they had now been drawn to meet old adversaries Rangers in the next round, the eighth meeting of the sides in cup competitions over the past six seasons.

Before that however there would be the return UEFA Cup game against Keflavik, Hibs' first ever visit to Iceland. The manager himself had visited the area some years before when in 1967 he had taken Aberdeen into European competition for the very first time, the game against Keflavik ending in a comprehensive 14–1 aggregate victory for the 'Dons'.

On this occasion Hibs had decided against chartering a private aircraft but to use a scheduled flight instead. The problem was that at that time there were no direct flights from Edinburgh to Iceland, the party eventually having to make its way from Glasgow. The return journey had created an even bigger problem. As there were no direct flights from Iceland to anywhere in Scotland on a Thursday, special arrangements had been made for the London-bound flight to be diverted to Abbotsinch, the Hibs party finally completing the journey back to Edinburgh by coach.

In an obvious attempt to attract a bigger crowd the game had now been changed from Keflavik to the national stadium in Reykjavic that was situated around 40 forty miles away. A fairly standard practice in the country for European games at that time, but even then a comparatively small crowd of only 3,154 had watched from the start, the poor attendance attributed to the late afternoon kick-off as the stadium at that time still lacked floodlights. Incessant rain the previous day had cast serious doubt on the game even going ahead, and although the heavily sanded pitch had eventually been declared playable, several of the Hibs players were later of the opinion that it had been the worst playing surface that they had ever encountered, conditions that obviously had made good football all but impossible. Before the kick-off Pat Stanton had been presented with a bouquet of flowers to mark Hibs 50th appearance in European competition, a surprise but nevertheless tremendous gesture that had been greatly appreciated.

As to the game itself, Hibs had somewhat surprisingly found themselves a goal behind at half-time although there had never at any time been any real danger of an upset, the second half almost all one-way traffic towards goalkeeper Olafsson's goal.

A second half strike by Stanton, his fourth goal in five weeks, had levelled the scores, only several tremendous saves by the goalkeeper keeping the final score down to a respectable level, the result in Edinburgh proving more than enough to have guaranteed Hibs a passage into the next round. In the early stages centre-forward Johansson had been guilty of putting himself about a bit and on one occasion a free kick into Hibs' box had been cleared when a dull thump could be heard, everyone turning to see Jim Black standing over the crumpled Johansson with the words 'Well I did tell you' leaving no one in any doubt as to what had just occurred.

At that time both Erich Schaedler and John Blackley had been called into the Scotland squad for the World Cup qualifier against Czechoslovakia. With the section already won after Scotland's historic 2–1 victory over the Czechs at Hampden, Blackley would win his first cap in the 1–0 defeat in Bratislava, Schaedler again having to watch from the sidelines. Blackley's inclusion in the starting line up however had been a richly deserved reward for his consistently reliable performances in the back four of the Tornadoes side. Signed from Gairdoch United by manager Bob Shankly in 1965 before being farmed out to Bo'ness Juniors, Blackley had potentially been just 24 hours from signing for Dunfermline when a promised trial had been cancelled almost at the last minute and would instead go on to give the Easter Road side many years of sterling service before eventually going on to manage the club. The first of his almost 400 appearances in all competitions over the following 11 seasons had been when deputising for the injured Pat Stanton in a 2–0 home victory against Dundee in October 1967, and it would not take him long to secure a regular place in the first team before eventually going on to become one of the best defenders in the country. Although the confident and creative player had possibly lacked a bit of pace he more than made up for this with his outstanding reading of the game and positional sense, and was another who had gone on to become a great favourite with the fans.

Although it was not yet November, even this early the following four away games inside just 12 days were to have a major bearing on the rest of the season. After a credible draw at Parkhead on the

A NEW CHALLENGE (1973–74)

Saturday, in midweek the party had made its way to Elland Road to face a Leeds side at that time considered not only the best in England but among the finest in Europe and one of the hot favourites to actually win the trophy. Taking advantage of some reverse psychology Turnbull had ordered a recent newspaper article by the former Leeds international and then Middlesbrough manager Jack Charlton advising the Scottish side 'to save the expense of their bus travel' to be pinned on the dressing room wall, and it was to have the desired effect. Apparently, a clearly infuriated Tom Hart had also sought out Charlton before the game to give the former England defender a piece of his mind, but unfortunately it is not known if his mission had been successful. Watched by a near 30,000 crowd, including the Scotland manager Willie Ormond who had been at the game to check on several players on either side, a confident Hibs had taken the game to their illustrious opponents straight from the first whistle and for large spells had been by far the better side. A Leeds team that would go on to win the championship at the end of the season just had no answer to the visitors' dominance in midfield, captain Pat Stanton in particularly outstanding form. Only several tremendous saves by the Scotland goalkeeper David Harvey had prevented Hibs from taking at least a two-goal lead into the break. In the second-half Hibs continued where they had left off but with just minutes left to play the game still remained goalless when Tony Higgins, who according to many had his best game yet in a green and white jersey, missed a glorious opportunity to give his side the victory that their performance had fully deserved. Sending a header over the bar from close range when it appeared far easier to score, the game finally ended 0–0. Although they had failed to achieve the win that their brilliant performance had merited, make no mistake that this was a tremendous moral victory for the Edinburgh side, the Leeds manager Don Revie himself admitting after the game that Hibs had been the better side for large parts of the game and had more than deserved to have emerged victorious. Their positive play had probably surprised Leeds when in their by now accepted custom in Europe they had gone onto the attack straight from the first whistle, and once again Turnbull had got his tactics just right.

Many neutral observers would later state that they had been somewhat surprised that a side containing several relatively inexperienced youngsters in Bremner, Higgins, Smith and McArthur, the latter making his European debut, could have been in such dominant form against an illustrious Leeds side, particularly at Elland Road. In truth few sides in Europe at that time would have been disappointed at leaving Leeds on level terms, the brief highlights shown on TV later that evening attracting many new admirers. There had been a slight concern for Hibs before the game however when goalkeeper McArthur had injured his hand in a light training session but although in some discomfort had managed to complete the entire 90 minutes.

For some reason clubs involved in midweek European action often seemed to struggle on the Saturday and unfortunately the tremendous result in Leeds would be followed by a 4–0 defeat at Ibrox, with a performance later described by Turnbull as the worse since his return to Easter Road. With the first leg of the League Cup quarter-finals due to take place back in Glasgow just a few days later, the manager had made it abundantly clear that he had been far from happy at the contributions of some of the more experienced players. O'Rourke, Cropley and Duncan in particular, giving performances in his opinion that had fallen well below the standard he had come to expect; the heavy defeat also extremely difficult to accept from a side with such ability and ambition. On the day, Hibs' midfield had made little impact on a game that Rangers had thoroughly deserved to win while the Hibs forwards had rarely created any real danger during the entire 90 minutes. Goalkeeper McArthur was Hibs' top performer on the day but still unable to do anything to stem the tide.

A few days later, the fans that had made their way to Ibrox for the League Cup quarter-final first leg against Rangers had not been slow in showing their displeasure, both during and after the game, as once again Hibs had failed to play to their undoubted potential. In a 2–0 defeat, the performance was another pale imitation of the tremendous display in Leeds just seven days earlier. After a one-sided first half, a tactical change by Turnbull had seen some slight improvement. They had been looking likely to equalise a first-half goal by Greig only for Erich Schaedler to send an attempted clearance high into his own net past a startled McArthur. The consummate professional Alex McDonald merely warned by the referee after his over-zealousness in congratulating the Hibs full-back when a booking might well have been in order. Although far from impossible, Hibs now faced an uphill battle in the return leg at Easter Road if they were to have any hope of retaining their hold on the trophy.

Before the return leg against Leeds in Edinburgh Tom Hart had once again been involved in controversy involving his own fans when raising the ticket prices for the game. The centre stand was raised from the normal 75p to £2.00 with proportional increases for other parts of the ground, a move that had once again been strongly condemned by the majority of the fans including the chairman of the Supporters Association as outrageous. This was not the first time that the chairman had angered his own supporters regarding ticket pricing. As mentioned earlier he had been guilty of the same before a Scottish Cup tie with Aberdeen two years earlier, just before the Sporting Lisbon game the previous season the supporters had again been outraged to learn that briefs for the main stand that were normally priced at 75p had now been increased to £1, a rise widely condemned as being far too high and nothing more than a cynical attempt to raise more revenue. The move once again resulting in a deluge of complaints to both the newspapers and the club.

Whether the price increases had any effect on the eventual attendance is open to speculation but a crowd of around 36,000, well below the anticipated 45,000 had been inside the ground at kick-off. However, regardless of the confidence gained from the inspiring performance at Elland Road just a few weeks earlier, the return leg at Easter Road would ultimately end in disappointment. Against an injury weakened United, Hibs had come up against Billy Bremner at his magnificent best when sweeping up behind the back four, and at times only the Scottish international had stood between the home side and the victory that their performance had otherwise warranted. Despite almost 90 minutes of pressure Hibs had struggled to force a breakthrough although it appeared that they had been denied a deserved victory when Alan Gordon headed past goalkeeper Letheran. Initially awarding the goal, to the bemusement of the crowd and the Hibs players themselves, the Austrian official then changed his mind after consulting his linesman and awarded Leeds a free kick instead, the linesman one of the very few inside the ground who thought Gordon offside. Despite the almost constant pressure and an arrogant but nevertheless admirable performance by the Leeds captain Bremner who had repeatedly denied the home side – at times almost single handedly – including several goal-line clearances, the 90 minutes ended goalless. Even with the benefit of extra time it was now on to penalty kicks, the first time that either side had faced the situation in a competitive game.

Nominated to take the first of the kicks that took place at the Dunbar end of the ground Pat Stanton could only watch in horror as his otherwise well struck shot sent the goalkeeper the wrong way but struck the junction of the post and bar before rebounding to safety. All the others would be converted; Cropley, Blackley, Bremner and Hazel for Hibs, and Leeds were through to the next round where they would ultimately be defeated over two legs by the Portuguese side Setubal. In the dressing room after the game a still clearly disappointed John Blackley had reminded Jim McArthur that he could have been a hero had he managed to save a couple of the spot kicks, only for the goalkeeper to reply that it was the outfield players that had missed the chance to make a name for themselves by failing to find the back of the net. Interviewed after the game the Leeds captain Billy Bremner had nothing but praise for the battling Easter Road side:

> Hibs did everything but score, and if luck had been on their side they would have won by three or four goals and we could not have complained. They are a brilliant side and I cannot praise them highly enough.

As the penalty kicks were being taken the Leeds manager Don Revie and his assistant Les Cocker had remained on the field alongside the players which was strictly against the rules prompting an immediate complaint by Tom Hart to the official observer at the game followed by a telegram to the UEFA authorities in Switzerland the following morning demanding a replay. Incredibly, despite

A NEW CHALLENGE (1973-74)

Revie and Leeds being found guilty at a later hearing and the manager banned from the dugout for the next European game, the committee also decided that Revie's presence had not unduly influenced his players and that Hibs' request for a replay had been rejected. Unbelievably, although their protest had otherwise been successful Hibs had still been required to forfeit the compulsory deposit of 500 Swiss francs that had been received by the authorities on receipt of the complaint.

On the domestic front, the return League Cup fixture against Rangers at Easter Road a few weeks later had been highly unusual because of its midweek afternoon kick-off. Due to industrial action by electricity workers, random areas of the country had been liable to fall victim to 'surprise blackouts' at any time and in the interest of safety games under lights had been temporarily suspended. Despite its 1.30pm start when most of the regular supporters should still have been at work, a more than credible 19,245 had been inside the ground at the kick-off. Almost ten months after his horrendous leg break against East Fife, and almost a year to the day since he had scored the winning goal against Rangers in the League Cup semi-final, just a few days earlier John Brownlie had made a surprise return to first team action in a 2–1 home defeat of Dundee. Keeping his place for the game against Rangers he had received a rapturous welcome from the Hibs fans as he lined up in his usual position. Unfortunately, against a Rangers side that had been totally committed to defence with ten men behind the ball at all times in an attempt to hold on to their earlier lead, once again Hibs had been a mere shadow of the side that had performed so well in both UEFA Cup games against Leeds. On the day few of the Hibs players had played to their true capabilities, Duncan, O'Rourke and Cropley again producing contributions well below what had come to be expected. The eventual goalless draw, the third blank against the Ibrox side in just a few weeks, ending any hopes of Hibs retaining the trophy. After the game there had been reports that some of the Rangers supporters' buses had been stoned and windows smashed by some thugs as they left the ground. Although the culprits had been arrested by the police Tom Hart had been vehement in his condemnation in stating that this type of action would not be tolerated at Easter Road. 'We do not want supporters of this type following the team. Our fans have a good reputation both at home and away: keep it that way.'

In the league however things were still going well. Apart from the earlier defeat by Hearts that had provided the Gorgie side and its supporters with a degree of satisfaction after the New Year's Day mauling, between then and just before the turn of the year only the 4–0 defeat at Ibrox had interrupted a more than impressive run of eight victories and three draws. With 28 goals scored against just the nine conceded, these were results that included 5–0 home wins over both Clyde and Morton that would see Hibs second top of the table. Of the 28 goals, 14 had been shared by both O'Rourke and Gordon, evidence that there were still very few concerns in that department. In the 5–0 defeat of Clyde, Pat Stanton had scored his first, and as it would turn out the only hat-trick of his professional career, one from the penalty spot. In the 5–0 victory against Morton a few weeks later this time it would be O'Rourke's turn to score three, his first treble of the season and the ninth during his time at Easter Road.

This impressive run came to an abrupt end a few days after Christmas with a 1–0 defeat by Partick Thistle at Firhill. Although Hibs had undoubtedly missed the injured Alan Gordon, in no way could this have been an excuse for the overall poor display. Few of the players had performed to the level expected the result a performance that had culminated in Blackley missing the opportunity to equalise from the penalty spot.

One newspaper he following morning was of the opinion, perhaps rather harshly considering that it had been only the sides third league defeat of the season:

> Hibs will be bitterly disappointed not only at the result but especially the performance after their recent tremendous displays, and on this showing it appears that they still have some way to go before they can be considered genuine title challengers.

Harsh or not, during the previous few seasons the club had established a fantastic reputation for attacking and entertaining football

A NEW CHALLENGE (1973-74)

so it was perhaps understandable that the critics, like the fans, would now be that much harder to please.

At that time both the second and third teams had also been in impressive form, Stan Vincent's East of Scotland side topping the table, the second team overseen by John Fraser that regularly included the potential first team players, Robertson, McKenzie, Spalding, Murray, Higgins, McGregor, McGhee and Hazel also doing well.

1 January 1974 would be the start of Hearts' centenary year, but any celebrations at Tynecastle would have to be temporarily put on hold as Hibs continued their recent dominance of the holiday fixture with a convincing 3-1 victory at Easter Road. Cropley himself was continuing his own personal recent habit against the Edinburgh rivals by scoring twice before Duncan guaranteed victory with a third. All three had been scored in the opening 45 minutes, as had Hearts' solitary counter by Donald Ford with the result that the second half had been something of an anti-climax. During the previous ten seasons, games between the Edinburgh rivals had now resulted in ten victories for the home side with only four defeats, six ending all square, 36 goals scored by Hibs during this time compared with the 18 conceded.

With attendances throughout the country still continuing to fall it was now more obvious than ever that a change of format had been needed, and again both Edinburgh sides, Dundee, Rangers, Celtic and Aberdeen had all met to discuss the situation, only this time with the approval of the league management committee. Previously the committee's resistance to change had proved a major stumbling block but the perseverance of the so-called 'big six' now at least appeared to be paying some kind of dividend. The authorities had now agreed to canvas all the senior sides in the country for their views regarding the proposal for three leagues of ten and one of 18, a package designed primarily to entice back the missing fans. The problem remained however that this still required a two thirds majority to implement any change, but one way or another change would have come.

For a third successive year Hibs had declared a substantial loss at their AGM. Despite an increase of over £52,000 in gate receipts during the previous financial year, expenses had also increased by a colossal £63,000 and it was evident that even the majority of the so-called bigger clubs were now finding it impossible to survive on gate receipts alone. However, after the promised consultation the management committee had now agreed that from the beginning of the 1975–76 season a ten team Premier League would come into operation, each side playing each other four times a season, twice at home and twice away. The other sides would be split into two leagues of 14 playing each other once home and away, the addition of an extra cup competition hopefully compensating for any loss of revenue caused by the fewer number of games.

In that year's Scottish Cup Hibs had been drawn against Second Division Kilmarnock at Easter Road in the opening round, the first time the sides had faced each other in the competition for almost 35 years. Several English managers were said to have been in the crowd to cast an eye over the potential transfer targets Alex Cropley and John Blackley but they would not have been all that impressed by the early play of the home side who soon found themselves two goals behind but a tremendous fightback by a team that now appeared back to something like its best would eventually end in a 5–2 victory. The result, but particularly the second-half performance, no doubt pleasing manager Turnbull, a win that had also drastically shortened Hibs' odds on winning the trophy for the first time in 72 years. While several of the other sides had elected to play their cup games on the Sunday, Hibs' game went ahead on the Saturday as usual, the forward-thinking Tom Hart of the view that playing games on a Sunday had been unfair on the players and their families.

Alan Gordon's absence from the side in the earlier defeat by Partick Thistle due to injury had possibly highlighted a lack of experienced cover in the goalscoring department. Perhaps believing an injection of new blood to be the answer, in a surprise move and despite strong competition from Aberdeen who would be well aware of the player's goalscoring capabilities, Turnbull had travelled to Liverpool to sign the former Aberdeen centre-forward Joe Harper from Everton; a player he knew well from his time at Pittodrie. An initial £100,000 fee had already been agreed when Aberdeen came in with an increased offer, Hibs finally having to fork out £120,000 to secure the player's signature, a then club record.

A NEW CHALLENGE (1973–74)

It was a move that would eventually go some way in spelling the end of the fan favourites Alan Gordon and Jimmy O'Rourke's time at the club, and although little blame could be attached to Harper himself it would be seen by many as only the start of the gradual decline at Easter Road.

Harper's career so far had been somewhat chequered. Starting his professional career at Morton, the then 18-year-old had scored 29 league goals from just 30 games in season 1966–67 before joining Second Division Huddersfield Town. However, after failing to settle in England he would soon return to Morton before signing for the then Aberdeen manager Eddie Turnbull in 1969, scoring one of the 'Dons' goals in the Scottish Cup final victory over Celtic that same season. In December 1972 Aberdeen had accepted a bid of £180,000 from Everton for the player making a huge £140,000 profit on their original investment but once again Harper had failed to settle in England and was said to have been 'absolutely delighted' to be renewing his acquaintance with Eddie Turnbull at Easter Road. His relationship with his former manager, who according to some had appeared 'to be all over him' had possibly created something of a slightly unsettling atmosphere at the previously happy club, as had the suspicion that he had been on more money than the rest of the players, a rumour that had always been denied by Turnbull. The manager himself must have detected the slight unrest in the dressing room and had consequently demanded that 'this player must be accepted' perhaps drawing attention to a problem that had not been nearly as big an issue as made out. The instruction probably did Harper no favours and if anything may well have strengthened any slight resentment. According to at least one teammate, although Harper had been popular enough in the dressing room, he was not a great mixer, and as far as he personally was concerned what had been a 'tremendous team spirit had appeared to go out the window on his arrival'. Some were also said to have been suspicious of his close relationship with the manager and they had now started to watch what was being said that bit more.

Visibly overweight and well short of match fitness Harper had still been serving a suspension received at Everton when he signed for the club and consequently would not be considered for first team duty for several weeks. His first game in a green and white jersey would see him scoring a hat-trick for the reserves in a 4–1 victory against Motherwell at Fir Park.

The acquisition of the player had now presented Turnbull with the problem as to who Harper would replace in the starting 11. This would be answered, temporarily at least, when Alan Gordon, the club's top goal scorer during the past few seasons had found himself on the substitute's bench at Brockville at the beginning of February with Harper making his first team debut. In a dour and unimaginative goalless draw, during which time the Falkirk goalkeeper Ally Donaldson had not been called upon to make a single save of note, again none of the Hibs players had played to anything like their best and in truth had deserved no more than a share of the points. Near the end a still clearly unfit Harper had the opportunity to open the scoring from almost on the goal line only to scuff his attempt before the ball was eventually cleared to safety. To be fair to the player it sometimes takes time for a new signing to settle into the side, but Harper had done little to impress the watching Hibs fans, the biggest cheer of the afternoon reserved for the appearance of substitute Alan Gordon when he replaced the former Everton player near the end.

In the Scottish Cup yet another determined performance had been needed against a stuffy St Johnstone in Perth, Jimmy O'Rourke taking full advantage of the pace and unpredictability of Arthur Duncan in the opposition penalty area to score his second hat-trick of the season. Perhaps surprisingly, despite his prolific partnership with Alan Gordon the previous season when the pair had scored a phenomenal total of 76 goals between them in all competitions – O'Rourke bagging 34 including six hat-tricks – the player had found himself completely out of the picture at the beginning of the season. His position was filled either by new signing Iain Munro, Tony Higgins or Bobby Smith, and it was perhaps difficult to understand why despite his phenomenal strike rate that the manager didn't seem to really rate the player. A brief reintroduction into the first team had resulted in O'Rourke failing to score in half a dozen games and it would be back to the substitute bench for him, or even worse the second team. Recalled for a 2–1 victory against Dundee in mid-November he had celebrated his recall by scoring both Hibs goals in the 2–1 victory. Despite earlier failing to secure a regular place in the side, a hat-trick in the Scottish Cup against St Johnstone at Muirton had taken his total to 18 in just 14 appearances.

However, a 4–2 victory at Easter Road at the end of February had now increased Celtic's lead at the top of the table to five points. Dixie Deans had opened the scoring in the very first minute of the game, his side leading 2–1 at half-time only for O'Rourke to level things ten minutes after the restart before Celtic scored another twice to eventually establish a credible 4–2 victory. While neither the player nor the fans could have known it at the time, after 12 seasons and 119 goals in all games it would turn out to be the last goal that O'Rourke would score for the club. Before the game Hibs had been the only side in Britain with a perfect home record, the defeat now allowing Liverpool to take the honour with the loss of just a single point.

Seven days later Turnbull would have a surprise in store for the watching fans with his team selection for the game against Rangers. After spending the previous two games as an unused substitute Joe Harper would finally make his home debut wearing the number seven jersey in a new look side that had included only Gordon and Duncan from the recognised front five with the recalled Munro at inside left. But by far the biggest surprise of the afternoon had been the appearance of Stanton at inside right. Against an at times uninspired-looking Rangers attack and shaky defence the new formation had proved itself by running out comfortable 3–1 winners. Up front the recalled Alan Gordon had been particularly impressive in scoring twice, ably assisted by Duncan and Stanton. At the back Spalding, Black and Blackley had looked in unbeatable mood, Harper himself making a more than satisfactory home debut to keep Hibs in second place in the table.

The earlier comprehensive Scottish Cup win over Kilmarnock and the impressive away victory against St Johnstone, had been followed by a 3–3 draw against Dundee at Easter Road in the next round, Alan Gordon this time scoring a hat-trick. One behind at half-time, in what turned out to be a tremendously exciting cup tie, five goals had been scored in 14 second-half minutes including Gordon's hat-trick to draw the sides level and he could well have won it in the very last minute only to send his header narrowly past the post with the former Hibs goalkeeper Thomson Allan helpless. Unfortunately, in the replay at Dens Park in midweek Hibs had produced what turned out to be yet another incredibly disappointing performance in front of a large travelling support, the game finally ending in a 3–0 defeat. The lacklustre display that had meant Hibs bowing out of the competition almost without a whimper now left only the championship itself or the consolation of a UEFA Cup place to play for.

Meanwhile, after several call ups to the Scotland squad although he had remained unused, in what would also turn to be Pat Stanton's 16th and last appearance for the full side Erich Schaedler would finally win his first, and as it would turn out only full cap in a 2–1 defeat by West Germany in Frankfurt; Alex Cropley an unused substitute.

After several call ups to the international squad only to watch from the sidelines Schaedler had needed to show patience, his inclusion in the side for the game against Wales a deserved reward for his consistently reliable performances at Easter Road since signing from Stirling Albion in 1969.

A home game against Motherwell that had been postponed earlier due to a waterlogged pitch had finally gone ahead in midweek a few weeks later. However, after just 15 minutes and Hibs already leading by a goal from the penalty spot, the referee had been forced to bring the proceedings to a temporary halt after the thick blanket of fog that had been hanging over the city all day steadily worsened as the game went on, eventually making visibility all but impossible, both for the players and the fans on the terracing. After a wait of several minutes while the Met Office had been consulted, and after being assured that the conditions were unlikely to improve the referee had eventually been left with no other option but to abandon the game.

If the fans had been disappointed at the game being cancelled then they would have been absolutely furious to learn that there was to be no refund or even a voucher entitling them to free entry when the game was eventually replayed. Apparently, according to the Scottish League Management Committee there had been nothing in the rules to cover the situation and the now twice postponed game would eventually go ahead the following midweek. Often criticised in the past by his own supporters regarding his pricing policies, this time it had been Tom Hart's intention to allow the fans entry to all parts of the ground at greatly reduced rates for the replay only to learn that while admirable, this would also be contrary to league rules. After further consultation with Motherwell, admission prices for both the stand and enclosure over which the authorities had no jurisdiction would be at the normal terracing price of 35p. Perhaps the actions of an association that had not always been known for making intelligent or popular decisions in the past should not have come as too much of a surprise. When the game did eventually go ahead a Bobby Smith goal had been enough to give Hibs both points and a welcome victory, and after conceding 22 goals in the previous nine games goalkeeper McArthur would no doubt have found the shut-out even more enjoyable.

An embarrassing 3–2 defeat by mid-table Arbroath at Gayfield would finally put an end to any lingering hopes of the championship and leave Hibs fourth in the table behind Celtic, Rangers and Aberdeen, although still with two games in hand. The points dropped during the season against the so-called smaller sides had proved particularly expensive.

The season however would end on a more positive note with five of the remaining seven games won, the others drawn, as Hibs finally managed to finish second in the table. Four points behind champions Celtic and a solitary point ahead of third-placed Rangers, the club's highest league position since 1953, the second-place finish also guaranteed automatic qualification for the following season's UEFA Cup.

Included in this late run had been a game against Arbroath at Easter Road that had been postponed earlier in the season, the 2–1 victory avenging the defeat at Gayfield just days earlier. Although initially encountering great difficulty in breaking down a resolute, hard-working visiting defence that had played almost the entire game with eight or nine men behind the ball, in a dramatic climax all three goals had been scored inside a three-minute spell near the end. With Edwards pulling the strings from midfield Bremner had opened the scoring only for Arbroath to equalise just seconds after courtesy of a Schaedler own goal, before Harper wrapped up the points just a minute later with a tremendous solo goal that delighted the home support.

While the second-place finish had been a remarkable achievement with several impressive performances along the way, only rarely had the scintillating form of the previous few seasons been on display. However, in just under three years Eddie Turnbull could be well satisfied by what he had already achieved in creating one of the most exciting sides in the club's history that had reached four cup finals playing scintillating football that had not been seen at Easter Road for many years; the accent on a fast, fine flowing attractive game.

Of the 34 league games played 20 had ended in victory with nine drawn, the 75 goals scored bettered only by champions Celtic and more than enough to qualify for the following season's Drybrough Cup. In Turnbull's first season as manager Hibs had ended in fourth place, third the following season and now second, leaving the supporters wondering if they dare allow themselves to dream of going one step further in the coming season. Yet again well over 100 goals had been scored in all competitions, the majority once again by Alan Gordon and Jimmy O'Rourke.

Although several promising youngsters had been blooded, with all due respect it would perhaps have been asking too much at that stage of their career to have expected an inexperienced young player to replace real quality. With the exception of Derek Spalding who had been the find of the season, Higgins, Smith and Murray had all failed to make any real impact on the starting 11. Willie Murray of whom so much had been expected after his promising goalscoring start during the pre-season tour of Ireland a couple of seasons earlier would have been particularly disappointed to have managed just the one appearance for the first team during the season just ended. Though, in fairness to the player, as already mentioned it would have been an extremely difficult task for any youngster to have broken into this Hibs side during the previous few seasons.

Turnbull's acknowledged success in the past had been simply in playing the right players in the right positions. The manager's quandary over who should drop out to accommodate Joe Harper

A NEW CHALLENGE (1973-74)

had finally appeared to be settled when after 305 games in all competitions, including substitute appearances and over a hundred goals, Jimmy O'Rourke, then the longest serving player at Easter Road and one of the most popular ever to wear the green and white of Hibs, had requested a transfer. Although this had initially been turned down it now seemed obvious that the player's days at Easter Road were already numbered. Despite scoring 18 goals in just 14 appearances during the season just ended, the Hibs fanatic had been finding it extremely difficult to hold down a regular first team place, particularly in the early part of the season and now saw his future away from Easter Road. In the final game of the season, a 4-1 victory at Tannadice, the Hibs fans had been surprised to say the least to find that Alan Gordon had not been included in the starting line up. They would be even more astounded later that evening to learn that the prolific goal scorer had now been placed on the 'open to transfer' list along with Jim Black who had recently lost his place at the heart of the defence, first to Stanton and then Spalding.

For a second consecutive season Gordon had ended as top goal scorer with 16 in the league and 25 in all competitions, although well below the overall 37 the previous year. O'Rourke had scored 14 in the league compared to Harper's nine although in slightly more games. Most of the supporters were again failing to see the logic that the club's top two goal scorers were now apparently surplus to requirements.

Although the player himself had done nothing wrong, the signing of Harper had not only been considered unnecessary at that time, but also appeared to have upset the balance of the side, an opinion shared by the fans who had been more than satisfied at what they had been watching during the past couple of seasons. Harper's game was far more direct than the intelligent link-up play of Gordon from midfield, as was his lack of height in the penalty area, Gordon's lethal prowess in the air and his often quoted 'See you at back post' regularly causing all kinds of havoc in the opponents' box.

After his early promising start John Hazel had also struggled to establish a regular place in the first team with just three appearances and another two as substitute during the season. Now, after over 60 games in all competitions including appearances in both the Scottish Cup and Drybrough Cup finals the previous season, realising that his future probably lay elsewhere, just before the end of the season he had joined his former teammates Roy Baines and Alex McGhee at Morton. After failing to force himself back into the first team set-up after his earlier injury against Celtic reserves, the talented Kenny Davidson had also been freed and would soon sign for Dunfermline before finally ending his playing career at Meadowbank Thistle.

In a change from the normal routine, despite offers from New Zealand and Greece there would be no end of season tour, the players allowed to recharge their batteries after a tough season at home.

A Traditional Period (1974–75)

DURING THE SUMMER there had been little rest for both John Blackley and Erich Schaedler who had been called into the Scotland squad for the home internationals, Blackley winning his second full cap in the 2–0 defeat of England at Hampden, Schaedler once again watching from the sidelines.

Although he would take no part in the actual competition itself, Erich had become an innocent party in the now infamous boating incident at Largs. A few days earlier Scotland had defeated Wales 2–0 at Hampden. After the game the players had been allowed out for a few drinks and around midnight they were making their way back to their hotel when a slightly under the weather Jimmy Johnstone had decided to commandeer a nearby empty rowing boat for a prank, only for one of the players to kick the craft further out into the river. Only then did Johnstone realise that the boat had no oars and was drifting further out to sea. Quickly grasping the potential seriousness of the situation, both Celtic's David Hay and Schaedler had jumped into another boat in an attempt to rescue Johnstone only to find that theirs had sprung a leak. Forced to return to shore, Johnstone was left to be rescued by the coastguards that fortunately had already been called out by some of the other players. Perhaps even more fortunately, the Scotland manager Willie Ormond's thoughts regarding the incident are not known.

Both Schaedler and Blackley however would be part of the squad that would make its way to Germany for the World Cup finals a few weeks later. In winning his fourth full cap in Scotland's opening game, a 2–0 victory against Zaire, John Blackley became the first Hibs player to appear in a World Cup finals since Eddie Turnbull in Sweden in 1958. After a goalless draw with Brazil, Billy Bremner missing perhaps the best chance of the game from close range in the final minutes when the ball had bounced off his shin and past the post, a 1–1 draw with Yugoslavia a few days later would mean Scotland exiting the competition at the first stage but only on goal average. It would turn out to be Blackley's only appearance in the finals and he would not play for Scotland again for almost two years. Schaedler however had again remained unused and would never figure in the international set-up again.

On the football front, despite losing their hold in the League Cup the previous season and the early exit from the Scottish Cup at the hands of Dundee, a second-place finish in the table for the first time since the heady days of the Famous Five had suggested that Hibs were still well on course to achieve Eddie Turnbull's objective of winning the title.

Once again the club had decided on a tour of Norway and Sweden as a precursor to the coming season, the three-game tour ending with victories against both Levanger and Rosenberg and a draw with Osterland. By a remarkable coincidence, just 24 hours after the Rosenberg game Hibs had been informed that the Norwegian side were to be their opponents in the opening round of that season's UEFA Cup.

Before that had been the defence of the Drybrough Cup and the club's 100% record in the competition not to mention a £6,000 bonus for reaching the final. Yet again the experimental offside ruling had come into operation, not only for the Drybrough Cup but now also the League Cup. A proposal that meant what had initially been merely an experimental ruling could possibly also be introduced permanently in all competitions in the near future including the championship itself had concerned the majority of the leading clubs including Hibs who had been firmly against any such move. Perhaps sensibly, at the next management committee meeting the proposed new ruling, that as far as most clubs had been concerned would have encouraged the use of the long ball to the detriment of skilful football, had been rejected.

In the opening Drybrough Cup game, a 2–1 home victory against the recently promoted Kilmarnock, the centre half position had been filled by the promising young prospect Derek Spalding. Since making his first team debut against Berwick Rangers in the East of Scotland Shield a couple of seasons earlier, a player who had come through the ranks at Easter Road had now developed

A TRADITIONAL PERIOD (1974–75)

into an outstanding prospect. He had been something of a first team regular in the final few games of the previous season when replacing the injured Stanton. On the captain's return, Spalding had kept his place in the side at the expense of the experienced Jim Black who understandably had been unhappy at losing his position and had now handed in a transfer request.

The victory had set up yet another meeting with old adversaries Rangers in the semi-final at Easter Road, now the 12th occasion including replays that the sides had faced each other in cup competitions during the previous seven seasons. A game that could, and should, have been over inside the opening 20 minutes, only for a dominant home side to scorn several gilt-edged chances to open the scoring, had allowed a Rangers side now featuring the future Scotland goalkeeper Stewart Kennedy to take the lead midway through the half with a goal by Alex MacDonald. Another by Parlane just before half-time had doubled the Ibrox side's lead leaving Hibs with it all to do. However, in a tremendous second-half fightback two goals by Joe Harper had brought Hibs right back into contention and were now looking much the stronger side, for the future Hibs signing Graham Fyfe to score a third in the late stages inflicting the Easter Road side's first ever defeat in the competition after eight games.

Harper's goals had already taken his total to five in five games including the pre-season tour of Scandinavia, but he was to go even better a few days later by scoring all five in Hibs' 5–0 victory over the Dutch side Nijmegen in a friendly at Easter Road. Despite Harper's impressive scoring burst, by far the biggest ovation of the evening had again been reserved for the immensely popular Alan Gordon when he replaced Cropley midway through the second half. Harper would later joke that he had scored all five goals and still been booed off at the end, but in fact this had merely been the fans' reaction to their favourite Gordon being left out of the side. Harper's scoring spree however had raised the question as to who had been the last Hibs player to score five or more goals in the same game. The most obvious answer for many of the older fans would have been Joe Baker who had famously scored nine in Hibs 15–1 Scottish Cup victory against Peebles Rovers in 1961, but in fact it had occurred twice since then. During the club's tour of North America in 1965 Neil Martin had scored five in the 15–1 victory over Concordia, Willie Hamilton going even further on the same trip when scoring seven consecutively in Hibs 15–1 victory against Ottawa All Stars to earn the man of the match salver. A notoriously light traveller as far as luggage was concerned; it is now well known that not having a suitcase large enough to hold the award, Hamilton had simply bent it in half.

Now back to only the winners going through to the qualifying stages, a League Cup section that included the Scottish Cup holders Rangers, St Johnstone and the then League Cup holders Dundee, would be won far easier than probably would have been expected with just a single defeat at Dens Park. So far that season Jimmy O'Rourke had yet to feature in the first team and again there would be no place for the popular player in the line up against Rangers on the opening day when a 3–1 victory would give Hibs revenge for the Drybrough Cup defeat just a few days earlier. Despite missing several early chances, goals by Duncan and the recalled Alan Gordon would give Hibs a two goal lead to take into the interval, another just a minute after the restart by Harper, finishing the game as a contest. An admittedly under-strength Rangers side had been second best all afternoon, a late goal by the future Hibs player Ally Scott a mere consolation in Hibs' eventual 3–1 victory. The return of Alan Gordon had also brought poise to the midfield although always available to move into attack where he could utilise his lethal prowess in the air.

Only that morning, after five seasons as a first team regular and well over 200 first team appearances including four cup finals, centre-half Jim Black had rejoined his former side Airdrie in a deal reputedly worth around £8,000. It would now appear that with the impressive form shown so far by Derek Spalding that Turnbull was now pinning his hopes on the promising youngster. Black, who had been the club's record signing in 1969, had spent the remaining weeks of the previous season in the reserves. It seemed even then that he no longer figured in the manager's future plans although, somewhat ironically, the previous season he had been voted the Hibs Supporters Association's player of the year. Although possibly lacking a bit of pace, Black was tremendous in the air. A good passer of the ball he had also formed a great partnership with Blackley at the back although the pair could often be seen having fierce on-field arguments. On one occasion the centre-half threatening to grab Blackley by the throat, disagreements it has to be said that were quickly forgotten as soon as the final whistle sounded, and his contribution to the side particularly under Turnbull should not be underrated.

For some time Tom Hart had been extremely concerned that football was now in real danger of being seriously over exposed on TV and the effect that the cameras were having on attendances throughout the country. Unhappy that the previous Drybrough Cup finals had also been beamed out live against his wishes, the single-minded Hart had now banned the cameras from covering the game against Rangers. A decision however that had proved somewhat inconclusive when just 23,539 had turned up for the game, compared to the almost 28,000 for the Drybrough Cup game between the sides just a few days earlier.

After the victory against Rangers, home and away wins against St Johnstone and just the single defeat by Dundee at Dens Park, Hibs now needed just a point from the final section game at Ibrox to secure a place in the quarter-finals. Once again Rangers had discovered that aggression was no substitute for skill and class, qualities that this Hibs side had in abundance, and despite their opponents customary aggression and energy there had been very few anxious moments in the Hibs penalty area during the entire 90 minutes. Although, it would take until the final minute to secure victory when a goal by substitute Cropley had been enough to ensure Hibs' place in the quarter-finals and another meeting with Kilmarnock.

Despite his occasional dispute with authority and sometimes his own fans there is no doubt that Tom Hart always had the best interests of the game at heart and it was around then that his contribution to the game was recognised by the football authorities when he was elected onto the League Management Committee, his fellow director Tommy Younger regaining his place on the International Selection board. In the first local derby of the season at Easter Road, what would turn out to be yet another tough and tense encounter would eventually be a game of three penalties. Goalkeeper Garland saving efforts from both Cropley and

Harper, Ford scoring from the spot for the visitors after an earlier own goal by Clunie and only a late counter by Duncan in an incredible finish allowing Hibs to collect both points. Yet again the game had failed to reach any great heights; Bremner and Spalding forming an impressive partnership at the back, although it has to be said, against a Hearts side that had shown little penetration all afternoon.

John Blackley had missed the game. After a long summer without a break including the World Cup finals in Germany, Blackley felt that he wasn't playing well at that time and was in need of a short break. An approach to the manager however had been ignored and he had continued to be selected. Another request resulted in Turnbull demonstrating his legendary stubbornness, with Blackley spending the next few weeks in the second team during which time Turnbull had refused to speak to him, regularly passing at the ground without even a glance.

Although Hibs had already rejected an earlier bid from Blackpool for Jimmy O'Rourke, to the great disappointment of the fans just a few weeks later the popular player would become the third member of the celebrated side to leave the club when he joined St Johnstone in a £15,000 deal, a move that probably could have been predicted. As so often happens O'Rourke would make his debut for his new club against his former teammates at Muirton. When having already received dozens of telegrams and cards from well-wishers, in Edinburgh he would also be on the end of a rousing reception from both sets of fans as he took the field before the game but would no doubt have been desperate to put one over on his former teammates to show that Turnbull had been wrong to let him go.

Since his debut against Utrecht in 1962 O'Rourke's all-action style had made him an immediate favourite, not only with the fans but also his teammates who recognised just what his industry and goalscoring abilities had brought to the side. Hibs had lost not only a popular player but a tremendous asset in the dressing room where his incredible enthusiasm, encouragement and humour had been an inspiration particularly among the younger players, all helping to create the tremendous team spirit that was running through the club. That afternoon in Perth however he had ended up on the losing side when goals by Stanton, Gordon and Edwards had

A TRADITIONAL PERIOD (1974-75)

given the visitors the points in a 3-1 victory. But things were to turn out rather differently when the pair met again at Easter Road just a few weeks later. Then, despite an article in the match programme warmly welcoming O'Rourke back to the scene of his former glories and yet another tremendous reception from the fans, he had repaid the gesture by scoring what would turn out to be the only goal of the game after just four minutes, giving Hibs their first league defeat of the season.

Qualification for the League Cup quarter-finals with a game to spare, particularly after the home and away victories against current league champions Rangers and only one defeat from the first five league games had suggested that the club was still on the right lines, although winning the championship inside the manager's initial three-year projection was still far from being realised.

After the difficulties encountered on the trip to Keflavik the previous season, the club had now decided to charter its own aircraft for the UEFA Cup game against Rosenborg in Norway, once again several dozen fans given the opportunity to travel with the official party at a much reduced rate.

With Blackley now back in the side, in a game far more one-sided than the final scoreline would suggest, Hibs had built up what was thought to have been a commanding three goal lead midway through the second half, only for Rosenberg to stage a spirited comeback with two late goals by danger man Iverson; goals that should never have been allowed. The first when he had clearly impeded goalkeeper McArthur before putting the ball into the net; the second in the very last minute when the referee had waved play on despite the linesman's flag being raised for offside, the official admitting after the game that on reflection both decisions had been wrong. Hibs' third goal scored by Cropley had been the clubs 100th in European competition. Despite the slender margin of the victory however, no problems had been anticipated in the return leg in Edinburgh and so it was to be proven.

At Easter Road the torrential rain that had been falling all day had also helped reduce the attendance to just over 12,000, but those that had ignored the atrocious conditions were to witness Hibs' almost complete domination of their amateur opponents.

Although Rosenberg had taken a surprise early lead the end result had never been in any doubt, the eventual 9–1 victory after doubles by Harper, Munro, Stanton; Cropley scoring twice from the spot; and Gordon with one, had been the clubs highest ever in a competitive European game.

On the Saturday Hibs started where they had left off in midweek with a comprehensive 6–2 home victory over Motherwell. The high scoring had again delighted the watching fans, but more importantly the performance had suggested that this was Hibs back to something like the side of previous seasons. In what had been a tremendous 90 minutes there had been no failures, Motherwell just having no answer to Hibs' almost relentless threat in their penalty area straight from the start. 5–1 ahead at the interval the visitors had been completely demoralised by a marvellous display of attacking football with every man again playing his part. Over on the other side of the city things were somewhat different, a 5–0 defeat by Dundee at Dens Park that same afternoon had left the Tynecastle side struggling at the foot of the table, results that would eventually lead to relegation and the resignation of manager Bobby Seith.

After a 3–3 draw with Kilmarnock at Rugby Park in the league, a 4–1 victory at Easter Road would be more than enough for Hibs to qualify for the semi-finals, the players leaving the field at the end to a well-deserved standing ovation. It had been the first game to take place under the new improved Easter Road lights. Utilising the existing pylons the new state of the art system that was said to have cost around £27,000 to install, a significant sum at that time, was said to have been four times stronger than before and twice as powerful as the minimum recommended by UEFA for European fixtures.

Floodlights were not a new phenomenon however, Hibs one of the first to experiment with the medium as far back as 1878. But along with Stenhousemuir they were considered the modern pioneers of football under lights in this country after a friendly at Ochilview in 1951. Played under what had basically been training lights with a few added lamps behind each goal, the match officials wearing semi-luminous outfits for the occasion and the use of a white ball which was just a normal brown one painted white, it had sometimes been difficult for both players and fans to follow play in the murky gloom but nevertheless it had alerted others to the advantage of football under lights. Hibs had first encountered modern floodlights during a tour of Germany, Austria and Switzerland during a friendly against Berne in 1950. The club had not been notified beforehand that part of the game was to take place under lights, and although initially angry, it did not take the astute Harry Swan long to recognise the benefit of games under floodlight, particularly the potential advantage for European football.

Although they had not been the first in Scotland to install their own lights, with Falkirk, Rangers, Kilmarnock and East Fife before them, most of these lights had been roof mounted along the stands, the players regularly complaining of losing the flight of the ball in the glare. The Hibs directors had travelled extensively seeking advice on the medium, only the best system considered good enough, and had eventually settled on four 100-foot-high pylons situated at each corner of the ground. When completed in 1954 they had been described as the brightest and best in Britain and the first 'real' floodlights in the entire country.

In the cup game against Kilmarnock the brilliance of the new lights were said to have impressed the fans, but the real shining light of the evening had been the magnificent performance of Alex Cropley. Watched from the terracing by both the Arsenal manager Bertie Mee and chief scout Gordon Clark, a former teammate of Cropley's dad at Aldershot, it is now common knowledge that contact had already been made with the player.

After the impressive performances against Motherwell and Kilmarnock the semi-final against Falkirk at Tynecastle would turn out to be something of an enormous anti-climax. With very few moments of real excitement from either side, with just 20 minutes remaining a tremendous drive by Joe Harper from well outside the penalty area had been enough to win the game. The Falkirk manager John Prentice had earlier described Hibs as the best side in Scotland at that time, and this could perhaps have gone some way in explaining his team's ultra negative defensive tactics throughout the entire 90 minutes that had appeared more to do with frustrating the Easter Road side than actually winning the tie. Harper's goal however had been enough to send Hibs into the cup final and a third meeting with Celtic at the ultimate stage of a national cup final in just under 18 months.

Still to come were eight days that would perhaps go some way in defining Hibs' season. Except for the earlier defeat by St Johnstone, they remained unbeaten in the league and the players had made their way to face Celtic at Parkhead in confident mood, aware that a victory would also see them top equal in the table on goal difference if other results went their way.

Considering their impressive displays in recent weeks it would eventually turn out to be a truly woeful display, the mere shadow of a side that many had tipped before the season as genuine championship contenders. Any realistic hopes of victory had been dashed after Celtic raced to a decisive first-half lead with three goals inside a nine-minute spell without reply. Any hopes of a spirited comeback had been shattered when Deans scored a fourth just a few minutes after the break, his third of the afternoon leaving the Easter Road side with a monumental if not impossible mountain to climb. Yet another by Johnstone just before the end merely putting the seal on what had been a truly horrendous afternoon for the Edinburgh side. Not only had the comprehensive 5–0 defeat been a huge setback to any genuine championship aspirations but had also provided their opponents with a tremendous psychological boost before the sides met again in the cup final seven days later.

Four days later Hibs welcomed the Italian giants Juventus to Easter Road for the second round of the UEFA Cup. Apart from centre-forward Pietro Anastasi, then the most expensive player in the world who had cost the Italian club the then equivalent of £440,000, the Juventus side also contained another eight internationals including an 'old friend' in the former Napoli goalkeeper Dino Zoff who had conceded five goals on his last visit to Easter Road with Napoli in 1967.

Roared on by almost 30,000 mostly partisan fans, Hibs had started the game well, Harper missing a great chance to open the scoring midway through the half, only to find themselves a goal behind just a minute before half-time. After the restart Juventus pushed forward in a bid to increase their lead only for Stanton to score an equaliser with a header past Zoff after good leading

A TRADITIONAL PERIOD (1974–75)

up work by Brownlie and Edwards. Now spurred on by a highly excitable crowd just five minutes later Cropley put Hibs further ahead when scoring from his favourite distance of just a few inches after a Harper drive had come crashing back from the bar. The lead however was to last just minutes. Determined to go looking for more goals instead of possibly attempting to hold on to a lead to take into the second leg in Italy had probably been the wrong decision, and with Juventus now a real threat with their constant counter attacks into the Hibs penalty area, the ageing but still brilliant Altafini who had come on as a second half substitute scored the first of his two goals. Cuccureddu put his side further ahead before Altafini scored his second of the evening, the final 4–2 score while not impossible would now prove an incredibly difficult task to overturn in Italy. After the fourth goal goalkeeper McArthur had been aware of a shout from the crowd behind him demanding that Turnbull bring on substitute Higgins – and put him in goals!

After 27 home games in Europe it had been only Hibs' fourth defeat and their heaviest yet at Easter Road. It would be a major understatement to describe the result against a side from a country previously renowned for defensive football to score four goals away from home as disappointing.

Only that morning it had been announced that the game would be the first to take place in front of the recently erected three-foot-high anti-hooligan fences that had been mounted along the top of the perimeter wall surrounding the pitch. Designed to prevent supporters from entering the field of play, something that had now been occurring with increasing regularity throughout the country, Hibs had been the first club in Scotland to make the move. Trouble at football matches was nothing new, occurring at least since the late 1880s occasionally resulting in games either being disrupted or on occasion abandoned. The problem however had been gradually increasing in frequency since the 1960s and in 1980 would lead to the passing of the Criminal Justice (Scotland) Act that prohibited alcohol being consumed, not only inside the stadium but also on supporters' coaches, football specials and similar, also making it an offence to be found under the influence of drink inside the stadium. Trouble at games had also been of major concern to UEFA for some time. Not long before, a strongly worded letter had been sent to all the sides competing in each of the three European competitions reminding them not only as to the conduct of their players but also that of their fans with the added warning that any future punishment could include results being forfeited, stadiums closed or even exclusion for any club under their authority.

Just days later it was on to Hampden to face Celtic in the League Cup Final, the third meeting of the sides at the ultimate stage of the competition at the national stadium in five years. Once again a great number of Hibs fans had made their way through from Edinburgh by coach, car and rail, but unfortunately, once again the Easter Road defence completely failed to contain a rampant Celtic attack particularly centre-forward 'Dixie' Deans who helped himself to yet another hat-trick. In the opening minutes Edwards had a great chance to open the scoring only to send his close range shot past the post. Thereafter the Hibs defence had failed to curtail a rampant Celtic attack who scored twice midway through the half before Harper pulled one back to make the half-time score 2–1. Although Harper had managed to score another twice in the second half, his second just five minutes before the end, this would mean little as Celtic themselves had already scored another four. Although by far the better side throughout, several of the Celtic goals in the eventual 6–3 victory had been assisted by a touch of good fortune. None more so than Jimmy Johnstone's thunderbolt cross from the right that appeared to be going out of play but had simply struck Deans on the head before crashing past the helpless McArthur for Celtic's fourth. Blackley's comments to the bemused goalkeeper: 'You're allowed to stop them Jim', probably not appreciated by McArthur at the time. The final whistle after what had been yet another hugely humiliating defeat, the second time in just over two years that Hibs had conceded six goals in a cup final against Celtic, would come as a welcome relief, both for the players and supporters. Many fans having already left the stadium long before the end, the embarrassing scoreline finally brought to an end what had surely been the club's most disastrous eight days for many years. In scoring all three of his side's goals, only a tremendous save by Hunter in the very last minute had prevented Harper from scoring a fourth. As it was, he had possibly been the only player to score a hat-trick in a national cup final and still end up on the losing side.

For some inexplicable reason this highly skilful Hibs side that could usually take care of both Hearts and Rangers, often struggled against Celtic.

Curiously, for the remainder of the season the statistics in the official Hibs programme had continued to credit Harper with only two of the goals, the other mistakenly given as an own goal by the Celtic centre-half Billy McNeil.

Hibs: McArthur, Brownlie and Bremner, Stanton, Spalding and Blackley, Edwards, Cropley, Harper, Munro and Duncan (subs) Smith and Murray
Celtic: Hunter, McGrain and Brogan, Murray, McNeil and McCluskey, Johnstone, Dalglish, Deans, Hood and Wilson (subs) Lennox and McDonald
Referee: J Gordon (Newport-on-Tay)

The recent rich goalscoring form of the Celtic striker Deans had not gone unnoticed by the selectors and just a few days after the cup final he would win the first of his two full international caps in Scotland's 3–0 victory over East Germany at Hampden.

Any concerns of just how the Hibs players might react mentally after the disastrous events of just a few days before had been dispelled after a 5–0 home victory over Morton the following Saturday. It could well have been more, Cropley missing a penalty late in the game. Goalless at the interval, a scintillating second half display against a side that had been fully committed to defence throughout the entire 90 minutes would perhaps be the perfect tonic before the forthcoming return leg against Juventus in Italy.

In what was always going to be an uphill struggle against a Juventus side that had cost millions, Hibs had been by far the better side in the first half, creating more chances than their renowned opponents. With a bit of luck Stanton could well have had a hat-trick, only a poor decision by the referee allowing an Anastasi goal to stand despite the centre-forward appearing to be well offside, allowing Juventus to take a half-time lead. With the home side now having the advantage of a three goal overall lead, defeat already looked inevitable. With 30 minutes remaining a result that had already been all but over for some time was finally confirmed when centre-forward Anastasi scored with a tremendous overhead kick from all of 25 yards that gave goalkeeper McArthur no chance. The ageing but still brilliant substitute Altafina who had done so much damage in the first leg at Easter Road scoring twice more in the remaining minutes. It had perhaps been no disgrace exiting the competition at the hands of one of the classiest sides in Europe at that time but the eventual 4–0 scoreline had greatly flattered a side that would go on to win the Seria A championship for a 19th time at the end of the season.

After the heavy defeat in Turin, Hibs had embarked on a nine-game unbeaten run, winning six and drawing three. At the beginning of November a goal by Alan Gordon in a 1–1 draw with Dunfermline at East End Park would turn out to be not only his last goal for the club but also his last ever appearance for the first team, and he would spend the rest of his time at Easter Road languishing in the reserves. Later Gordon would turn down a move to Motherwell as part of an exchange deal as well as an approach by the then Patrick Thistle manager Bertie Auld who would have been well aware of his former colleagues goalscoring abilities. St Johnstone had also shown an interest possibly with the view of reuniting him with his former goalscoring partner Jimmy O'Rourke. However the player would eventually decide to join Dundee in a £13,000 deal, Hibs making a £1,000 profit on the transaction and Gordon becoming one of the very few players to have played for both the Edinburgh and Dundee sides. In just under three years at Easter Road he had scored 83 goals from 153 appearances in all games, three more than during all his time at Hearts but in a far shorter period. During training sessions at Easter Road the highly intelligent Gordon would often question the manager during team talks. Although usually genuinely interested, occasionally he would be at the wind up. Eddie, fully aware when he was being made a fool of in front of the other players had once come out with the now famous quote: 'The trouble with you Gordon is that all your brains are in your f*****g heid.'

A TRADITIONAL PERIOD (1974-75)

Also included in the unbeaten run had been a 1-0 victory at Ibrox when a Joe Harper goal had brought Rangers' reign as the only unbeaten side in Britain to an end, the first time that Hibs had defeated the Ibrox side three times in the same season since the Jock Stein era ten years earlier. Although the midfield trio of Stanton, Munro and Smith had all been in devastating form in repulsing Rangers' dangerous raids, it had been a real team effort. A performance that would later be described by one sports writer as a 'superb display of skilful and entertaining football played in quite dreadful conditions', and a victory that had also been crucial in keeping Hibs' championship aspirations alive.

Despite an earlier announcement by Eddie Turnbull that he was building a side not dismantling one and that no Hibs player was for sale, just a few weeks later the supporters would be devastated to learn that Alex Cropley had now become the sixth member of the cup winning side of just two years before to leave the club when joining Arsenal for a club record £150,000. During the summer Cropley had been surprised to be contacted by Eddie Turnbull and asked to meet him and the chairman at Tom Hart's home in the city. He arrived to find not only the Hibs manager and chairman as expected, but also the Chelsea manager Dave Sexton and it appeared obvious from their demeanour that his transfer had already been agreed. Caught totally off guard, the recently married Cropley had asked for time to think it over. Sexton however had needed an immediate answer and at that the meeting was at an end.

Probably having already seen the writing on the wall, Cropley had been keen on a move for some time, but whether it had anything to do with his rejecting the move to Chelsea, for the following few weeks he would have to content himself with a seat on the bench. Unknown to anyone at that time, for well over a year the player had been in regular contact with Arsenal through numerous telephone calls, home visits and the occasional meeting with a scout in city. While the London club had been extremely keen to sign the player, the major obstacle had been Turnbull. After several meetings with the Hibs manager the Arsenal chief scout Gordon Clark would describe Turnbull as possibly the most ignorant man he had ever encountered who had done nothing but swear at him. As far as both the player and Arsenal were concerned it had been extremely difficult to understand why if Hibs had been agreeable, even eager, on his move to Chelsea why they had been so strongly opposed to his transfer to Arsenal.

The day before Cropley's move to London, the former St Mirren player Ally MacLeod had been signed from Southampton for a fee of around £25,000 making Hibs much the winners in the transaction financially. At Love Street MacLeod had been a prolific goal scorer with over 60 goals in just three seasons. He had really only come to prominence however when scoring all four of the then Second Division side's goals in a 4–1 League Cup defeat of Rangers at Ibrox in 1972, an achievement that had also brought MacLeod to the attention of several English sides. As was their then habit of attempting to buy a player who had performed well against them, Rangers themselves had been interested in signing MacLeod but instead he had decided to try his luck in England with First Division Southampton. Unfortunately, competition from the likes of Mick Channon and Peter Osgood had severely limited his prospects of a regular first team place at The Dell, managing to make just a handful of appearances before a loan spell at Huddersfield. Far too good a player to be wasting his undoubted talents in the reserves, despite a late attempt by the then St Mirren manager Alex Ferguson to entice him back to Love Street MacLeod had decided to return to Scotland and sign for Hibs.

As Cropley was making his debut for Arsenal at Carlisle, substitute MacLeod had been replacing the injured Spalding at half-time in a game against Airdrie at Broomfield. The signing of a player who would go on to score almost 100 goals during the following nine seasons would turn out to be yet another tremendous bit of business for the club. Although possibly lacking a bit of pace, with his superb reading of the game, incredible ball control and goalscoring ability it would not take MacLeod long to become yet another huge favourite with the Hibs fans.

Just weeks after returning from a 28-day suspension and a £350 fine after picking up four bookings, Alex Edwards had been sent off for a sixth time during a 1–0 defeat by Aberdeen at Pittodrie. In the late stages of what had been a stormy

Eddie Turnbull.

Hibs board of directors c1972.
Back row left to right: Tommy Younger, Eddie Turnbull and Jimmy Kerr.
Front: John Christie, Tom Hart and Cecil Graham.

Turnbull's first team line up as manager of Hibs.
Back row left to right: Shevlane, Stanton, Black, Baines, Blackley, Brownlie and McEwan.
Middle: Baker, Graham, Auld, Turnbull, Hazel, Pringle, Davidson and Cropley.
Front: Physio McNiven, Stevenson, Hamilton and trainer Fraser.

Programme for the 1972 League Cup final.

Official Jewellers to:—
Scottish Football League
Scottish Badminton Union
Scottish Amateur Athletic Association
Cowal Highland Gathering

T. S. CUTHBERT
Norman and Gordon Crosthwaite
48 Buchanan Street, 7 Princes Square,
Glasgow, G1 3JR
Telephone 041-221 3717 and 4359
(Illustrations, Designs and Estimates prepared free of charge)

IT'S THEIR THIRD HAMPDEN FINAL IN SEVEN MONTHS

CELTIC

3. J. BROGAN	10. K. DALGLISH	Referee: A. MacKENZIE (Larbert)	
11. T. CALLAGHAN			
6. D. HAY	9. L. MACARI	Linesmen: J. V. BOARDMAN (Bo'ness) R. C. JOHNSTON (Strathaven)	
1. E. WILLIAMS			
5. W. McNEILL	8. D. DEANS	**IF IT IS A DRAW**	
4. G. CONNELLY		... at the end of 90 minutes play, an extra period of 30 minutes will be played. If there is still no decision, another game will be played at Hampden Park on Wednesday, December 13, kick-off 7.30 p.m.	
2. D. McGRAIN	7. J. JOHNSTONE		
Substitute: H. HOOD			

HIBERNIAN

A. EDWARDS 7.   J. BROWNLIE 2.
P. STANTON 4.
J. O'ROURKE 8.   J. BLACK 5.
J. HERRIOT 1.
A. GORDON 9.   J. BLACKLEY 6.
A. CROPLEY 10.
A. DUNCAN 11.   E. SCHAEDLER 3.
Substitute: J. HAZEL

HE BEAT ABERDEEN

Tommy Callaghan (left), signed from Dunfermline in November, 1968, for £35,000, was the man who scored the winner for Celtic in the semi-final against Aberdeen.

A spectacular goal in the 80th minute, hit with considerable venom from the outside of the penalty area. It gave Celtic a 3-2 win and gave Callaghan his first League Cup goal of the season!

Tommy, or "Tid" as he is known to his team-mates, has been one of Scotland's most consistent mid-field players this season. After he played against Ujpest Dozsa in the European Cup, the great Hungarian striker Ferenc Bene said of him: "I cannot recall seeing a player with such speed and stamina. I rate him one of the best I have ever seen."

Praise indeed!

Tommy Callaghan

HE BEAT RANGERS

John Brownlie (right), with a current value of around £150,000, scored the only goal of the semi-final with Rangers—and a brilliant match-winner it proved to be.

He broke quickly from defence on to a superb pass from Alex Edwards, caught the Rangers defence completely out of step, before unleashing a great shot which beat Peter McCloy low on his left side.

The goal came in 72 minutes and capped a superb display of football from Brownlie, who is 21 years of age, and just about the best right-back in British football at the moment.

Scotland team manager Tommy Docherty is fully aware of his worth, and has used John in both World Cup qualifying matches against Denmark. He could be the 'national right back for years to come.

John Brownlie

The team line ups for the 1972 final.

Players in the NB Hotel after the game.
Back row left to right: Humphries, Cropley, McNiven, Edwards, Black, Gordon, Stanton and Schaedler.
Middle: Turnbull, Hazel, Duncan, Brownlie, Hamilton and Herriot.
Sitting: O'Rourke.

Souvenir programme for Ayr United game. Front cover: Pat Stanton with both the Drybrough and League Cups.

Hearts 0, Hibernian 7.

Arthur Duncan.

Alex Cropley's 1972 and 1974 League Cup final medals.

John Blackley.

Programme for Pat Stanton's testimonial.

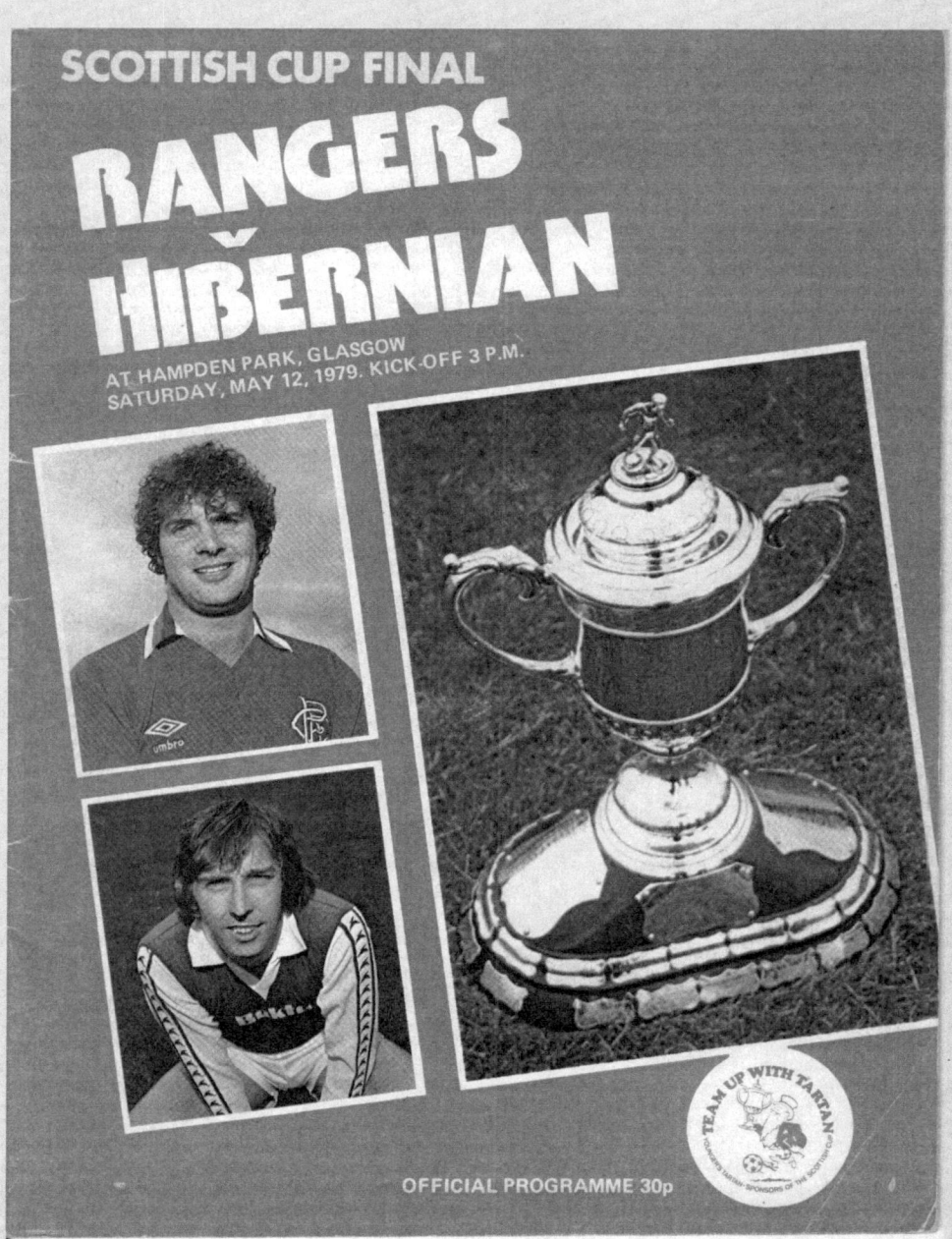

Programme for 1979 Scottish Cup final.

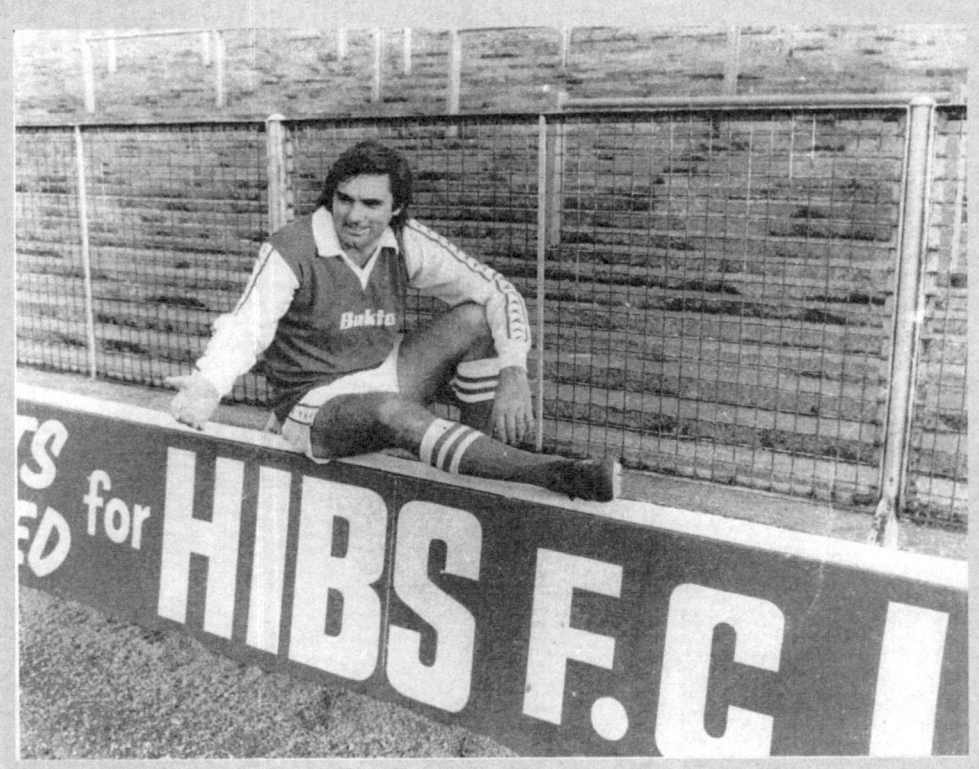

George Best's first day at Easter Road, 1979.

Best's debut against St Mirren at Love Street, Saturday 24 November 1979.

Jackie McNamara tackling Celtic's Frank McGarvey in the 5–0 Scottish Cup semi-final defeat. Turnbull's last game.

Turnbull's former Famous Five teammate Willie Ormond who would replace him as manager.

Turnbull in later years being interviewed for a video.

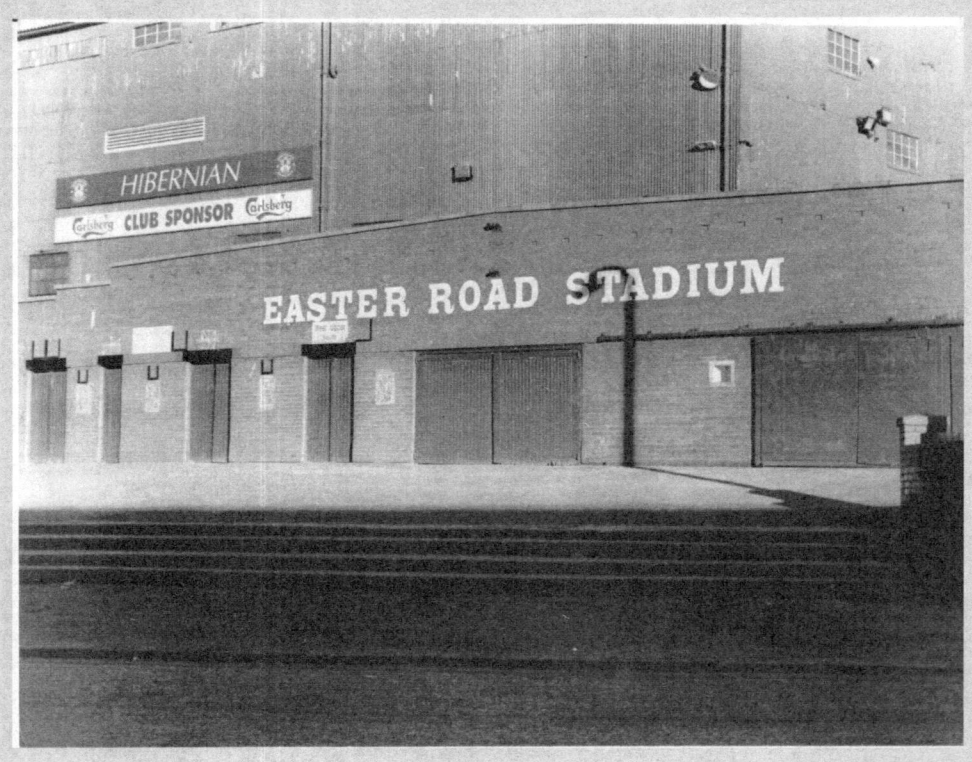

The old Easter Road frontage.

affair throughout, Iain Munro missing a penalty in the first few minutes, Edwards had been fouled by the Aberdeen full-back McClelland. Although by this time he should surely have known better he had foolishly retaliated, leaving referee Marshall no option but to send both players off, the actions of the gifted Edwards no doubt leaving manager Turnbull once again shaking his head.

1 January 1975 was the start of Hibs' centenary year and a crowd of almost 40,000 had packed inside Tynecastle for the traditional 'Neerday' game between the local rivals. With the impending arrival of the Premier League at the end of the season it would turn out to be the last ever league game between the sides. Unfortunately for anyone in the huge crowd that had been anticipating something special to commemorate the occasion, it had turned out to be just the latest of the drab and uninspiring goalless draws that the fans had become accustomed to in recent years. The only excitement reserved for the dying minutes when a shot from the Hearts centre-forward Donald Ford struck the post with goalkeeper McArthur beaten before the ball was eventually cleared to safety. The valuable point gained however had been enough to keep Hibs third in the table and still well in the hunt for the championship.

At that year's AGM a huge pre-tax loss of almost £150,000 had been declared for the financial year compared to the £40,000 deficit the previous season, alarming figures that seemingly had not even included the Joe Harper transfer fee. Again, wages, running costs and other expenses had risen alarmingly while income had dropped significantly. A situation that had obviously not been helped by the early exits from both the League Cup and UEFA Cup competitions that had also led to a decrease in the number of fans coming through the gates. At the meeting it had now been disclosed that around £4,000 was now needed each week just to keep the club's head above water, a figure unsustainable in the current climate and obviously extremely concerning. Also on the agenda had been the now regular issue of the guarantees for visiting sides; a situation that had generally been of most benefit to the so-called 'smaller sides' although the anticipated arrival of the Premier League in the summer when clubs would now be allowed to keep 100% of their takings would at least go some way in addressing the financial concerns.

Although considered something of a gamble at the time, Turnbull had given the 19-year-old goalkeeper Hugh Whyte and a 17-year-old Pat Carroll their debuts in the game against Dundee United at Tannadice. Showing few signs of nerves during what would turn out to be an impressive 3–1 victory, both youngsters had performed well in what had been another real team effort. Both part-timer Whyte who was then studying at university to be doctor and the former provisional signing and member of the Easter Road ground staff Carroll who had earlier earned rave reviews in the Scottish Schoolboys side against England at Wembley, had looked genuine prospects.

Whyte kept his place for the Scottish Cup tie against Celtic at Easter Road a few weeks later when a certain 'Dixie' Deans had again inflicted much of the damage in the 2–0 defeat when opening the scoring in the first half. Hibs fans must have hated the sight of him by this time. The goalkeeper however had appeared at fault after a dangerous in-swinging corner had rebounded from his chest straight to the Celtic centre-forward who wasted no time in rifling the ball into the net. Although to be fair to the youngster the ball had been hit with a fair bit of pace. Between the opener and Celtic's second and decisive goal, Hibs had again failed to take advantage of several good chances to equalise, particularly when Bremner hit the post with the Celtic goalkeeper Hunter stranded. Spalding in particular had a been in impressive form in keeping the ever-dangerous Dalglish quiet, but unfortunately the visitors had plenty of others on the field that afternoon who could take advantage of the situation. The defeat would now be leaving the Hibs supporters waiting for at least another year in the quest for the by now almost mythical Scottish Cup.

Probably disillusioned after watching a procession of players leaving Easter Road and perhaps another who had seen the writing on the wall, shortly after the cup defeat Blackley had made yet another request for a transfer, and consequently would spend the majority of the remainder of the season in the reserves.

With Black now at Airdrie, Spalding's skills now being utilised more in midfield and Blackley currently in the second team,

A TRADITIONAL PERIOD (1974-75)

Turnbull had moved to sign the Edinburgh-born centre-half Roy Barry from Crystal Palace. After eight seasons at Tynecastle where he had been a member of the 1962 League Cup winning team, Barry had joined Dunfermline during the 1966-67 season and along with teammate Alex Edwards had been in the Scottish Cup winning side that defeated Hearts the following season. After several seasons at Coventry City during which time he had suffered a serious leg break that kept him out of the game for several months he had signed for the recently relegated Crystal Palace who were then managed by the charismatic Malcolm Allison. While at Palace he had been about take up a short-term coaching position in America when contacted by Turnbull. A Hibs supporter in his youth, Barry recalls the occasion when as a registered Hearts player he had watched Hibs famous victory over Barcelona in 1961 from one of the Easter Road floodlight pylons resplendent in a Hibs jersey. Signed to add a bit of steel to the defence, the experienced Barry would make his debut in a 2-1 home victory over a Dundee side that included Alan Gordon. A goal behind at the interval, with just 15 minutes remaining Pat Stanton had equalised with what would be the clubs 100th goal of the season, Higgins scoring the winner in the closing stages.

Of the remaining ten games still to play, eight would be won with only two defeats. A 2-0 victory over Arbroath on the final day of the season enough for Hibs to again finish second behind champions Rangers who perhaps surprisingly had been winning the title for the first time since 1964. Of the 34 league games played 20 had been won with nine drawn, the 69 goals scored however the lowest among the top four although only champions Rangers had conceded less than Hibs' 37.

The slight slump around Christmas that had resulted in just five points from ten plus the Scottish Cup defeat by Celtic that according to Turnbull had been difficult to explain for such a talented side, had made it obvious to the majority of the supporters that the fairly recent sale of the prolific goalscoring partnership of Gordon and O'Rourke had been a major contributing factor. At that particular time there had been signs that Celtic had been in the process of a major rebuilding programme and that Turnbull had probably broken up what had been a supremely talented side far too early. Although clearly not the team of the previous few seasons, on their day Hibs had still been more than capable of providing some marvellously entertaining football and the reason for the decline as far as many had been concerned, not just the fans but several of the players themselves, could probably be traced back to the signing of Joe Harper, the last thing the club appeared to have needed at that particular time. A goal scorer of proven ability, Harpers acquisition had initially been welcomed, but the supporters would soon come to realise that his signing would in all probability spell the end for either the popular Gordon or O'Rourke, or both as it would ultimately turn out. Although again it must be stressed that no blame can be laid at the door of the player himself who had done little wrong, the fans had been in no doubt that his signing had been the catalyst for the beginning of the end for a side that would go down in Scottish football folklore. Apart from a hat-trick in Hibs' 6–1 defeat of Airdrie in April, of the final 19 games of the season including the Scottish Cup defeat by Celtic, perhaps surprisingly Harper had managed to score just once in a 5–1 defeat of Dunfermline, this time Iain Munro scoring a hat-trick.

He would however be on target in a 3–0 defeat of Berwick Rangers in the East of Scotland Shield and twice in a 6–0 end of season friendly in the Highlands against Des Bremner's previous side Deveronvale. Arranged sometime before, ironically, Bremner would miss the game as he had been on Under-23 duty for Scotland against Wales along with teammate Arthur Duncan, only his second international call up although he had remained an unused substitute.

Near the end of the season a mystery consortium of Edinburgh businessmen who for some time had been unhappy at Tom Hart's handling of the club had made an offer to purchase the managing directors shares in Hibs. Somewhat diplomatically the reason given was that they felt it unhealthy that the majority of the shares were then held by only three major shareholders, Hart himself with 63%. The initial approach had been made through a third party but was believed to have been initiated by members of the private 50 Club, that rented premises in the stadium. An angry Hart immediately requested a meeting with what he called these 'faceless people'. The consortium however had refused to reveal its identity and as Hart was not prepared to deal with anyone not prepared to show their hand in public, the matter was now at an end.

During the season the youngsters Murray, Higgins, Smith, Muir, McGhee and Dunn had all made occasional first team appearances, but like several others before them had all failed to establish a decent run in the side. When manager of Aberdeen Turnbull had spent a great deal of time and patience nurturing several young players through to the first team, but for some reason had appeared unwilling to devote the same effort at Easter Road. Now never appearing as comfortable in dealing with the youngsters as with the more experienced players, the manager had often been found to be dogmatic and lacking in patience, his by now well-known lack of man management skills often leaving much to be desired. It was no secret that many of the younger players didn't care much for him, some even frightened of his outbursts, several later describing him as a terrorist in a tracksuit.

At the end of the season both goalkeeper Roddie McKenzie and Gerry Adair had been among the list of those given free transfers. McKenzie would soon join Clydebank and Adair Dunfermline.

The Premier League and Nightmare at Montrose (1975–76)

THE 1975–76 SEASON would herald in an exciting new age for the Scottish game with the creation of the ten team Premier League, probably the first major reorganisation of the league tables since the formation of the Second Division in 1893. Now playing each other four times a season, twice at home and twice away, the majority of the so-called bigger clubs had all been in favour of a competition that had been specifically designed to create a greater challenge, attract bigger crowds and consequently raise more much needed finance. The fans however would take some time to get used to the new system as would some of the players, several not all that enamoured to the thought of now having to play each other four times in the same season. Also, given that it was highly unlikely that either Rangers or Celtic would ever finish in the bottom two of the ten team league this would leave a quarter of the remaining sides fighting to avoid relegation. Many also felt that the new set-up would encourage defensive play with managers reluctant to promote talented but inexperienced youngsters into the first team, and the fans had initially shown their disproval by staying away in numbers. The new three-league set-up would also fail to be overly popular, with the lower league sides extremely concerned at the prospect of now having to play just 26 league games a season as opposed to the 36 before. Even the financial promise of an additional Spring Cup competition failed to completely satisfy their possibly justifiable concerns.

Just before the start of the new season the football world had been stunned at the breaking news that Jock Stein and Bob Shankly, both former Hibs managers, had been involved in a serious car crash on the M74 when returning from a holiday in Menorca with family and friends. Although both Shankly and bookmaker Tony Queen who had also been a passenger in the car had been seriously hurt, Stein's injuries had been so severe that surgeons had to battle for over an hour to save his life and consequently he would be out of football for almost a year. Both Shankly and Stein had been great friends for many years, Shankly, as already mentioned, taking over as manager at Easter Road after Stein's premature departure at the end of a game against Rangers in February 1965.

Just as concerning had been the news that during the summer Eddie Turnbull had undergone a series of operations for a serious stomach complaint, quite probably a reoccurrence of an earlier problem, that had forced the then Aberdeen manager to miss the Grampian side's defeat by Celtic in the 1967 Scottish Cup final. Although the procedures had been a complete success, Turnbull would later spend several weeks recuperating at the family home in the north of Scotland and would miss the start of the new campaign.

Once again Hibs had decided on a short pre-season trip to Ireland in preparation for the coming season. Some of the more imaginative fans however sensed the decision was an omen as the League Cup had been won shortly after the club's previous trip to the Emerald Isle a couple of seasons before.

During Turnbull's time at Easter Road several players had attempted to grow facial hair but all had removed the offending growth after being 'requested' to do so, and although the manager was absent from the ground at the time his influence was still very much in evidence. Perhaps hoping to take advantage of Turnbull's unavailability, Joe Harper had arrived for the first day's training sporting a beard that he had immediately been ordered to remove by the now caretaker manager Wilson Humphries, a decision fully backed by Tom Hart. As far as the Hibs chairman had been concerned, Harper was fully entitled to grow a beard but he would not play for the club while doing so, including the forthcoming trip to Ireland. The dispute would drag on for several days, an appeal to his teammates that they should back him up falling on deaf ears, and just prior to the trip a now chastened Harper had turned up for training clean shaven.

The games in Ireland against Cork Hibs, Waterford and Bohemians had all ended in victory but perhaps the most pleasing aspect of the trip had been the fact that the defence had not conceded a single goal while scoring nine, Harper claiming three. As usual these games had been an ideal opportunity to provide the youngsters with more match experience, Willie Murray, Pat Carroll, Bobby Smith and Tony Higgins all making at least one appearance. After leaving Hibs two years earlier to join Morton, Alex McGhee had now returned to Easter Road and although included in the party that made its way to Ireland he would not feature in any of the games. The promising former schoolboy cap Lindsay Muir however would make his first start in a 6–0 victory over Waterford and had already shown enough promise to keep his place in the 1–0 victory against the Irish League champions Bohemians.

Near the end of the previous season both Turnbull and Hart had attended the UEFA Cup semi-final between Barcelona and Leeds United at Elland Road hoping to bring the Spanish giants to Easter Road as part of the club's centenary celebrations. Unfortunately, due to prior commitments neither Barcelona nor Real Madrid who had been approached later, had been able to accept the invitation. Instead League Champions Derby County who were then managed by the legendary former Hearts player Dave MacKay were said to have been delighted to accept the invitation. Although billed as a friendly, unfortunately the game against a side featuring such well-known names as Roy McFarland, David Nish, Colin Todd and the Scotland players Bruce Rioch and Archie Gemmill would turn out to be anything but glamorous. Watched by a decent crowd of over 17,000 including the still recuperating Eddie Turnbull, that with the exception of the forthcoming home games against Rangers, Celtic and Hearts would turn out to be Hibs' biggest attendance of the season, the only goal of a dull and uninspiring 90 minutes had been scored by the visitors just after the restart, and already there were signs that it was possibly going to be a long hard season.

With the Drybrough Cup competition now discontinued the season proper had started with the League Cup and in a section comprising of Dunfermline, Ayr United and Dundee, Hibs had eventually topped the group with ten points, three ahead of their nearest challengers Ayr United, only a 2–1 defeat in Ayrshire spoiling a sequence of five straight victories. In the home game against

THE PREMIER LEAGUE AND NIGHTMARE AT MONTROSE (1975–76)

Dunfermline Pat Stanton had received his marching orders for only the second time in his senior career after questioning a dubious decision by the referee that had gone against him. Stanton would later claim that he had not spoken out of turn to the official during the incident and confident that he had committed no offence would now be appealing the decision. Regardless, Hibs were through to the quarter-finals where they would now meet a hard-working Montrose side that had finished the previous season third in the First Division.

Before that however there would be the game against city rivals Hearts at Easter Road, the first ever meeting between the sides in the newly formed Premier League. Despite the initial optimism that the new format would provide more entertainment and attract bigger crowds, just 23,646 had paid at the gate, approximately the same as had attended the games between the pair at the corresponding stage the during the previous few seasons. However, continuing his goal-a-game ratio a tremendous 20-yard strike by Joe Harper just before the interval that gave the Hearts goalkeeper Jim Cruickshank no chance had been enough to give Hibs the points and a winning start to the Premier League. On top for most of the game, Hibs could well have scored more against the Hearts side, led by the future Hibs player Jim Brown who, while inferior in skill on the day, had fought hard to stay in contention during what could a highly competitive 90 minutes. The game, well handled by the referee Eddie Thomson, meant Thomson becoming the first ever Edinburgh referee to take charge of a championship game between Hibs and Hearts. On the day every Hibs player had performed well, no one better than the goal scorer Harper and the former Hearts player Roy Barry who without doubt would have taken even more satisfaction from the final result.

Meanwhile on the international front four of the current first team squad had now been called up for either the full or under-23 Scotland squads for the forthcoming internationals against Denmark. For Joe Harper it would be his third appearance for the full side, as it would turn out his only time as a Hibs player, and incredibly all three had been against Denmark. His international debut in the World Cup qualifier in Copenhagen in 1972 had started in embarrassing if not slightly humorous circumstances. Initially informed by the then Scotland manager Tommy Docherty that he would be on the bench only for experience and would not be called upon to play, to say he had been surprised when told to get stripped as he would be replacing the injured Jimmy Bone late in the game would be something of an understatement. However, suddenly finding himself in desperate need of the toilet, Harper had hurried inside the unfamiliar stadium and after relieving himself had inadvertently rushed through what turned out to be a security door only to find himself locked outside in the street still in his football kit. Only his frantic banging eventually attracting the attention of a steward for re-admittance to the stadium.

This time on from the start Harper had scored the only goal of the game to keep Scotland well in the running for qualification for the following year's European Championships, his teammate Arthur Duncan making his sixth appearance for the full side when replacing the injured Tommy Hutchison for the last 20 minutes. In the Under-23 game the previous evening Des Bremner had been included in the side defeated 1–0, his first international call up since Scotland's 2–0 victory against Denmark in 1972, John Brownlie seeing the game out on the bench as an unused substitute.

For Harper, the elation of scoring the winning goal would fail to end in such otherwise amusing circumstances as on his first visit to the Danish capital a few years earlier. In high spirits after what had been an important victory Harper and several of his teammates had decided to visit a night club in the city centre when in the early hours of the morning they had become involved in a disturbance with some of the locals that had led to the police being called. An investigation into the incident by the Scottish football authorities would later lead to Harper and his teammates, Leeds Billy Bremner, Celtic's Pat McCluskey and the Aberdeen pair Willie Young and Arthur Graham all receiving life bans from the international set-up. Although the suspensions would later be lifted, it would come too late for some, although Harper was to win one more cap as a substitute in a 1–1 draw with Iran in 1978, by then wearing the colours of Aberdeen.

THE PREMIER LEAGUE AND NIGHTMARE AT MONTROSE (1975–76)

The League Cup quarter-final against lower league Montrose at Easter Road a few days later had been watched by an otherwise healthy crowd of over 7,500 including the now back to full fitness Eddie Turnbull, but if anyone in the crowd had been anticipating an easy passage into the semi-finals then they were to be sadly mistaken. Possibly guilty of taking the spirited lower league side far too lightly, in a pathetic overall display against a no nonsense Angus side that had refused to allow Hibs to settle, not one Hibs player had lived up to expectation. The now impatient home fans had been made to wait until just six minutes from the end for Harper to score the only goal of the game. In the very last minute Duncan had squandered the chance to put the game, and possibly even this early the tie, beyond doubt when after rounding the goalkeeper and the empty goal gaping he had somehow managed to overrun the ball and the chance was lost. It would turn out to be an expensive miss, the final result however now ensuring a big turnout in the return leg at Links Park.

In the UEFA Cup Hibs had now been drawn against Liverpool and they had the opportunity to avenge the Fairs Cup defeat by the Anfield side almost five years earlier, the first game to take place in Edinburgh. Although Tommy Smith had been forced to miss the game because of injury, with players of the calibre of the former Hibs player Peter Cormack, Emlyn Hughes and Kevin Keegan they were still a side not to be taken lightly. Interviewed before the game regarding his side's chances, manager Bob Paisley who had only recently replaced the legendary Bill Shankly at Anfield, would only reply, perhaps tellingly, 'Liverpool respect all opponents but fear none.'

The torrential rain that had been falling all day had undoubtedly helped to keep the crowd for such a glamorous fixture down to around 20,000 diehard fans who had been brave enough to face the atrocious weather, far less than would have been expected had the conditions been perfect. Unfortunately, the treacherous underfoot conditions had also made good football almost impossible for both sides, the torrential rain on occasion even threatening to almost obliterate the pitch markings and making it extremely difficult for the officials to keep up with play.

Kicking down the famous slope Hibs had started the game well, opening the scoring after just 20 minutes with a long through ball from Munro collected by Duncan. The outside-left wasted no time in sending over an inch perfect cross that was met on the run by the inrushing Harper who proceeded to send a thunderous shot past Clemence and into the corner of the net without breaking stride. It had been a goal worthy of winning any game and one that had been met by rapturous applause from the now absolutely drenched Hibs fans on the terracing. Although Liverpool had been proving dangerous on the break it was the home side that came closest to scoring when a brilliant Stanton header flew inches past the post before Smith brought a tremendous save out of Clemence. Early in the second half Liverpool thought they had equalised when Neal had the ball in the net only for the strike to be rightly ruled out for offside despite the furious protest of the visiting players. With just ten minutes remaining the rampaging Duncan had been brought down in the box by Neal leaving the referee with no option but to award a penalty. However, although he had already scored with his previous four attempts from the spot that season Brownlie's woefully weak shot had allowed Clemence to save easily, the game finally ending 1–0. Despite the narrow win, Hibs' first ever against English opposition in a European competition, the victory had been fully deserved. At the end of the previous season Liverpool had only narrowly failed to win their ninth league title when losing to Middlesbrough on the final day of the season. This perhaps put Hibs' tremendous performance against such formidable opponents who were then rated one of the best sides in Europe into perspective.

The following midweek both the players and fans made their way to a wet and windy Links Park for the return leg against Montrose in confident mood. Already a goal ahead from the first game, another by Duncan after just 30 seconds had doubled Hibs' overall lead and although there had still been 89 minutes to play, a place in the semi-finals already seemed all but assured. Montrose however had other ideas and two second-half goals by the hard-working First Division side had levelled the tie after 90 minutes. It was now on to extra time where a freak goal by full-back Barr would seal Hibs' exit from the competition. In a rain-lashed Links

THE PREMIER LEAGUE AND NIGHTMARE AT MONTROSE (1975-76)

Park with a strong wind at his back Barr had lobbed a speculative clearance from just inside his own half that completely deceived goalkeeper McArthur. Just seconds earlier McArthur had been slightly distracted by trainer Tom McNiven asking if he was okay after receiving a head knock in saving a short pass-back from Schaedler, and possibly still dazed he had allowed the ball to bounce over his head and into the back of the net for what would turn out to be the winning goal. Stung, Hibs fought back furiously, Smith hitting the post in the very last minute but to no avail and at the end of what had been an all-round pathetic performance, the players had left the field with their heads bowed to a background of jeers from the fans that had made their way from Edinburgh for the game. All fully aware that it had been a most embarrassing result, the fans were left to make the long weary journey back to Edinburgh wondering just what might have been.

As Hibs were facing St Johnstone at Easter Road on the Saturday, Pat Stanton had been making his way to Perth with the reserve side for the corresponding game at Muirton. It would appear that although he had been no worse than anyone on the park Stanton had now been made the scapegoat for the humiliating defeat at Montrose in midweek and had immediately posted a transfer request. Perhaps the first public indication of a clash of personalities between the manager and player that unknown to the fans had been simmering behind the scenes for some time.

Considering the current situation, a major concern for the Hibs fans making their way to Liverpool for the return EUFA Cup tie in midweek was in wondering whether Stanton would be included in the starting line up. As far as they were concerned it would be absolutely inconceivable that a vastly experienced player who had already featured in several dozen competitive European fixtures since his first game against Valencia in 1965 would be missing from the side in one of the biggest games in the club's history. As it would turn out, although he had travelled south with the team the inspirational captain had not been included in the starting 11 and had watched the game from the bench. His exclusion was completely baffling to the supporters who had been more than aware of his defensive capabilities, particularly against a player as lethal in the air as John Toshack. In their by now customary habit in away European games, Hibs went on the attack from the very start but found themselves a goal behind after just 20 minutes following a cross from Keegan that had been met by the head of Toshack giving McArthur no chance from close range. Now roared on by the mostly partisan home crowd Liverpool went into all-out attack but were stunned when Edwards gave his side the overall lead on the night. After collecting a tremendous through ball from Bremner, the diminutive Fifer had proceeded to place the ball past Clemence for a rare but vital away goal that now meant that the away goals ruling could not come into operation and also that there could now be no extra time, the tie decided on the night. Straight from the restart Liverpool had redoubled their efforts to regain the lead and two further headed goals by Toshack now meant Hibs' exit from a European competition at the first-round stage for the first time since Valencia ten years earlier. There could be no disgrace in the defeat however, Hibs display in both games earning lavish praise from all quarters. At no time overawed, they had matched Liverpool throughout the entire 90 minutes and in Edwards they had the best player on the field. Interviewed after the game Turnbull had been disappointed at the bad goals lost by his side, all Toshack headers, the Welshman's first ever hat-trick for the club after five seasons at Anfield, leaving the vast majority of the Hibs fans to question if the inclusion of Stanton with his vast experience and his defensive qualities, particularly his ability in the air might just have made a difference.

The cup defeats, particularly the completely unexpected and extremely disappointing defeat by Montrose would have tremendous financial implications for the club and had perhaps been early signs that the heady days of just a few seasons earlier were now a thing of the past. The results would also have a severe impact, not only on the rest of the season, but arguably on the rest of the manager's time at Easter Road, and for him things would never be quite the same again.

Just days earlier, an emergency board meeting had been called to discuss the Stanton situation when somewhat surprisingly, but apparently unanimously, the directors had agreed to accept the players request for a transfer. The forthcoming announcement came much to the consternation of the fans, again resulting in a great many

THE PREMIER LEAGUE AND NIGHTMARE AT MONTROSE (1975–76)

letters of complaint sent to both the club and the papers, all vigorously condemning the decision.

In the league game against Motherwell at Fir Park the following Saturday Alex Edwards had been left out of the side for the first time that season. The demotion of the influential player who had missed much of the previous campaign because of injury and suspension resulting in yet another transfer request. The unsettled Edwards who as well as playing so well in the recent game against Liverpool had recently been voted the supporters player of the year had demanded a meeting with the manager to discuss the situation when he would again confirm his desire for a move. Apparently he had been unhappy at Easter Road for some time and along with Pat Stanton was now the second of the legendary 'Tornadoes' on the transfer list, a situation clearly suggesting that all was not well behind the scenes. According to several of the players, Easter Road had not been a happy place at that particular time with disharmony and low morale running through the club, not helped by a manager who now appeared to have little rapport with the players while also finding it easy to fall out with anyone without reason.

Against Motherwell a brilliant Harper goal after he had cleverly wrong footed a couple of defenders before calmly placing the ball past goalkeeper Rennie had initially appeared good enough to secure the points only for Pettigrew to equalise midway through the second half, Stevens scoring the winner for the home side in the very last minute after a mistake by goalkeeper McArthur.

After the cup defeats by Montrose and Liverpool and a draw against Dundee, the result at Fir Park had hardly been ideal preparation before facing league leaders Celtic at Parkhead when once again the visiting fans would be disappointed to discover that Edwards would again be missing from the side. There had been some encouraging news though when it was announced that after several games for the reserves Stanton had now been recalled to the first team and his transfer request withdrawn. On the surface it would now appear that the differences between the manager and player had been resolved, but unfortunately behind the scenes very little had changed.

As the teams took the field at a fog shrouded Parkhead there had been little sign of the forthcoming controversial events that were to deny Hibs their first league victory in the east end of Glasgow for six years. In a tremendous 90 minute performance when again there had been no failures Hibs had been leading at half-time after a goal by Bremner. A few minutes before the end Harper had doubled the lead, the goal immediately leading to the game being held up for several minutes after a number of home fans in the 'Jungle' had spilled out onto the pitch. Order was eventually restored only for the referee to now determine that the visibility was insufficient for the proceedings to continue. Possibly influenced by the Celtic supporters behind McArthur's goal chanting almost in unison that they 'couldn't see a f****** thing', he had now decided to abandon the game, Eddie Turnbull taking little consolation from the Celtic coach Sean Fallon as the players were leaving the pitch at the end that it had been God's will. Ironically just a few minutes after the sides had left the field the fog had lifted somewhat but by then it was far too late. At the League Management Committee meeting in mid-week it was decided that despite the Easter Road side being well in front at the time and with just minutes remaining the game would have to be replayed. A decision that understandably had infuriated everyone at Easter Road who felt that in the circumstances they should have been awarded the points, leaving many to wonder if the outcome would have been the same had the scores been reversed at the time. According to the authorities, if the proceedings had been abandoned on account of the Celtic fans invading the pitch near the end then the result would have stood, but as there had been no mention of the incident in the referees report, as far as the committee were concerned it was only right that the game should be replayed. The pitch invasion was evidently not even worth a mention in referee Bobby Davidson's account.

In mid-October the club had celebrated its centenary year with a dinner at the North British Hotel in Princes Street attended by well over 200 distinguished guests including the Lord Provost John Millar, representatives from all the league clubs in Scotland and many former players. Among the latter had been the 84-year-old Johnny Lamb, Hibs' oldest surviving player who had signed for the club in 1909; Willie Harper from the 1920s side; all

THE PREMIER LEAGUE AND NIGHTMARE AT MONTROSE (1975–76)

the Famous Five with the exception of Bobby Johnstone who had been unable to attend; and Willie Bauld and Jimmy Wardhaugh from Hearts, everyone present receiving an inscribed pewter tankard to commemorate the occasion. Of the modern players, Peter Cormack, then with Liverpool had been invited as had Arsenal's Alex Cropley who unfortunately had also been unable to attend, but somewhat incredibly none of the present squad including the club captain Pat Stanton. Making an extremely rare appearance had been the Edinburgh Association Cup that had first been won by the club in 1879 and borrowed from St Patrick's Church in the Cowgate for the evening. The Summer Cup won in the 1941 final against Rangers at Hampden had also been on display. It had been the then Hibs chairman Harry Swan's suggestion that a Summer Cup competition would help raise badly needed finance for the clubs during the war years, and after Hibs' victory in the inaugural final the trophy had been presented personally to Swan by the Hibs directors in appreciation of his efforts in inspiring the trophy. Shortly before the dinner Swan's family had received what they had considered a somewhat insensitive letter from the club asking if they could borrow the Summer Cup for the evening, but had been less than enamoured to discover that the directors had also requested the return of 'any trophy that belonged to the football club and not the family'. Although Swan was now dead, as a gesture of appreciation for his tremendous service over the years, his family had usually received tickets to the boardroom for each game. Sometime earlier however they had been notified that while it was no longer possible to guarantee tickets for every game they could be applied for on a match-by-match basis. Disgusted, the family would never again set foot in Easter Road.

To celebrate the centenary a civic reception had also been held in the City Chambers attended by the Lord Provost and other dignitaries, this time with all the current players present, while the Supporters Association had also organised a sell-out Centenary Rally at Leith Town Hall. Also released to coincide with the occasion had been an excellent book written by the keen Hibs supporters Phil Thomson and Gerry Docherty entitled *100 Years of Hibs*. Believed to have been the first ever complete history of the club to have appeared in print, the book had been an immediate hit with the supporters selling out almost immediately and is now a highly sought after collector's piece.

It was also around this time that the now fully recovered Eddie Turnbull had been made a director of the club in recognition of his service as a player, trainer and now manager.

After the earlier controversy at Parkhead, the game against Hearts at Tynecastle a few weeks later would once again end in contentious circumstances but this time in Hibs' favour. After an opening 45 minutes that had been almost completely dominated by a Hearts side still seeking its first Premier League victory over their local rivals, the maroons could, and perhaps should, have been several goals ahead only for the first 45 minutes to end goalless. After the break Hibs had started to come more into the game looking the likelier to score when after an hour the future Easter Road player Ralph Callaghan gave his side a lead that looked enough to have secured the points. However, in the dying seconds, what seemed a certain victory had been snatched from the home side. Stanton, who according to TV highlights later that evening might just have been in an offside position, headed a tremendous Brownlie cross from the right wing past Cruikshank to level the scores, his first goal against Hearts for over three years and his first ever in the Premier League. As far as the Gorgie faithful were concerned however, the main point of contention had been the timing of the goal. In those days, if injury time was indeed played it would usually just be a few seconds and Stanton's goal, even according to the majority of the jubilant Hibs fans leaving the stadium at the end, appeared to have been scored well after the game should have been over. At that time there was no all-day drinking, the pubs reopening for the evening session at five o'clock, and to this very day there are still Hearts fans who will swear that the first pints were being poured in Gorgie when the Hibs captain scored what has now become a famous goal – a strike that had also prevented Hearts from occupying joint top place in the table equal on points with Celtic.

In the Tynecastle boardroom before the game the Hearts chairman Bobby Parker and his fellow directors had presented Tom Hart with a silver rose bowl to commemorate Hibs' centenary, a gesture fully appreciated by everyone at Easter Road, and just one of many similar tributes received from clubs throughout the country.

Missing from the side since the defeat by Motherwell almost two months earlier, Alex Edwards would make a return to the first team just in time to face Rangers at Easter Road. In Hibs' 2–1 victory, once again Pat Stanton had taken the honours by scoring twice with magnificent headers. It was Arthur Duncan though who really took the eye with his constant dangerous probing runs deep into the opponents' penalty area. Yet again, Rangers' by now customary physical approach to the beautiful game had been no match for the fast intelligent play of the home side who had totally outplayed their opponents throughout the entire game, the victory lifting Hibs into second place in the table just two points behind leaders Celtic.

A disappointing 2–0 defeat by Dundee at Dens Park however would mean Hibs dropping to third place. After a bright start during which they had completely dominated the proceedings, an incredible mix-up between goalkeeper McArthur and centre half Roy Barry midway through the second half had allowed Caldwell the easiest of chances to open the scoring with the first of his two goals that afternoon. As well as ruining the game, Dundee's infuriating offside tactics had appeared to unnerve the Hibs players, Blackley's frustration coming to the fore when he was sent off just a few a minutes from the end after a clash with an opponent.

Just a few days later Hibs would again make their way through to Glasgow for the rearranged game with Celtic that had been abandoned earlier because of fog. Goalless at half-time, after an opener for the home side by Deans, a tremendous 40 yard free kick by Erich Schaedler, his first goal for almost three years, had secured a richly deserved equaliser, the game finally ending 1–1. The better side for large parts of the game, according to Turnbull it would have been an injustice if Hibs had left Parkhead with anything less than at least a share of the points. The generous Hart had often popped into the dressing room at Easter Road after a particularly pleasing victory to hand out 'a few quid for a drink', but this time he would go even further by awarding the players the win bonus that as far as he was concerned they had been cheated out of after the abandoned game. A magnificent performance by Brownlie, the best defender on the field by far had probably led to his promotion from the under-23s side to the full Scotland squad for the forthcoming game against Romania at Hampden, his first call up to the full side for almost three years. Mention must also be made of Roy Barry and John Blackley who had both been immense against opponents that had often been forced to rely on quick counter attacks, and on this particular performance Hibs had demonstrated that they still had nothing to fear from any club in the country. A slight concern for the Easter Road support however in what had been the side's sixth consecutive game without defeat had been the performance of Joe Harper who now seemed to have lost his scoring touch and possibly his confidence, his last goal against Motherwell nine games before. Although he had scored in the abandoned game against Celtic a few weeks earlier this obviously had not counted as official.

A narrow 1–0 home victory over Motherwell on the Saturday had been enough to lift Hibs back into second place in the table but after his earlier lean spell it would not have come as too much of a surprise to find the unsettled Harper relegated to the substitute's bench. Now clearly unhappy at Easter Road, the player who would be ordered to report to Easter Road on the Monday morning for training while the rest of the players had the day off, had already handed in a transfer request. It now seemed almost certain that he would not remain long at the club. Yet again it had been left to Pat Stanton to secure the points when heading a perfectly flighted Edwards cross from the right past goalkeeper Rennie. To their credit however, Motherwell, including the former Hibs player Peter Marinello, a recent £35,000 signing from Portsmouth, had fought hard to take something from the game. There had also been a particularly an impressive performance by the former Hibs provisional signing Willie Pettigrew up front, but in the end it would be a victory fully deserved.

Just before the turn of the year Alex Edwards had been sent off for the seventh time in his senior career during a 2–2 draw with Aberdeen at Pittodrie, only this time it would appear that the highly talented but often unpredictable player had been a victim of his reputation. Booked earlier by an overzealous referee

THE PREMIER LEAGUE AND NIGHTMARE AT MONTROSE (1975–76)

after simply attempting to take a throw-in that had been awarded to the home side, Edwards would later receive a red card after what appeared to be an innocuous tackle on Eddie Thomson, the Aberdeen player even appealing to the referee on Edwards' behalf. Thomson's appeal however would fall on deaf ears leaving Edwards facing yet another lengthy suspension and Hibs to lodge an official protest at what was considered to have been an extremely harsh decision. Somewhat ironically it had been a year and all but a day since Edwards' last dismissal, also against Aberdeen. In an exciting and evenly balanced contest Hibs had been leading 2–1 early in the second half after goals by Bremner and Duncan when full-back Erich Schaedler, who had been outstanding in curtailing the attentions of the dangerous Jocky Scott, had been forced to leave the field after picking up an injury, to be replaced by Spalding. The change however appeared to have upset a previously composed Hibs defence. Now battling to force an equaliser, Aberdeen had even missed a penalty before Williamson equalised, but in the circumstances particularly as Hibs had played part of the game with ten men, both sides would probably have been happy enough with a hard-fought share of the points.

Just prior to the home game against Celtic at Christmas, chairman Tom Hart, not always universally popular with many of his own supporters, had once again infuriated the fans when announcing that in future there was to be no Boys' gate. Initially just for the fixtures against Hearts, Rangers and Celtic, it would eventually spread to cover all games, a decision Hart felt would soon be copied by others. According to the chairman a close watch kept on the turnstiles used by the younger supporters had found that a great many attempting to gain entry had looked much older than the required age limit. Instead there would now to be a few parent and child gates situated in the car park area with reduced rates for concessions although pensioners would still be required to show proof of status. This had been nothing new. Several years earlier a similar scheme had been in operation at many of the senior grounds when only in the 'interests of safety' there been no Boys' gate for the 'big' games although ironically despite any impending threat of danger a youngster could still obtain entry if willing to pay the full price. The move would also put an end to the traditional lift-over's that for generations had encouraged youngsters to attend games and had often led to them becoming fervent fans in future years.

Before the New Year's Day game with Hearts at Easter Road the players of both sides had taken the field at Easter Road wearing black armbands in respect of the former Hibs chairman Sir John Bruce who had passed away the previous day. Eighteen months earlier both Bruce and his wife had been seriously injured when his car had been in a collision in the Inverleith area of the city. The world-renowned surgeon had never completely recovered from his injuries and had died peacefully in the Western General Hospital aged 70.

In front of over 32,000 fans, Hibs' biggest crowd of the season so far, Hearts had the misfortune to catch their city rivals at the top of their game. Two first half goals by Arthur Duncan inside an eight-minute spell followed by another by Bobby Smith now meant that after just 25 minutes the game was already as good as over, Hibs thereafter seemingly content to play out time against a Hearts side that had been outplayed in every department throughout the entire 90 minutes. In the previous ten New Years Day fixtures three had been won by Hibs with six drawn, Hearts only victory a 3–2 win at Easter Road in 1966. Interviewed immediately after the game a clearly delighted Turnbull thought the performance, particularly in the first half 'could not have been bettered by any side in the country. The fast, intelligent attacking play allowing us to score three goals in a brief period to wrap up the points'.

In the Scottish Cup Hibs had been drawn against First Division Dunfermline at home. It had now been 74 years since Hibs last won the coveted trophy and many of the fans could possibly have been excused for thinking that they had been handed an easy start to the competition. The players themselves had possibly also been guilty of taking a then struggling Fife side that would be relegated at the end of the season far too easily. Already weakened by an earlier injury to Edwards and the three-week suspension handed out to Blackley in midweek after his earlier sending off at Dundee, Hibs had failed to dominate the proceedings against feisty opponents that had twice fought back to equalise goals by Stanton and Harper. Just as a replay at East End Park was beginning to look likely Bobby Smith scored what would turn out to be the winner in the final minutes when heading a Duncan cross past goalkeeper Barclay and ensuring an extremely relieved Hibs entry into the second round draw. While the treacherous underfoot conditions had been far from ideal in no way could this have been used as an excuse for the extremely scrappy performance by the home side handicapped to an extent by a first half injury to goalkeeper McArthur although he had managed to finish the game. All credit however should go to a struggling Dunfermline side that had battled manfully throughout the entire game.

An examination would later reveal that McArthur's injury was likely to keep him out of action for several weeks. With this in mind Eddie Turnbull had wasted no time in travelling to the Potteries to sign the giant 6ft3 former Clydebank goalkeeper Mike McDonald from Stoke City on a four-year contract for a fee said to have been in the region of £30,000. Signed from Clydebank in 1972 as understudy to the great Gordon Banks, McDonald had already made several appearances for the first team before receiving a serious injury that had kept him out of the game for around ten months. Obviously severely hindering his chances at the Victoria ground, after the recent signing of Peter Shilton he now found himself third in line. Reportedly delighted to be returning to Scotland the giant goalkeeper had made his debut in a convincing 5–0 home win against St Johnstone on the Saturday.

Before the game against Dundee at Easter Road seven days later the players of both sides took the field wearing black armbands this time in memory of the former Hibs manager Hugh Shaw who had passed away in midweek aged 80. Signed as a centre-forward from Clydebank Juniors during the final days of the First World War it was only after moving back to left half that he found his true position and was a member of the celebrated side of the 1920s that had reached consecutive Scottish Cup finals. After a dispute with the club, in the summer of 1926 he had joined Rangers but would remain at Ibrox only long enough to collect a League Championship medal before moving to city rivals Hearts at the start of the following season. After brief spells with East Fife, Leith Athletic and Elgin City, Shaw had returned to Easter Road as trainer under manager Willie McCartney before succeeding the latter after his death in 1948. He would lead the club to three League Championships inside five seasons, runners-up only on goal difference on another occasion and also take the club into the inaugural European Cup in 1955 and remains Hibs' most successful manager to this very day. Leaving Easter Road to manage Raith Rovers in 1961 allegedly after a fall out with chairman Harry Swan, Shaw remained a popular and well-respected figure in the game until the end.

In the Scottish Cup Hibs had now been drawn at home against a Dundee United side that although then struggling at the foot of the table were to prove surprisingly challenging opponents. After a goalless first half, a determined United had taken the lead midway through the second 45 minutes leaving Hibs in real danger of crashing out of the competition only for a late headed goal by Brenner to give his side a second chance at Tannadice while also soothing the fraying nerves of the Hibs fans on the terracing.

Watched by a far bigger crowd than usual, a great number making their way from the capital, the replay would take place in quite dreadful conditions, the players at times forced to fight their way through ankle deep mud. However, taking advantage of the strong wind the game appeared to be all but over after just 25 minutes when goals by Spalding and Edwards had given Hibs a seemingly commanding lead. Despite goalkeeper McDonald being called upon to make several decent saves near the end against what had proved to be resolute opponents, there would be no more scoring, and Hibs were now through to face a Motherwell side that had surprisingly defeated the cup holders Celtic in the earlier round.

Meanwhile, never too far from controversy and rarely intimidated by reputations, Tom Hart had once again not been slow in speaking his mind when accusing both Rangers and Celtic of cowardice after they had apparently refused to play each other. At that time both Glasgow sides had been separated at the top of the table by just a single point only for their forthcoming derby fixture to be called off because of a 'flu epidemic' in one of the camps. Hart however had been convinced that with the clubs so near each other in the table that neither had been prepared to risk defeat at the hands of the other at that particular time. Although no action would be taken against the outspoken Hibs chairman, he would later apologise after being informed that a rule was then in existence that allowed a fixture to be cancelled if five or more players from one side had been forced to miss a game because of illness.

In the Scottish Cup, a spirited second-half performance had been required against a stuffy Motherwell at Fir Park after Hibs had fallen two behind early in the game. Recalled to the side in place of the suspended Blackley, Derek Spalding celebrated his return to the first team by scoring his first goal of the season with a tremendous drive from just outside the box to reduce the leeway. Duncan's equaliser ten minutes from time guaranteeing yet another big crowd at Easter Road in midweek.

In the replay goalkeeper McDonald had started to repay his transfer fee by making several outstanding saves from Pettigrew to keep Hibs in the competition against a confident Motherwell side that had been well on top throughout the 90 minutes, and how they must have regretted the missed chances. Goalless at the interval yet again Hibs had relied on Pat Stanton to come to the rescue after an earlier goal by Bobby Graham but despite an extra 30 minutes there was to be no more scoring, both sides having to settle for a third game playoff at Ibrox the following week.

Before that however would be the final derby of the season at Tynecastle when Arthur Duncan, making his 300th appearance for the club, had opened the scoring after just three minutes with what coincidentally had also been his 100th goal for the first team. Despite at times threatening to exact another heavy defeat on a hard-working Hearts side, that would turn out to be the final score. In a new look forward line Turnbull had taken the opportunity to give the youngsters Willie Murray, Alex McGhee and Pat Carroll a rare run in the first team, all doing little wrong as Hibs continued their recent supremacy in the fixture having now conceded just one goal against the six scored in the previous four games between the sides.

Both Carroll and Murray had kept their place in the side for the second replay at Ibrox in midweek when a goal by Harper, the last he was to score for the club, had given his side a half-time lead only for Motherwell to score twice inside nine minutes in the second half, the first from the penalty spot by substitute Peter

Marinello. In a late attempt to save the game Hibs threw everyone forward, Brownlie hitting the post with a long-range effort before Blackley fired wide from close range when it appeared easier to score. Sadly, in the end it would all be to no avail and Motherwell were through to face Rangers in the semi-final where they would eventually be defeated 3–2 at Hampden.

Of the remaining ten games only four would end in victory including a 2–0 defeat at Somerset Park by relegation-haunted Ayr United that would also turn out to be Joe Harper's last game for the club. During this run there had been an impressive 2–0 win against title contenders Celtic at Easter Road, a result that had put an end to any hopes the Parkhead side still retained of winning the championship, while also virtually guaranteeing third-placed Hibs a European spot the following season.

Since his move from Dunfermline almost three years earlier the cultured Iain Munro had been a valuable part of the first team but midway through the season he had lost his place to the rapidly improving Bobby Smith and would spend the rest of his time at Easter Road either on the substitute's bench or in the second team. During his time at the club Munro's intelligent and refined play had attracted many admirers including Rangers who were now suggesting a swap deal with the former Hibs player Colin Stein. Stein however firmly rejected a return to Easter Road, and instead Munro moved to Ibrox in exchange for Ally Scott and Graham Fyfe, both then on the fringes of the Rangers first team. Because the move had taken place after the transfer deadline all would have to be content with a place in their respective reserve sides in the meantime. Munro however who had already made several appearances for St Mirren while on loan from Hibs would not be long at Ibrox before a permanent move to Love Street where he would eventually receive several full caps for Scotland before a brief return to Easter Road later in his career.

Just days later it would come as no great surprise to learn that the unsettled Joe Harper who had earlier asked for a transfer had rejoined Aberdeen for around £50,000, Hibs losing almost £70,000 on the deal. Both clubs had already agreed the terms with Davie Robb coming to Easter Road in part exchange, but like Colin Stein this had also been rejected by Robb and the deal

THE PREMIER LEAGUE AND NIGHTMARE AT MONTROSE (1975–76)

finally concluded on a strictly cash only basis. During his three seasons at Easter Road Harper had often failed to produce his earlier Aberdeen form. Although 44 goals from 90 appearances in all competitions still represented an impressive strike rate, after his 26 the previous season including the hat-trick in the League Cup final, during the current campaign so far he had managed to find the net only around a dozen times, his last, as mentioned earlier, in the quarter-final tie with Motherwell at Ibrox several weeks before. Although popular enough with the other players, and once quoted as saying that Hibs were the best side he had played in, the body language of the now clearly unsettled Harper during large parts of the season had perhaps suggested that he was well aware of his growing unpopularity among the majority of the support who had never completely accepted a player they felt responsible for the earlier breaking up of the side, particularly the prolific partnership of Alan Gordon and Jim O'Rourke. In later years Turnbull would confess that he had probably broken the side up far too early, but that his original intention had been to play all three, Harper, Gordon and O'Rourke, in the same side but that it had not worked out. This however seems unlikely as the then St Johnstone player O'Rourke had rarely been included in the starting 11 at the time.

The curtain would finally come down on what had been a sometimes inconsistent but otherwise relatively successful season with an away game against relegation-threatened Dundee United, a victory absolutely vital for the Tannadice side if they were to have any hope of avoiding the drop. For some reason Hibs usually struggled against the United side, who had already taken five points from the earlier league games between the sides, a record according to the *Evening News* that Hibs should have been ashamed off. The run of poor results continued after first-half goals by goalkeeper McAlpine from the penalty spot and a another by Hall had been enough for United to secure their Premier League status while condemning city rivals Dundee to the lower division along with bottom of the table St Johnstone. In many ways it had been a peculiar campaign, Aberdeen, who had never before been relegated in the club's long history had also spent much of the season struggling in the bottom half of the table. Only narrowly managing to escape the drop on goal average after a 3–0 victory over Hibs in the penultimate league game of the season.

The experienced Roy Barry now approaching the veteran stage of his career had been a regular in the first team until losing his place late in the season to the talented Derek Spalding. His last appearance in a green and white jersey a 3–0 home defeat by Rangers at the beginning of April and he would join Second Division East Fife during the summer. Over the previous 12 months several young players had been blooded including the promising Lindsay Muir and Willie Paterson. Ally Brazil, a recent signing from Currie Hearts, also made an early appearance as an unused substitute in the 2–0 victory against Motherwell while Pat Carroll had managed just the one outing after his breakthrough the previous season.

The energetic former Scotland Youth cap Willie Murray had been required to show patience since making his impressive first start against Waterford in 1972, particularly in competition for the number seven shirt with Alex Edwards, but in the season just past had managed to make around 16 starts for the first team in all games plus several more as substitute. However, after a promising breakthrough into the first team the previous season goalkeeper Hugh Whyte had managed just half a dozen outings in all games and was soon to join Dunfermline.

Although there had been several impressive performances during the season, there had not been nearly enough to suggest that all was well behind the scenes. While managing to end the season in an otherwise respectable third place behind champions Rangers, who perhaps surprisingly had been winning the title for only the second time in 12 years (having also won it the previous season) and depriving runners-up Celtic from winning ten-in-a row, Turnbull had often struggled to field a settled side due to injury, suspensions and loss of form. Once again it had probably been asking too much of any inexperienced youngster to step in only when needed.

From the 16 games against the bottom four sides, apart from the four straight wins against bottom of the table St Johnstone, only three of the other 12 against Aberdeen, Dundee United and relegated Dundee had been won, with 15 goals compared to the

THE PREMIER LEAGUE AND NIGHTMARE AT MONTROSE (1975–76)

story. Overall, the performances during the season had possibly started to paper over the thin cracks that were now starting to appear and it was even more obvious than before that a major rebuilding programme was required.

As well as the promise of more entertaining football, if the aim of the new ten team set-up had also been to provide more goals then as far as Hibs had been concerned it had failed in its aims. Managing to score just 55 league goals from the 36 games, the lowest among the top four sides as opposed to the 67 the previous season, while conceding 43, ten more than before, this could possibly be explained by the majority of the games now against consistently stronger opposition than before.

As far as the fans were concerned however optimism for the future still remained high and it was now onto next season.

A Shock Exit for Pat Stanton (1976–77)

AT THE END of the previous season Wilson Humphries had been forced to resign because of ill health to be replaced as first team coach by John Fraser, his former position now filled by the enthusiastic former Falkirk and St Johnstone player John Lambie who would be a welcome addition to the backroom team.

With Roy Barry now at East Fife, at the start of what was now a desperately needed rebuilding programme, centre-half George Stewart had been signed from the recently relegated Dundee for a reported fee of around £40,000. The Edinburgh-born Stewart had been preparing to spend the following season in the lower division when he had been approached by Eddie Turnbull, his signing for the club a self-confessed dream come true for the lifelong Hibs fan. He would go on to make over 150 appearances over the following five seasons before finally ending his playing days with Cowdenbeath.

After two seasons with St Johnstone where he had been an almost permanent fixture in the first team, just before the start of the new campaign Jimmy O'Rourke had joined Motherwell, but it was not the last we were to hear of the popular former player at Easter Road.

For the third time in five seasons Hibs again decided on a three-game tour of Ireland in preparation for the new season with games against Bohemians, Dundalk and Drogheda that had all ended in victory. With both Ally Scott and Graham Fyffe now eligible for first team selection, along with new signing Stewart they had all been included in the squad that made its way to the Emerald Isle. Ominously there had been no place for Pat Stanton in the starting line up for any of the games. He had also now been replaced as club captain by John Blackley, although he would make brief appearances from the bench against both Dundalk and Drogheda.

Drawn in a League Cup section along with Montrose, Rangers and St Johnstone, in the opening game against Montrose at

A SHOCK EXIT FOR PAT STANTON (1976–77)

Links Park Hibs had made all the early running with Ally Scott scoring his first goal for the club during the first half of what would be an eventual 1–0 victory, but yet again they had found the lower league side stuffy opponents. With memories of the last meeting at the same ground no doubt still fresh in the mind, with just minutes remaining Duncan had missed a tremendous opportunity to double Hibs' lead when after collecting a Scott pass he had rounded goalkeeper Gorman but with the goal gaping he had somehow managed to overrun the ball and the chance was lost. Once again there had been no place for Pat Stanton in the starting 11 and despite constant calls throughout the game for his introduction, he would see out the game on the sidelines. Overall however there had been several encouraging signs that suggested they would be a much tougher and harder side to beat in the coming season.

The home game against Rangers in midweek had turned out to be yet another physical but otherwise exciting affair. Although with little in the way of skill in evidence, both Ally Scott and Ian Munro scored for their respective sides in the eventual 1–1 draw. New signings Scott and George Stewart had both shown up well, Stewart reducing the ill-tempered Derek Johnstone to second best while Scott had more than matched his former teammate Tom Forsyth physically throughout the entire 90 minutes. According to both managers at the final whistle the game could well have gone either way although Jock Wallace had readily acknowledged that McCloy had been by far the busier goalkeeper. A representative from Sochaux, Hibs first-round opponents in the UEFA Cup, had watched from the director's box and would have been impressed both by the performance and determination of the home side and no doubt would have had plenty to report back on his return to France.

After a 2–1 victory over St Johnstone in Perth and a 3–0 defeat at Ibrox, the return game against St Johnstone at Easter Road would turn out to be memorable. Hibs had been leading 2–0 at half-time before blasting poor Saints with another five goals inside 12 second-half minutes, the game finally ending in a comprehensive 9–2 victory. As the score would suggest it had been no contest almost from the start, young Lindsay Muir scoring twice as the lower league side had been totally overrun and outplayed. However, despite the comprehensive victory, even with the home game against Montrose still to come Hibs would finally end the section in second place behind Rangers, the first time that the club had failed to qualify for the later stages of the competition for seven years. With just minutes remaining the injured George Stewart had been forced to leave the field to be replaced by substitute Pat Stanton. After 13 seasons at Easter Road it would turn out to be his last ever appearance for the club.

Any thoughts of the earlier convincing victory over St Johnstone however had been completely overshadowed by the breaking news on the morning of the home game against Montrose that Pat Stanton had joined Celtic in exchange for Jackie McNamara. The announcement completely stunning everyone connected with the club, players, staff and supporters, with the crowd at the game against Montrose later that evening not slow in making their feelings known. Hibs fans throughout the entire country had been united in their condemnation that a player who had achieved legendary status, not just at Easter Road but throughout the country, had been allowed to leave. In a statement released a short while later manager Turnbull had been complimentary in reminding the supporters that while he was fully aware of what a tremendous servant Pat had been to the club he was now trying to rebuild the side and that no one can go on forever. Pat himself had also found difficulty in coming to terms that he was no longer a Hibs player as he had fully expected to end his career at Easter Road.

He had been at home preparing to make his way to play in a reserve game at Tynecastle later that evening when he received a phone call from the manager. After some small talk Turnbull came straight to the point: 'I have a Mr Stein with me who would like a word.' Asked if he would be interested in signing for Celtic and now realising that he no longer had any future at Easter Road he had no hesitation in answering in the affirmative and motored through to Parkhead in the morning accompanied by Alan Gordon to sign on the dotted line, watched by Jock Stein. Pat would later joke that the biggest problem had been in how to tell his Hibs-supporting dad that he had signed for Celtic! As he was leaving the ground on his way back to Edinburgh he had passed

A SHOCK EXIT FOR PAT STANTON (1976–77)

Jackie McNamara who he knew slightly from previously playing against him and had nodded, completely unaware at the time that Jackie was to be his replacement at Easter Road. Pat would later tell of his disappointment when collecting his boots from Easter Road the following morning that only trainer Tom McNiven had been there to wish him well for the future, the entire situation leaving a sour taste that after all those years of loyal service that neither the manager nor any of the directors had even called to wish him well.

At the time McNamara himself had been completely unaware that he would be replacing, in his own words, a legend, joking that had he known he would have asked for more money! A near regular in the Celtic first team the previous season, for several months he had been playing through the pain barrier with a knee injury although still managing to finish games. Yet to feature during the present campaign Turnbull had been convinced that Stein had been trying to offload an injured player. However, well aware of McNamara's condition the astute Hibs manager had already been assured by a specialist that the player would recover fully after an operation. Looking back, despite the obvious fury of the supporters, the move had probably been in the best interests of all parties, Stanton going on to complete a full set of domestic medals at Parkhead while Hibs would be gaining nine seasons tremendous service from McNamara.

There would be even more concern for the supporters after an article appeared in the *Evening News* a few weeks later suggesting that both Brownlie and Blackley had been linked with a move to Newcastle United, a claim immediately refuted by Turnbull as simply paper talk. In the same interview Tom Hart had referred to Stanton's move to Parkhead. 'No one had forced Pat out of Easter Road. The player who has gained financially from the move was informed of Celtic's interest and asked if he wanted to go', a statement that seemed to conveniently paper over the ongoing tension between the parties. Not that long before Stanton had been pulled aside by Turnbull and asked why he had fallen out with the club, only to receive the curt reply: 'I have not fallen out with the club, I have fallen out with you and I will be at Easter Road when you are long gone,' a statement that brought no response from the manager who had simply walked away. According to several insiders Turnbull didn't appear to have time for anyone at the club that he felt was bigger than him. Pat had been widely acknowledged by the supporters as Mr Hibs and this apparently didn't go down too well with the manager who would receive more criticism over Stanton's move than any other, including that of Jimmy O'Rourke or Alan Gordon. It is perhaps worth repeating in full Turnbull's article in the *Pink News* later that evening:

> The midweek deal with Celtic has brought Hibs a lot of adverse publicity due to Stanton's standing with the supporters but the transfer was negotiated with the Hibs best interests in mind. I am well aware that that the fans would think that if he is good enough for Celtic, then he is good enough for us, which is fair comment, except that Celtic wanted an experienced man to play in the middle of the defence, while I have Stewart and Blackley playing there for Hibs. We brought McNamara to Easter Road because he has skill, pace, and works willingly. He is a different kind of player to Stanton and at eight years younger, he will have time to prove himself, and then the supporters will be better placed to pass judgement.

As Stanton was making his debut for Celtic in a 2–2 draw with Rangers at Parkhead on Saturday 4 September, that same afternoon McNamara had made what would be described as a useful first start for his new club at inside left in a 2–1 home defeat by Dundee United. However, the fans who had been eagerly awaiting the start of a new league campaign would have been entitled to expect much better against a side that had only just escaped relegation at the end of the previous season on goal average. According to one newspaper report it had been a quite dreadful start to the new campaign and a performance that the players should well have been ashamed of. Although more than enough chances had been created in the first 45 minutes alone to have already secured the points, it had required a Brownlie penalty to give Hibs a half-time lead. United had come more into the game in the second half against a hesitant home defence allowing goalkeeper McAlpine to equalise just after the break, also from the spot, although United would have to wait until the very last minute for Wallace to score the winner. Completely lacking any punch up front, particularly during the second 45 minutes, it was a failing that would have to be addressed quickly if Hibs were to have any hopes of making any real impact in the coming season.

In the UEFA Cup Hibs had been drawn against the French side Sochaux who were making only their second ever appearance in a European competition. Missing the experience of the injured Edwards, in the opening game in Edinburgh Hibs had come up against yet another side that had clearly come to defend and had succeeded in its aims. After almost 90 minutes of non-stop pressure when once again enough chances had been created to have made the return game in France a mere formality, in the end Hibs had to settle for a first half strike by Brownlie after the swirling wind had completely deceived the unfortunately named goalkeeper Bats, the ball ending in the back of the net for the only goal of the game. With McNamara ineligible as he had not been signed before the deadline, Hibs had also missed the experience and influence of the injured Ally MacLeod, only Duncan in the forward line having any real European experience. With both Lindsay Muir and Ally Scott making their European baptism and Murray and Smith having only limited game time in Europe it was obvious that Turnbull had once again been struggling to field a settled side. With the delight of the Sochaux players and officials at the final whistle, it was evident that they were now confident of overturning the result in the return leg.

It would not turn out to be however, the game in the Stade Auguste Bonal ending goalless, John Brownlie's strike at Easter Road enough to see Hibs safely through to the next round. Contrary to the result it had been anything but a dull game with plenty of attacking football. Only a good save by goalkeeper Bats in the very first minute had prevented Bremner from doubling Hibs' overall lead on the night, the recalled Alex Edwards showing that he had lost nothing of his poise or cunning as he produced a string of pinpoint passes from midfield that again could well have led to more goals, only good defending by the French side allied to poor finishing and bad luck preventing a three of four goal victory for the visitors. Throughout what had been a disciplined performance Hibs had been backed by enthusiastic vocal encouragement from a group of supporters that had made their way from Edinburgh after a long coach journey, the players receiving warm and well-deserved applause as they left the field at the end.

Surprisingly both Rangers and Celtic had exited Europe at the first-round stage, Rangers after a 2–1 aggregate defeat by FC Zurich and Celtic 4–2 after both legs to the Polish side Wisla Krakow, now leaving only Hibs and a Hearts side that had earlier defeated Locomotive Leipzig in the Cup Winners' Cup to carry Scotland's hopes into the next round.

Probably now realising that his earlier decision had been a mistake, and possibly to appease the supporters Tom Hart had now announced that he was to reintroduce the Boys gate for any youngster that had been unable to take advantage of the parent and son gate as they did not attend games with an adult. Although, as before it would not be in operation for games involving Hearts, Rangers or Celtic.

Although there had been plenty endeavour shown by both sides in the home game against Ally MacLeod's Aberdeen, it had otherwise turned out to be a dour and unexciting affair, the disappointingly small crowd receiving little in either entertainment value or goalscoring chances. At no time did either side look likely to finish the game with both points, the goalless draw now leaving Hibs after four games still seeking their first league victory of the season, a situation perhaps surprisingly also shared at the time by Hearts, Rangers and Celtic.

With no games in either of the top leagues in both England and Scotland due to international commitments, at the beginning of October a friendly had been arranged against Newcastle United at St James' Park when an Ally Scott goal would not be enough to prevent a 2–1 defeat. During the second half fighting had broken out on the terracing between rival fans forcing the referee to stop the game for several minutes until the police had restored order. That same afternoon in Birmingham during a 'friendly' between Aston Villa and Rangers events had been even worse. Shortly after the home side had taken a two-goal lead a distinct change of mood could be sensed inside the stadium. A bottle thrown from

A SHOCK EXIT FOR PAT STANTON (1976–77)

the crowd had just missed one of the Villa players defending a corner, when without warning hundreds of Rangers fans had invaded the pitch leaving the referee with no option but to cancel the game. As the players made their way to the safety of the dressing rooms the police were battling to control the madness taking place all around them on the pitch, trouble unfortunately that had continued in the surrounding streets and into the town centre later that evening. At that time Cropley had usually returned to Edinburgh after home games and had wisely decided to sit as far to the back of a train filled with Rangers supporters as possible to hopefully avoid being recognised.

In the UEFA Cup Hibs had now been drawn against the little-known Swedish side Östers, then managed by the legendary centre-forward Gunnar Nordahl who had previously set goalscoring records both in Sweden and later in Italy with AC Milan. Leaving nothing to chance both Eddie Turnbull and Tom Hart had made their way to Sweden to watch their future opponents in action and had left impressed by their all-action attacking style and had returned expecting a difficult encounter in Edinburgh.

The home leg at Easter Road had been watched by a crowd of less than 11,000, but again if anyone had been expecting an exciting game with both sides attacking from the start then they were to be disappointed when Östers immediately fell back into a packed defensive formation. With just six scored in the previous eight games it would probably have been no surprise to find that both Hibs goals in what had otherwise been a one-sided affair had been scored by defenders. Ten minutes from half-time Smith had cleverly beaten two men out on the left before sending over a tremendous cross that was met by the inrushing Blackley to bullet a header into the net for his first ever European goal. Brownlie doubling Hibs lead from the spot just 60 seconds later after a defender had handled a Bremner shot that had come back off the crossbar. After the break the supporters had sat back in expectation of yet another second half goals avalanche, but despite Hibs almost total domination this had failed to materialise and there was to be no more scoring. Considering the ultra-defensive play of the Swedish side many of the supporters were now of the opinion that even with the away leg still to come that the tie was effectively already as good as over, an opinion that would soon come back to haunt them.

After seven games Hibs finally managed their first league win of the season with a 3–2 victory over Ayr United at Somerset Park. In what turned out to be a game of three penalties the scores had been even at the interval after each side had scored from the spot. Midway through the second half the referee had awarded what must have been one of the worst decisions of the season. When chasing a loose ball in his own penalty area Schaedler had been crudely tackled from behind by the Ayr substitute McSherry both players falling to the ground. To the utter amazement of everyone inside the stadium and despite the furious protests of the Hibs players, referee McFaul awarded Ayr a penalty. Justice was done however when goalkeeper McDonald who had been booked during the ensuing melee managed to save the kick. Not long after, Smith put Hibs ahead, Duncan scoring a third with just two minutes remaining, Ayr's goal in injury time merely a consolation.

In midweek sad news had been received from Canada regarding the sudden death of the former player Willie Hamilton from a heart attack aged just 37. Once described by no less a judge than Jock Stein as perhaps the most naturally gifted player he had ever managed, the much-travelled Hamilton's outrageous lifestyle had at times threatened to overshadow his fantastic talents on the pitch. After spells in England with Sheffield United and Middlesbrough, Hamilton had joined Hearts in 1962 before a later move to Hibs where he would make over 60 appearances before joining Aston Villa. Later after a short spell training at Easter Road possibly with a view to being re-signed, he would later make a return to Tynecastle before short spells with several other sides including Hamilton Academicals, finally making his way to Canada and leaving supporters wherever he had played with sublime memories of his tremendous footballing skills. A highly talented but often wayward genius, the stories regarding the player are legendary and almost far too numerous to recall. Pat Stanton remembers the time they were sitting together in the Easter Road dressing room before a game when the bold Willie turned to say:'Pat, do you know that Gene Pitney, (a singer who at that time had a chart hit with the record '24 Hours to Tulsa') and I have something in

A SHOCK EXIT FOR PAT STANTON (1976–77)

common?' Only for the bemused Stanton to confess his ignorance of the matter, Hamilton replying: 'Neither of us has a Scotland cap!' A member of the Hibs side that defeated Real Madrid in a famous friendly in 1964, a few weeks later Hamilton would finally win his one and only full cap for Scotland when lining up alongside team mate Neil Martin in a 2–1 away victory against Finland, the single full appearance for his country an extremely scant reward for his outstanding talents. On another occasion as was their then habit before certain big games the Hibs players had been staying overnight at their usual Edinburgh hotel in Great King Street before a New Year's Day game against Hearts at Tynecastle. Just before midnight chairman Harrower had poured the players a drink to see in the New Year before they were packed off to bed. Eric Stevenson, who was not playing the following day, had been surprised to be roused from his sleep around 3am by trainer Tom McNiven and asked to accompany him downstairs where they found the bold Willie still sitting on his own drinking. Packed off to his bed, the following morning the rest of his teammates had not been overly pleased at Hamilton's antics and had let him know. During the game Hamilton had scored the only goal of the game from almost on the by-line, and later back at the hotel to collect their belongings, Hamilton could be heard loudly berating the players,'Aye you're no shouting at me now, I have just won you your bonus!'

In the first Edinburgh derby of the season at Easter Road, a goal by Willie Paterson had been enough to preserve Hibs' unbeaten Premier League record against their city rivals. A completely reorganised side now had Spalding replacing Schaedler at left-back, Edwards in the unfamiliar position of inside right and the young Willie Paterson making only his second appearance for the first team on the left wing in place of the injured Arthur Duncan. Paterson put Hibs ahead with a well-placed header inside just 35 seconds with his first and what would turn out to be his only goal for club. Despite Hearts' early pressure Hibs had looked comfortable enough until an injury to centre-half Stewart after just 30 minutes had forced Turnbull to reshuffle the side, after which Hearts started to come more into the game. As expected in a local derby it had turned to be yet another hard-fought encounter with every player battling for every ball. With just minutes remaining of an evenly contested second half Prentice equalised for the maroons with a goal that was probably just reward for Hearts' second half endeavours. In the end both sides would probably have been more than satisfied with a share of the spoils.

Despite the confidence of the Hibs fans, in the return game against Östers in Sweden, Hibs had displayed what must rank as perhaps their worst ever performance in Europe in front of just 1,175 spectators, probably the lowest that the club had played before in a European competition. Whether the lack of atmosphere could be used as an excuse, in a display that would later be described by the manager as an 'absolute disaster', few players had emerged from the game with any credit. With Edwards and Bremner making little impact in midfield, shambolic defending had allowed Östers to take a 2–0 half-time lead and although Smith had pulled one back in the second half to give them a chance, yet again poor defending had allowed the home side to score twice more. The final 4–1 victory sending Hibs crashing out of Europe as the Swedish side went forward to meet Barcelona in the money-spinning next round where they would eventually be defeated 8–1 on aggregate.

In a break from the rigours of what had already been shaping up to be an extremely disappointing season, in midweek the Hibs fans had the opportunity to watch the great Gordon Banks in action in a friendly against Stoke City, the game ending in a 1–0 victory for the visitors, a young Garth Crooks scoring the only goal. The career of the legendary goalkeeper Banks, a World Cup winner in 1966, had been cut short after losing an eye in a road accident a few years before. Now, while unable to take part in competitive games because of insurance issues, he had still been in great demand for friendlies and testimonial games and no doubt the fans would have been delighted to have watched in person a player once rated the best goalkeeper in the world.

Yet another draw, this time against the previous season's treble winners Rangers, the third between the sides so far that season, had been Hibs' eighth from the 11 league games played with just the single victory against Ayr United at Somerset Park. In the 1–1 draw, Rangers had fully deserved their early lead only

A SHOCK EXIT FOR PAT STANTON (1976–77)

for Hibs to equalise thanks to an own goal by Steele just before half-time. After which, Hibs had grown in confidence and had looked the likelier to take the lead but there was to be no more scoring. Interviewed after the game Eddie Turnbull had reportedly been satisfied, both with the performance and result, and that any point at Ibrox was an acceptable result particularly in the current situation. So far only 12 goals had been scored against the 13 conceded and although it was still early days the statistics would obviously have concerned the manager and he would already have been more that aware of just where the problem lay.

A 2–0 defeat by Motherwell in midweek had left Hibs still seeking their first home win of the season. In a success-based industry the falling attendances would have left the manager but particularly Tom Hart more aware than before that a major improvement had been needed, particularly in the goalscoring department, before the following weeks trip to Pittodrie to face the then league leaders and League Cup winners Aberdeen. At Pittodrie, Joe Harper would score the only goal of the game in the first-half after a tremendous solo run against his former teammates, a strike that perhaps for obvious reasons would have given him even greater pleasure. Despite a much improved performance from a spirited Hibs side that had battled manfully for an equaliser particularly in an entertaining and exciting last 45 minutes, unfortunately it had been to no avail, Harper's strike enough to give his side the points.

A few weeks later Graeme Fyfe scored his first and as it would turn out only goal for the first team in a 1–1 draw with Partick Thistle in Glasgow, Hibs' first point from the previous three games. Now after 14 games the club was left still seeking only its second league victory of the season and first at home. After a bright start when he had featured in all six League Cup section games, the highly rated Fyfe who had earlier made more than 100 appearances for Rangers had struggled to claim a regular first team place at Easter Road. After just 15 starts and another from the bench he would join Dumbarton at the beginning of the following season. His former Rangers teammate Ally Scott however had fared slightly better and would eventually make 37 appearances in all games, including several as substitute scoring three goals. One of which after only 30 seconds in a 2–2 draw with Motherwell in September that had been touted at the time as a candidate for the fastest goal of the season.

With the manager already not having his troubles to seek, there was to be even more bad news when it was revealed that Jackie McNamara, who had been something of a fixture in the first team since making his debut at the beginning of the season although often playing through the pain barrier, was now to undergo a cartilage operation. The side was certain to miss the passion and determination of a player Eddie Turnbull would later describe as the last real tackler in the game. The operation would obviously keep McNamara out of the game for several months and except for a single appearance from the bench late in the season he would spend the remainder of the time in the reserves.

Away from Easter Road, what had previously been under-23 internationals had now been replaced by the under-21s. Just a few weeks after joining Celtic, Pat Stanton, who had last featured in the Scotland set-up against West Germany in 1974, had been included in the side as one of the two over-age players for a game against Czechoslovakia that would ultimately end in a no-score draw.

Although Ayr United had been defeated at Somerset Park earlier in the season, after 14 league games Hibs were still looking for their first home victory having lost two and drawn four of the previous six, results that had again been reflected at the turnstiles. Of the 13 goals scored so far, only third bottom Partick Thistle had scored fewer, two coming from the penalty spot, two by defenders and an own goal, the problem more concerning as every week passed.

In the return game against an Ayr side that was then languishing near the foot of the table Hibs would finally achieve a home win although the narrow 1–0 victory had been courtesy of yet another own goal. The result however now leaving Second Division Forfar as the only club in the entire country without a home win. The game had also been fairly unusual in that it had taken place on Christmas Eve which could possibly have accounted for the extremely low turnout of just 3,875, at that time Hibs lowest home crowd of the season. Perhaps in an attempt to lure the fans

A SHOCK EXIT FOR PAT STANTON (1976–77)

away from late night Christmas shopping, admittance prices to the enclosure had been reduced to that of the terracing but even this had done little to encourage the supporters along to the game. Although the final scoreline would probably have suggested a close encounter, in reality it had been anything but. Despite dominating almost the entire 90 minutes, the Hibs players had perhaps understandably appeared either over anxious in front of goal or in shooting from distance, allowing goalkeeper Geoghegan to save easily, although they had grown in confidence after an own goal by Filippi midway through the second half. While the victory had been enthusiastically welcomed by the scattering of fans on the terracing all would be aware that their favourites were almost certain to face a far tougher challenge at Tynecastle a week later.

However, with an estimated 30,000 tickets already sold, the eagerly awaited New Year's derby had been postponed due to the blizzards that were then sweeping the country making the Tynecastle pitch unplayable and would not take place for several weeks. The harsh conditions had also meant the home game against Dundee United a few days later being postponed. This game would go ahead later in the week after the weather had eased somewhat, when in front of yet another poor home crowd Hibs would start 1977 with yet another draw, the game, probably to no one's complete surprise, once again ending without a goal.

On the positive side it had been a far better performance than of late. Only a tremendous performance by goalkeeper Hamish McAlpine, who at times had appeared unbeatable as his teammates struggled against Hibs' relentless pressure had allowed United to leave Edinburgh with a point. The result however still left Hibs seeking that elusive first victory against United in the seven games between the sides since the introduction of the Premier League almost two years before.

Thrice postponed, the New Year's game against Hearts at Tynecastle would finally go ahead at the end of January, the narrow 1–0 victory continuing Hibs recent dominance of the fixture. It had now been 22 years since their city rivals had won the New Year's holiday game on their own home ground.

Earlier in the week there had at last been some welcome news for the manager that the influential Ally MacLeod who had not played since the beginning of September was on his way back to full fitness after an operation on his injured knee and had already successfully come through a couple of reserve fixtures unscathed. Although it had been thought highly unlikely that he would be ready for the first team for a few weeks yet, just 24 hours after scoring a hat-trick in the second team's 5–0 League Cup semi-final victory against Airdrie, MacLeod had made a surprise appearance at Tynecastle, celebrating his return to first team action with a flash of brilliance. The goal allowing Hibs to secure both points. In an otherwise fairly poor game MacLeod had started the move himself from midfield before taking a return pass from McGhee to fire past Cruickshank, the victory allowing Hibs to exchange places in the table with their archrivals.

Just days before, news had been received that the former player Davie Shaw had died aged just 59. Captain of the Hibs side that lost to Aberdeen in the first post-war Scottish Cup final in 1947 and also the league winning side of 1947–48, during his 11 years at Easter Road Shaw had made eight appearances for Scotland, five while forming a full-back partnership with teammate Jock Govan and on another occasion alongside colleague Hugh Howie. Leaving to join Aberdeen in 1950, he had captained the Grampian side to League Cup success in 1953, and later as manager to the club's first ever league title in 1955, finally ending his time at Aberdeen as trainer under the then manager Eddie Turnbull in the 1960s.

In the seemingly never-ending quest for Scottish Cup success Hibs had drawn Partick Thistle at home in the opening round, a game unusual for the fact that it took place on a Sunday, and perhaps even more surprisingly just 24 hours after a 4–2 defeat by Celtic in Glasgow. Although Tom Hart had previously been reported as being firmly opposed to Sunday football, the game would still go ahead as planned. The novelty seemed to have caught the imagination of the Edinburgh public with almost 14,000 inside the ground at the start, the highest home attendance of the season except for games against Hearts and both the Old Firm sides. Goalless at the interval thanks only to several brilliant saves by the Scotland goalkeeper Alan Rough, the custodian could do little to stop Hibs from scoring three times in 18 second-half minutes to progress into the next round and prolong the supporters' expectations of Scottish Cup glory. Most of credit for the victory however had belonged to Ally MacLeod who had now scored in each of his last three games, a clear sign of what the side had been missing in his absence.

After a highly unlikely run of four games without a draw while winning two, Hibs would be back to their now familiar routine in a home game against Rangers that had also been postponed earlier because of the poor weather, the no-scoring encounter now extending the number of Hibs' drawn league games to an incredible 13 from just 23 starts. Although played in midweek when traditionally games normally attracted much smaller crowds than would be expected on a Saturday afternoon, the 12,542 had still been considered an extremely disappointing turnout when compared to the 25,000 that had attended the League Cup tie between the sides at the beginning of the season. It was perhaps a further indication that the supporters were not all that happy at what they were then witnessing on the park and subsequently voting with their feet. In what turned out to be yet another drab affair almost totally lacking in entertainment, the main talking point of the evening had been the inept performance of referee Muirhead who according to the papers the following morning had the proverbial nightmare. The highlight of a totally unsatisfactory performance being when the already booked Alex McDonald of Rangers, not always the most sporting of players, had been involved in an incident with Alec Edwards near the stand side touchline when he had attempted to prevent the Hibs player from rising to his feet after a tackle by wrestling him to the ground. Muirhead had made his way to the scene of the incident appearing to point his finger in condemnation towards the Rangers player when to the surprise of almost everyone in the ground he then proceeded to book Edwards while taking absolutely no action against the real transgressor McDonald, completely lacking the courage to send the Rangers player from the field, sadly a situation that had all become far too familiar throughout the years.

In the Scottish Cup Hibs had now been drawn away against First Division Arbroath. With attendances still dropping alarmingly a good cup run was now essential and although there was always the danger of underestimating lower league opponents it was not thought that the then middle of the table First Division side would cause any real concerns in stopping Hibs from progressing into the next round. However, in a game that was never at any stage dominated by the Premier League side, Hibs would have to wait until 20 minutes from the end for a Blackley goal to spare the their blushes, after a far more determined Arbroath had taken the lead ten minutes after half-time and could well have scored more against a hesitant Hibs defence, more than deserving a replay in midweek.

At Easter Road on the Wednesday Hibs had been leading at half-time after yet another goal by Ally MacLeod only to make a disastrous exit from the competition when poor defending had allowed their First Division opponents to score twice inside two second-half minutes, one an own goal by George Stewart. In the end Hibs had no one to blame but themselves, poor finishing and dreadful defending at fault for a humiliating defeat that had been even worse as it had been at home. It had been the club's first Scottish Cup defeat at Easter Road by a lower league side since the embarrassing 3–2 defeat by Edinburgh City in 1938 that had been switched from City Park to Easter Road in anticipation of a much bigger gate. Sadly, defeat to a lower league side was now no longer a new experience and at the final whistle Turnbull had been jeered from the field by the few fans that had bothered to stay until the end of what had been a hugely embarrassing defeat. Perhaps these were the first real tangible signs that the heady days of just a few seasons earlier were now quite definitely over.

Previously mainly the domain of the Old Firm fans, incidents involving hooliganism were sadly becoming much more common throughout the game. After the embarrassing defeat by Arbroath a number of Hibs fans who quite simply could not accept defeat had embarked on a trail of wanton vandalism all the way from the ground into the centre of town smashing shop windows and other needless damage along the way. Edinburgh Councillor Cooke later calling for both the football authorities and the Hibs board to be held responsible for damages that had amounted to well over £1,000 in the High Street area alone. Just a few weeks earlier during a game against Hearts at Tynecastle trouble between rival supporters had led to several arrests with dozens more ejected from the ground, more evidence that trouble at football games was on the increase.

After the embarrassing cup defeat by Arbroath, the *Evening News* journalist John Gibson, a well-known Hibs supporter, had suggested jokingly that Hibs should perhaps try hiring a hypnotist. This comment later leading to the well-known hypnotist Robert Halpern who was popular in the city at that time offering his services, an offer however that had been politely refused. In his column a few days later Gibson had gone even further by stating that perhaps Hibs had players at that time who were well capable of defeating the efforts of any hypnotist.

Around that time the private members 50 Club that had previously rented premises inside the stadium had now opened new clubrooms immediately across the road from the main Easter Road stand. The official opening was perhaps surprisingly performed by chairman Tom Hart with the announcement that he was pleased that the earlier differences between the parties had now been overcome, a reference to the earlier attempted takeover bid.

In the middle of March Hibs had made their way to Tannadice still seeking their first Premier League victory over Dundee United after seven attempts but once again had been destined to leave empty handed. Again it had been obvious that their weakness in front goal had been the main problem, Brownlie even missing the chance to equalise a first half United goal from the penalty spot midway through the second half. The fans left wondering if MacLeod who had missed the game because of injury would have made a difference against a United defence that had been far from convincing throughout the entire 90 minutes.

Despite their often inconsistent form, in midweek Hibs had continued their recent good run against their city rivals with a more than credible 3–1 victory at Easter Road, when according to the *Evening News* the following day there should perhaps now be an enquiry as to how a shot-shy Hibs could manage to score three goals in a league game for only the second time that season. In front of yet another disappointingly small crowd of just 13,625, the lowest for an Edinburgh derby for some years, Hibs had been well on top against a Hearts side that was then struggling near the foot of the table, the victory providing some small comfort for the now clearly frustrated home fans.

Pat Stanton had made his first appearance back at Easter Road since his transfer to Celtic earlier in the season a game that incredibly would eventually end in yet another draw. After Glavin had opened the scoring for the visitors in the first-half who else but MacLeod would score the equaliser for Hibs. The point gained now meaning that Celtic could win the championship with a victory on their return to Easter Road in a few weeks' time when according to one sports writer there would surely be a far bigger turnout than the disappointing 11,841 tonight. With the advantage of the strong wind at their backs in the first half Hibs could well have been several goals ahead, only for the now expected habit of poor finishing allowing the sides to change over at half-time with the scores still level. With the elements now in their favour in the second half, the Celtic fans had sat back expecting a convincing victory for their favourites only for the game to still end level after a tremendous rearguard display by the entire Hibs defence.

Hibs and Hearts would meet again just over two weeks later this time at Tynecastle when Des Bremner would take the opportunity to score both Hibs goals in the eventual 2–2 draw. Gibson had opened the scoring for Hearts only for Bremner to level the proceedings with a tremendous 30-yard drive before scoring his second of the afternoon in the second half. Only a controversial last-minute equaliser by the future Hibs player Jim Brown would prevent his side from dropping further into the relegation zone. Appearing well offside when he received the ball inside the Hibs penalty area the linesman had immediately raised his flag, only for referee Gordon to allow Brown to slip the ball past goalkeeper McDonald much to the fury of the Hibs support. The result however had provided Hearts with some breathing space from the worry of relegation and Hibs the dubious record of having gone into the history books with their 17th draw in just 32 league games.

On Saturday 16 April Celtic made their second visit to Easter Road inside just a few weeks. Already seven points ahead of second placed Rangers, a solitary goal by Craig had been more than enough give the visitors the league title for the first time in three years and Pat Stanton his first championship medal. Once again Tom Hart had banned the cameras from covering the event, repeating his earlier claim that the game was in danger of being overexposed on the TV screens. Several other clubs were now starting to show concern regarding the TV menace but so far the forthright Hibs chairman had been the only one with the courage to act. He would later go a step further by calling on the football authorities to ban the cameras from all games under their jurisdiction if only for a trial period, an appeal however that would ultimately fall on deaf ears. Meanwhile, but perhaps predictably the BBC had now turned their cameras in the direction of Ibrox where Rangers had defeated a struggling Ayr United 4–1.

Although the championship had now been wrapped up the victory had not been achieved easily against a dogged Hibs side that had battled hard for a result. The purist would perhaps have expected better in what would eventually become a dour hard-fought battle, but for 90 minutes there had been little to separate the sides though by then the final result would have only been of any real interest to Celtic. As could be expected Pat Stanton had again received a rousing welcome from both sets of fans as he took the field before the game and at the final whistle he had been warmly congratulated by his former team mates and back room staff particularly trainer Tom McNiven, the absence of manager Turnbull or any of the directors –particularly Tom Hart – to congratulate a player who had given so much to the club over the years extremely noticeable.

Just a few days later Hibs' fourth victory of the season against a struggling Ayr United would be watched by just 2,835, the club's lowest attendance of the entire campaign, even less than the 3,875 that had attended the game against the Ayrshire side in December, to be followed by yet another drab no-score draw at Rugby Park.

As far as the supporters were concerned and by that stage probably even the players themselves, the end of the season just couldn't come quickly enough. The curtain would finally come down on what had been yet another hugely disappointing campaign with a 1–0 defeat by Partick Thistle at Firhill, a result that had allowed the Glasgow side to overtake Hibs into fifth place in the table.

Over on the other side of the city however things were even worse. At the end of January Hearts had been lying fifth in the table two places above Hibs, but since the 3–1 home defeat by their Edinburgh rivals in March they had gone on a horrendous run of results that would eventually see them finish second bottom of the table and facing relegation for the first time in the club's history. Even the home win against Motherwell on the final day, their first victory in the previous nine games, was not nearly enough to save them from the drop and the eventual sacking of manager John Haggart. Several well-known names had seemingly been in the running to replace Haggart in the Tynecastle hot seat but the position would eventually be offered to the former Hibs player Willie Ormond who had only recently resigned as manager of Scotland after a successful spell with St Johnstone.

While Hibs had eventually managed to end in sixth place it would be something of an understatement to say that the season had turned out to be a major disappointment. Of the 36 games played only eight had ended with a win, all against the bottom three sides with doubles against Ayr United, Hearts and Kilmarnock. Of the remainder an incredible 20 had been drawn, a then record, results that would also mean that for the first time in six seasons there would be no European football at Easter Road the following season.

In a season of highs and lows the lowest point had undoubtedly been the home defeat by First Division Arbroath in the Scottish Cup. Perhaps in an attempt to revive the flagging spirits of the Hibs support, in an end of season interview Turnbull had been extremely positive in praising the team's defensive record that indeed had been impressive with just 35 goals conceded. With the exception of Second Division Stirling Albion it had been the lowest of any of the sides in the entire three leagues. But again it would not be difficult to see exactly where the main problem lay with just 34 scored, again with the exception of relegated Kilmarnock the lowest in the entire Scottish League. Even Falkirk who had been demoted from the First Division had scored more, the

A SHOCK EXIT FOR PAT STANTON (1976–77)

supporters perhaps understandably failing to fully appreciate the manager's apparent confidence for the coming season.

Bobby Smith had ended the campaign as top goal scorer in league games with a measly seven, while MacLeod who had missed a large part of the season through injury had ended overall top scorer in all games with just 12. Once again several youngsters, Ally Brazil, Willie Paterson, Lindsay Muir, Mike Wilson and Alex McGhee had all made appearances in the first team but only Brazil and to a lesser extent Muir would have a prominent part to play in the future. For Willie Murray however it had been his best season yet making 16 outings for the first team including two starts against Sochaux in the UEFA Cup plus several more as an unused substitute scoring once.

Ian Campbell who had yet to feature in the first team had been among the seven players freed along with the talented inside-forward Mike Wilson who had been signed straight from school aged 15 but had since managed just three games for the first team during this time, only one during the season just ended and would soon sign for Dunipace Juniors. At the end of the season Tony Higgins had been yet another who had struggled to hold down a regular first team place and had now been made available for transfer.

Since the signing of George Stewart earlier in the season the promising Derek Spalding had also found difficulty in claiming a regular position in the first team and although the club still retained his registration he would soon move to play in the North American League with Chicago Sting.

Not everyone had been convinced that the Premier League had been for the better, often failing completely in its aims of providing more entertainment, increased attendances and improved finance. Instead, in many ways it had turned out to be quite the reverse with most sides still recording falling gates accompanied by the obvious loss of revenue. Although a league of just ten sides had perhaps looked good on paper, in reality the predicted improvements had failed to materialise, resulting in a league that according to some had become one ruled by fear. With 20 per cent of the sides outside either Celtic or Rangers facing relegation at the end of the season, the odds had often made it extremely difficult for managers to encourage attacking football, and now with no easy games many had also been reluctant to introduce inexperienced youngsters into the fray.

Erich Schaedler had started the season out of favour but with Bobby Smith later moving into the forward line in an attempt to generate more fire power, the full-back had been restored to the side. Briefly losing his place again, this time to Spalding, he would ultimately end the season in his usual position. The injured MacLeod and later McNamara had undoubtedly been a huge miss in an otherwise fairly inexperienced side, and it was now all too obvious that the exciting, free-scoring days of just a few seasons earlier were now a thing of the past. A fact that was not wasted on the supporters.

Just a few weeks after winning the championship at Easter Road, Pat Stanton would complete a full set of domestic honours after Celtic's 1–0 victory over Rangers in the Scottish Cup final at Hampden, the first time the showpiece had been shown live on TV since Clyde's victory over Celtic in 1955. It would also turn out to be Jock Stein's 25th trophy as a manager and his last.

Sponsorship and a Battle with the Cameras (1977–78)

IN YET ANOTHER attempt to appease the now clearly dissatisfied supporters, in a pre-season interview the manager had apparently again been pleased with the club's defensive record during the previous season but had also been aware that the team would need to start winning more games, recapture the clubs reputation for scoring goals and give the supporters the type of entertainment they had come to expect in recent seasons. Encouraging words, but a statement nevertheless that would have had little impact on the fans who at the very least had probably expected some badly needed new signings during the summer.

By now the players were back training much nearer home at Holyrood Park. At that particular time very few if any of the Scottish clubs actually owned their own training facilities, many usually making use of regular venues. Over the years Hibs had trained at several different locations throughout the city, Hawkhill, Piershill, Wardie, the Jack Kane Centre and more recently the Civil Service grounds at Silverknowes, all on a temporary basis, even at times the beach at Seafield where on one particular occasion they had been about to take part in small sided game only to discover that they had forgotten to bring a ball. Now under the watchful eye of coach John Fraser, after completing the warmup exercises, a new generation of players would then experience the traditional run around the Queen's Drive that had been endured by generations of players before them, on several occasions even asked to make the lung bursting slog to the top of Arthur's Seat before returning to the ground for a welcome and well-deserved shower.

The summer of 1977 would also herald the dawn of an entirely new era in British football. In an exciting new age of sponsorship Hibs would become the very first senior side in the entire country to feature a sponsor's name on their jerseys: the name of the sportswear manufacturers Bukta emblazoned in prominent four-inch-high white letters across the chest accompanied by the company logo on a wide green bands down the side of each sleeve.

At a time when sponsorship in the game had still been an extremely sensitive subject, in 1970 the brewers Watney Mann had been the very first commercial enterprise to financially back a competitive professional football tournament and would be followed just a year later by the Drybrough Cup, the first ever commercial competition exclusively for Scottish clubs. With attendances still dropping throughout the country the football authorities in Scotland had not been slow in recognising the obvious benefits of commercial involvement in the game and it would clearly be only a matter of time before its logical progression into other sports.

At that time several prominent European sides were already benefiting financially from shirt sponsorship. Quickly recognising the opportunity to provide a much needed boost to its finances, the then struggling English non-league side Kettering Town managed by the former Wolves and Ireland international Derek Dougan had decided to adopt the innovation and feature the name of the local firm Ketterington Tyres on their shirts. This however had not been to the liking of the Football Association. Individual sponsorship had been banned in England since at least the early years of the decade, and Kettering would soon be contacted by the football authorities to be reminded that the move had been in direct contravention of the association rules and threatened with further action if the offending wording was not removed. In an imaginative attempt to circumvent the regulation the club had then changed it to feature only the initials KT in large letters, the T obviously standing for either Town or Tyres, the creative innovation however only leading to a further warning that the club risked being fined £1,000 if the offending letters were not removed.

Although Kettering had the support of several First Division sides including Liverpool and Derby County who would soon go down the same road themselves, at that time given the circumstances, there was only going to be one winner and the disputed logo had been removed. At a time when finance was desperately

SPONSORSHIP AND A BATTLE WITH THE CAMERAS (1977–78)

needed throughout the game, particularly in the lower leagues, the FAs decision was generally seen as a backward step.

Although Hibs themselves already had the backing of both the Scottish League and the SFA, the move had not been well received by either the BBC or STV, both claiming that the size of the lettering clearly breached the advertising code. Hinting at a possible camera ban on any game involving the Edinburgh side if the offending wording was not removed, the irony of the situation would no doubt not have been lost on Tom Hart who had been advocating such a move for some time. The attitude of the television companies however had provoked a commendable response from the Scottish League when stating that if this was indeed to be the case then it would lead to blanket coverage of any game falling under its jurisdiction. Now taking full advantage of the situation, both football authorities had felt the time right to once again raise the subject of broadcasting fees for games covered by the cameras, seeking a substantial increase from the current contract that was described as derisory, perhaps even double. The subject of repeats had also been raised. At that time both channels had been allowed to repeat any game or highlights as often as they desired free of charge, an obviously unfair situation that would soon change.

The row would continue for some time, Hibs now officially informed by STV that according to the Independent Broadcasting Authority rules, coverage of any game involving a team displaying any kind of shirt advertising was prohibited. Later, a month-long truce had been agreed by all parties that Hibs would not feature on either channel until a solution could be found. The ongoing dispute that had been financially harmful to all sides would drag on for several weeks until Tom Hart came up with a temporary solution to the problem. After consultation with Bukta, Hibs had agreed at least for the time being that the club would wear an alternative strip for any match covered by the cameras, although making it clear that he planned to appeal to the House of Commons through the well-known Hibs supporter MP Alex Fletcher. Fletcher would later raise the subject in parliament wondering why if Hibs had been prohibited from wearing a sponsor's logo on their jerseys, how the brewing giants Scottish and Newcastle had been allowed to sponsor the Scottish Cup for £250,000.

Regardless, a solution would eventually be found to the ongoing saga and Hibs' innovative move would soon be adopted by other clubs. Today it would be almost impossible to find a sports shirt anywhere in the world that did not feature advertising of some sort.

In a change to the recent custom of visiting Ireland in preparation for the forthcoming season the club had instead decided on a short three-game tour of the Highlands with games against Deveronvale, Inverness Thistle and Elgin City, all ending in victory, Des Bremner scoring twice in the 6–0 win against his former side Deveronvale that included his brother in the line up. In all 16 goals had been scored against just the two conceded and although they would undoubtedly face much stiffer opposition in the coming season, after the lack of goals during the previous campaign the players would have found it a welcome boost to their confidence.

There would be even more good news for the fans with the news that Jackie McNamara was now back to full fitness and with John Brownlie about to serve a suspension that had been carried over from the previous season, the versatile former Celtic player had temporarily replaced the Scottish international at right-back, a position he had occupied in all three games during the short tour of the Highlands.

The new season would now kick off with three home games inside the opening eight days, but bizarrely in three different competitions. Inaugurated just a few years earlier, this would be Hibs' first ever appearance in the sponsored Anglo Scottish Cup competition that had now replaced the Texaco Cup. Competed by clubs from both Scotland and England it was set in eight groups of four in a straight knockout home and away format. The opening rounds consisted only of clubs from their own particular home country, the top two in the Scottish section then going forward to face English opposition in the next round. However, similar to its predecessors the Watney, Drybrough and Texaco Cups, while the new competition would prove initially popular with the fans, interest would gradually diminish and eventually lead to the competition's demise in 1981.

SPONSORSHIP AND A BATTLE WITH THE CAMERAS (1977-78)

The opening round against Ayr United at Somerset Park had eventually turned into a bruising affair poorly handled by a referee who had failed completely to control the tough tackling of the home side, particularly when George Stewart had required attention after appearing to have been deliberately stamped on by an opponent as he lay on the ground. Hibs had been well on top during the opening 45 minutes, a goal by Smith giving them a deserved interval lead. In the second half however it would be a vastly different story. As an Ayr side that would be relegated at the end of the season started to take complete control of the proceedings, it had been no surprise when they equalised midway through the half, Ally Scott scoring the winner for Hibs near the end very much against the run of play.

A few days later it would be back to league action against Motherwell and what would turn out to be yet another scrappy affair. Although the swirling wind had made it extremely difficult for either side to produce much flowing football, according to one newspaper the following morning few fans would have been excited at the prospect of another nine months of this sort of fare. In another bad-tempered 90 minutes with little in the way of good football, defences had been well on top, the no-scoring draw predictable long before the end. A surprise for the fans however had been the appearance of the 19-year-old substitute Gordon Rae who had been signed only the previous day from Whitehill Welfare. The youngster was probably just as surprised as the fans, although he had been informed that while he would be on the bench the following day he would not be called upon.

That same afternoon in a game against Dundee United at Parkhead, Pat Stanton had been forced to leave the field at half-time with a knee injury that would eventually require surgery. Unfortunately, the injury would fail to heal completely and Stanton would never play competitive football again, bringing a sad and premature end to 15 distinguished seasons as a well-respected professional.

In midweek Hibs were now to face First Division Queen of the South in a new look League Cup competition. In recent years the fans had become weary of the same old start to the season with the usual four, sometimes five sides in the qualifying sections, a format that had been in place since the tournament's inception 31 years earlier. In an attempt to create more interest it would now take place on a straight one-off knockout home and away format. Watched by fewer than 5,000 now fairly disinterested supporters it would turn out to be Hibs' lowest home attendance of the entire season. Well aware of their steadily growing frustrations Turnbull had appealed for the supporters to get behind the players, particularly the younger ones. In yet another attempt to find a solution to the lack of goals the teenager Gordon Rae, a prolific goal scorer with both his former amateur sides had started the game, the youngster doing his future prospects no harm when scoring what appeared to be a perfectly legitimate goal only for it to be disallowed by an over officious referee. An Ally MacLeod goal in the first half had been cancelled out by an O'Hara strike before Hibs conceded a soft penalty late in the game that few referees would have penalised when Stewart was adjudged to have pushed an opponent inside the box, Dixon scoring what would turn out to be the winner from the spot. Although they had not played all that badly the supporters had been particularly unhappy that Hibs could not even manage to defeat a side from a lower division at home, sadly not a new experience after Arbroath and Montrose in previous seasons. Unfortunately, the poor result had led to a number of fans who could not take defeat once again rampaging through the city in a wave of vandalism, smashing shop windows all the way into the centre of town, incidents that would later lead to the chairman of the supporters club demanding that severe action be taken against all those involved.

Some belief would be restored at Ibrox a few days later when young Gordon Rae making only his second first team start took advantage of a mistake by the Rangers goalkeeper McCloy to open the scoring after just four minutes, with a strike that went in off his knee to give his side an unexpected half-time lead. The goal however appeared to settle Hibs who could well have scored more, particularly a MacLeod effort just before half-time that had only just been scrambled to safety. In the second half Rangers had reinforced their efforts to take something from the game but although having most of the pressure had rarely looked like scoring and were stunned in the very last minute when Bremner doubled the

SPONSORSHIP AND A BATTLE WITH THE CAMERAS (1977–78)

visitors lead to give Hibs its first victory at Ibrox in three seasons. At that particular time Bremner was playing the best football of his career, his reading of the game and work rate an inspiration to his teammates and for some time rumours had been circulating linking him with a move to Celtic. Gossip however that would eventually come to nothing.

In the return game against Ayr United at Somerset Park, goals by Bremner and Smith in a 2–2 draw had been enough for Hibs to qualify for the second round of the Anglo Scottish Cup where they would now face Blackburn Rovers away in the first leg. Before that however there would be the return League Cup tie against Queen of the South at Palmerston, a victory vital if Hibs were to progress into the next round. Just before kick-off the players had been surprised to say the least to discover that the long-serving and highly respected trainer and physiotherapist Tom McNiven had suddenly tendered his resignation.

When joining Third Lanark in 1958 McNiven had been the youngest trainer in the game aged just 24. Arriving at Easter Road in the summer of 1963 as a direct replacement for Eddie Turnbull after the latter's surprise resignation, and coincidentally on the very same day as the legendary Pat Stanton, McNiven had already agreed to sign for Morton when he became aware of Hibs interest. Fortunately for a generation of Hibs and Scotland players Morton did not stand in the way of him joining Hibs. With a particular talent for strapping or massaging an injury and the patience required in helping a player recover mentally from an injury, something that was often overlooked in those days, perhaps just as importantly he could be trusted not to pass on any of the rumours or gossip generally associated with a treatment room. Widely considered to have been well before his time, his talents would often only be truly appreciated after a player had experienced what was on offer elsewhere. McNiven's abilities had also been recognised by the SFA and for several years he had been a valuable member of the international set-up, not only the full Scotland side but also the inter-league and under-18 teams. Although refusing to be drawn on the reason for his sudden resignation, behind the scenes it had been known for some time that a long-standing personality clash with the manager who was said to have been unhappy at the time McNiven was spending with Scotland had brought the situation to a head. Popular with the players, McNiven had been described as possibly the nicest person you could ever wish to meet. Although it had not been common knowledge at the time, during his time at Easter Road Rangers had tried on several occasions to tempt him to Ibrox with far better conditions and wages, but McNiven had remained loyal to Hibs. It was not the last we would hear of him at Easter Road.

The announcement however would have done little to improve the already low moral running through the club at that time. It had also done little to inspire some badly needed confidence in the camp when for the third time in three seasons Hibs would exit a cup competition at the hands of a lower league side, the no-scoring draw in the return against Queen's at Palmerston allowing the Second Division side to go forward into the next round. On a rain swept pitch Hibs had battled hard for the goal that might well have kept them in the tournament, only for the old problem of failing to take their chances coming back to haunt them. Despite relentless pressure on the opponent's goal particularly in the final 20 minutes the game eventually ended scoreless, the home side even managing to miss a second-half penalty. The cup exit would also prove expensive financially, particularly at a time when attendances were still dropping throughout the country. In reality, the game had been lost at Easter Road and once again even this early it appeared as though it would turn out to be another long hard season.

In yet another attempt to introduce more fire power into the attack, centre-forward Jim McKay was signed on a month-long trial from the Highland League side Brora Rangers. Making his debut as a substitute in a 3–0 defeat of Newcastle United in a friendly at Easter Road at the beginning of the month he had already done enough to impress the manager who was keen to sign him on a permanent deal. McKay, a prolific goal scorer in the Highland League, had earlier spent a week training at Easter Road during pre-season but an attempt to sign him at that time had failed to materialise when Hibs' valuation of the player had fallen well below that of Brora's. Turnbull however had kept an eye on

SPONSORSHIP AND A BATTLE WITH THE CAMERAS (1977–78)

the 21-year-old's progress and had now got his man, albeit on a temporary basis.

At Tannadice a few days later Dundee United had continued its unbeaten Premier League record against the Easter Road side with a 2–0 victory. Although achieved with very little trouble it had required a wonder solo goal by Kirkwood and a hotly disputed penalty after goalkeeper McDonald had been judged to have brought down Sturrock inside the box to achieve victory against a Hibs side that despite working hard had never at any time looked like scoring.

In a break from the pressures of domestic football, in midweek Hibs had faced the English Second Division side Blackburn Rovers at Easter Road in the second round of the Anglo Scottish Cup. Several years earlier both clubs had been involved in a major transfer deal when just days after scoring four goals in a comprehensive 8–0 Scottish Cup defeat of Alloa at Recreation Park in 1947, centre-forward Jock Weir had turned up for training at Easter Road on the Monday as usual only to be informed that he was wanted upstairs, returning a short while later clutching a railway warrant and carrying his already parcelled boots. It turned out that whether he had wanted to leave or not he had been transferred to Blackburn Rovers in a deal worth £10,000, a then record equalling fee between Scottish and English clubs, the transaction completed in the Caledonian Hotel later that evening. According to the press sometime later the Blackburn forward line; i.e. five players, had cost an astronomical £35,000 to assemble. Changed days indeed.

The game against Blackburn had already appeared to be over when Hibs took a two-goal lead after just ten minutes; both scored inside 60 seconds, McKay with his first for the club. However, with the fans sitting back to await a goal avalanche they were to be disappointed as Hibs failed to add to their lead against a visiting defence that had been exposed throughout. Although Brotherston managed to pull one back for Blackburn well against the run of play, in the end the final scoreline had failed to reflect the Edinburgh side's almost total dominance of the 90 minutes when after their tremendous start they had fallen into their now familiar routine of failing to capitalise on their domination of a game. Often guilty of attempting to beat one man too many, it had required a tremendous save by McDonald in the closing stages to ensure victory. One newspaper headline the following morning perhaps summing it up best: 'Slapdash Hibs let Blackburn of the hook'.

Meanwhile with attendances still continuing to fall throughout the country with the accompanying loss of revenue, after the first-round exit from the League Cup there would be even more concern for the club when a routine safety check had now revealed that certain areas of the ground were unsafe, including the exits leading from the north stand into Albion Road, and were in need of immediate attention. The main cause for concern however had been the discovery that a couple of stairways on the east terracing, particularly the one leading out onto Albion Road and Hawkhill Avenue should be temporarily closed until urgent reconstruction work had been carried out, the Lothian Regional Council now setting a crowd limit of just over 29,000. In the wake of the disaster at Ibrox not all that long before, safety checks had become even more stringent than ever and while crowd safety should always be a priority, the recent revelation would not help a club already haemorrhaging money.

In the return at Ewood Park, a 25-yard drive by Tony Higgins midway through the second half would be more than enough to see Hibs safely into the next round where they would now face Bristol City. In a well-deserved victory against a punchless Blackburn attack that had shown little threat throughout, Hibs could well have scored more, chances that once again may well have come back to haunt them. Only a tremendous save by McDonald had prevented Blackburn from taking an undeserved early lead well against the run of play. Watched by a crowd of just over 6,000, the poor turnout could perhaps have been explained by Blackburn having won just one of their previous five games including the defeat by Hibs at Easter Road a couple of weeks earlier.

Before the home game against Celtic a few days later, the supporters had been surprised to see Hibs taking the field at the start wearing new look purple jerseys now featuring the sponsor's name much reduced in size, obviously for the benefit of the TV cameras. Controversy however never seemed to be all that

SPONSORSHIP AND A BATTLE WITH THE CAMERAS (1977-78)

far away in games against the Old Firm. Just before half-time Edvaldson had opened the scoring for Celtic with a header, the irate Hibs players immediately surrounding the referee protesting that he had already blown his whistle before the ball entered the net, the protests as could well be expected waved aside. The decision appeared to sting Hibs into action. They started the second half in determined mood, only to concede another twice inside two minutes before McKay scored a consolation a few minutes from the end, his second and last goal for the club. It would also turn out to be John Blackley's last game in the Hibs side, at least for the moment, when in a surprise move that stunned the supporters with its lightning speed he had joined Newcastle United in midweek for a fee said to be in the region of £100,000.

Since signing for the club from Gairdoch Juveniles in 1965 Blackley had gone on to make 424 appearances in all games for the first team scoring 12 goals, while also winning seven full Scotland caps along the way including an appearance against Zaire in the 1974 World Cup finals in Munich. An integral member of the Tornadoes side that won two Drybrough Cups and the League Cup in 1972, although happy enough at Easter Road, after watching a procession of his teammates making the journey south over the years he had been keen to try his luck in England for some time. As a youngster he had been due to have a trial with Dunfermline only for it to be cancelled almost at the last minute and had been delighted to join the Easter Road side where he believed that youngsters would get their chance. Rumoured to have been earlier approached, although unofficially, by both Celtic and Manchester United, at one time terms had all but been agreed with Everton only for Hibs to pull out at the very last minute, proceedings that had apparently been so far advanced that the English side at one stage had considered legal action. The defender's wholehearted and determined play had instantly made him a great favourite of the Easter Road fans but despite the supporters' anger towards the board regarding his move to Newcastle, the financial circumstances at Easter Road at that particular time had probably made his transfer inevitable, the fee received probably going straight to the bank and Blackley going on to enjoy his time on Tyneside at a great club with a tremendous set of supporters.

The Celtic game had also brought Jim McKay's month-long loan deal to an end. Attempts had already been made to extend the deal for another month but with several other clubs said to be showing an interest in the player the move had understandably been rejected. In midweek Turnbull had even made his way to Brora himself to see if a deal could still be done only to find that they were now asking £10,000 for McKay's transfer, more than double Hibs' valuation of the player. Despite further discussions no agreement could be reached, and it would be back to the Highland League for McKay and Hibs to continue their search for a goal scorer.

A 2-1 home defeat by an Ayr United side that would be relegated at the end of the season would see Hibs drop to seventh in the table, or third bottom, and with only three wins from the last eight league games they were already in danger of relegation. Goalless at the interval, Hibs eventually took the lead courtesy of an own goal early in the second half of a game that had been described in the press as truly appalling with little football. Neither side had looked capable of finding the net until Cramond scored a surprise equaliser before a dreadful mistake by Brazil near the end had allowed Ayr to claim the vital points. Although he had been lining up at right-back since the beginning of the season, McNamara had now replaced Blackley in the centre of the defence allowing Brownlie who so far had made just the one appearance to resume in his normal full-back position. Blackley's exit however now meant that with Edwards then in the reserves, only Brownlie, Schaedler and Duncan had remained in the starting line up from the League Cup winning side of 1972.

The home leg of the Anglo Scottish Cup semi-final against a Bristol City was to end in controversy. With the former Hibs player Peter Cormack playing a prominent part in the proceedings Bristol had taken a deserved half-time lead only for Duncan to equalise two minutes after the interval with a header. With Hibs now well on top and Bristol at times forced into desperate and sometimes ruthless defending against a rampant home side, near the end the former Leeds and England defender Norman Hunter had been sent off after just the latest in a series of bad tackles on

SPONSORSHIP AND A BATTLE WITH THE CAMERAS (1977-78)

MacLeod. For some reason this decision appeared to have upset Cormack, who as the Hibs supporters knew from experience could be a hot-headed individual, and just few minutes later he would join his teammate in the bath after cynically head-butting Bremner. With just six minutes remaining Hibs missed a glorious opportunity to take a lead however slender into the return leg in Bristol after Higgins had been brought down in the box only for MacLeod to miss from the resulting penalty.

After the game a furious Tom Hart had been desperately unhappy at what he considered to have been an over robust performance by the visitors throughout the entire 90 minutes, particularly the incidents involving the double red cards near the end. Concerned for the safety of his players in the return leg at Ashton Gate he had immediately contacted the Scottish League seeking permission to withdraw from the competition, even prepared to pay the £2,000 fine. Understandably, Hart's comments didn't go down too well with the Bristol manager Alan Dicks and his directors who were determined that the second game should still go ahead, or they would be seeking £12,000 compensation for any loss of revenue.

In a game against Rangers at Easter Road once again the supporters would be surprised to see their favourites take the field in unfamiliar kit, this time canary yellow jerseys with green trim, and again with a much reduced sponsor's name across the chest. Obviously chosen because the purple jerseys worn earlier against Celtic would have clashed against the dark blue of Rangers on the TV screens, the yellow shirts had been designed specifically to avoid a colour clash. However, despite a vigorous search of the sports shops for an appropriate replacement, nothing considered suitable could be found and Bukta had been forced to create its own brand-new kit. In what would eventually turn out to be a game of two penalty decisions, in the first half Hibs had a sound claim for a spot kick after Higgins had been brought down inside the box by Forsyth, the furious appeals of the Hibs players ignored by the referee, wrongly according to most neutral observers. The referee however had no hesitation in awarding a penalty after ignoring a similar incident at the other end of the pitch leaving Jardine to score what would turn out to be the only goal of the game from the spot, the narrow defeat now leaving Hibs second bottom of the table.

Regardless of any previous animosity between the sides the away game against Bristol City would eventually go ahead two weeks later although obviously without the services of either Hunter or Cormack. In front of an extremely poor crowd, many probably discouraged from attending the game by the atrocious weather that had turned the pitch into a sea of mud, Bristol would ultimately prove the superior side. The eventual 5–3 victory sending them through to the final where they would now face St Mirren and eventually win the trophy 3–2 on aggregate. Fortunately, after Tom Hart's earlier comments there had been little hostility between the rival supporters on the terracing, and as a gesture of goodwill the Hibs chairman had been presented with a bottle of sherry by the Bristol directors in the boardroom after the game.

Some weeks earlier in yet another attempt to solve the ongoing goalscoring crisis Turnbull had moved to sign centre-forward Martin Henderson on loan from Rangers, the youngster making his debut in a 2–1 victory over Aberdeen at Pittodrie. Henderson unfortunately would not be the answer, managing to score just once in the 5–3 defeat by Bristol Rovers and after just a handful of games would soon be on his way to America to sign for Philadelphia Fury.

It was now even more obvious that the main problem had clearly been the lack of goals. As a result Turnbull turned his attention towards Dundee in an attempt to sign striker Bobby Hutchison, a player he had long admired, in an exchange deal involving the long-serving full-back Erich Schaedler. At that time Schaedler had been facing fierce competition for the left-back position from Bobby Smith and had been unsettled at Easter Road for some time having already posted several transfer requests, the most recent just a few weeks before. Several attempts to complete the deal had all been rejected by Dundee, but Turnbull's persistence eventually paid off. As Schaedler was making his first start for his new side in a goalless draw at Dumbarton, Hutchison made his Hibs debut in a 3–2 home defeat by Partick Thistle, the disappointing result now leaving Hibs rooted in second bottom place.

SPONSORSHIP AND A BATTLE WITH THE CAMERAS (1977–78)

Schaedler's departure now left only Brownlie and Duncan from the League Cup winning side currently still featuring in the first team. Many years later the former Hibs player Mickey Weir had been asked to name his hardest ever opponent, and without even the slightest hesitation had answered: Erich Schaedler. That was just during training, the committed defender as wholehearted in practice matches as he had been on the pitch. Jim McArthur also recalls an incident during a previous game against Hearts when Schaedler had tackled Kenny Aird with far more force than necessary ending with the Hearts player in amongst the crowd and having to leave the field for treatment, the incident surprisingly resulting in a mere ticking-off from the referee. When asked later why he had been so forceful, Schaedler had simply replied: 'Well he kicked me three years ago!'

However, for Hibs things were about to get even worse. A no-score draw with Dundee United and a 3–2 reverse at home by Partick Thistle would be followed by a 3–0 defeat by St Mirren at Love Street the following Saturday. A result that had prevented Hibs from potentially opening up a gap over fellow strugglers Ayr United and Clydebank at the foot of the table. Now with just the single point from their previous six league games, perhaps for the first time the threat of relegation was a genuine reality. Reportedly unhappy that his players had been forced to play on a pitch resembling a skating rink (admittedly the farcical conditions had applied to both sides with the St Mirren players adapting to the treacherous underfoot conditions far better than the visitors), an already frustrated Turnbull would have been even more unhappy to find his side two behind after just ten minutes, a third goal by Reid in the second half meaning little. Although Hutchison's energetic style had made him popular enough with the fans there had been little improvement in the goalscoring stakes and he would fail to find the net in his first nine games.

It was around that time that a highly critical article by the former fan favourite Joe Baker had appeared in the *Evening News*. Deeply concerned at the current state of affairs at Easter Road, Baker had accused Tom Hart of running a one man show. As far as he was concerned there was a lack of communication between the board and the fans that he still expected to turn up on a Saturday. The manager himself was not exempt from the criticism. Baker was still in contact with several of the current players who assured him that Turnbull's attitude to them had not changed since he himself had been given a hard time both on and off the field, the manager's manner towards reporters abrasive to say the least, and it appeared as though things were not about to change for the better. In comparing the current side to that of just a few years earlier, Baker wondered how a potentially great forward line had been allowed to leave without adequate replacements in place. What was the reason behind the departure of Gordon and O'Rourke and why had the outstanding, talented Alex Edwards been left on the bench for so long? The Stanton situation had been yet another area of major concern, a player who had given his all for the club, yet nobody has found out why he had been allowed to leave. Also, why Tom McNiven, without doubt the best physiotherapist in the entire country, had seemingly been forced to quit? Looking to the future Baker was convinced that a younger more approachable manager was needed, someone perhaps like Stanton, and a totally new outlook required at Easter Road. In his regular column in the *Evening News* Stewart Brown had been in complete agreement with Baker in wondering just how a club that had been runners-up only three years before could now find itself in mid-season already strong candidates for relegation. Why had no much needed major signings had been made at the beginning of the season after such a disappointing previous campaign? Had this merely been to balance the books?

Perhaps unsurprisingly Baker's comments had been followed by a flood of letters to the newspaper from the fans, almost all agreeing with the former English international. Many saw the signing of Harper as the start of the problem, others accusing the manager of being content to settle for second best. As far as some had been concerned Tom Hart's lack of PR had always been obvious, at times appearing to pursue a policy deliberately designed to antagonise and alienate the fans including his continual raising of the prices for big games.

Support for the chairman however would come from an unlikely source when a letter from the former Hibs player Bobby Kinloch appeared in the *Pink News* just before the turn of the year. In the

SPONSORSHIP AND A BATTLE WITH THE CAMERAS (1977–78)

article Kinloch had wondered just how many of the supporters would have been prepared to invest in the club without the slightest guarantee that they would get their money back, an obvious reference to Hart's personal financial input. Football is just like any other business and the books must be balanced. A businessman with a good product can be financed through various avenues but few if any would be prepared to financially back a football club, so where does the money come from week to week? Only two avenues are open when things go wrong – either selling players or investing even more resources personally.

In the game against Ayr at Somerset Park just before Christmas, a solitary second-half goal by Arthur Duncan, only his second of the season in all games, had been enough to secure both points against a battling United side. This not only gave Hibs their first victory from the previous ten games but also lifted the side into eighth place in the table, and the start of a seven-game unbeaten run.

In midweek Martin Henderson's three-month loan period had come to an end and he would return to Ibrox. Failing to live up to his early promise when he had made over two dozen first team appearances while scoring ten goals during Rangers 1975–76 championship winning season, during his time at Easter Road the youngster had managed to make just six first team appearances, two as substitute without managing to find the net and had spent the previous few weeks in the reserves.

A 2–0 home victory over second placed Aberdeen the following week had turned out to be only Hibs' second consecutive victory of the season and a league double over the Grampian side. With Jackie McNamara and George Stewart commanding at the centre of the defence against it has to be said an extremely disappointing Aberdeen side that was then challenging for the championship, first-half goals by Willie Murray and Arthur Duncan had been more than enough to give Hibs an extremely welcome and well-deserved victory. Now eighth place in the table, or third bottom, the players were cheered from the field at the end, an extremely rare occurrence in recent weeks.

Probably now realising the folly of his earlier decision to sell Jimmy O'Rourke, Turnbull had already made several approaches to Motherwell in an attempt to bring the former fan favourite back to Easter Road. The offers however had all been rejected out of hand by a Fir Park side then just two points above Hibs in seventh place in the table and perhaps understandably unwilling to part with a regular member of the first team squad to a potential fellow relegation struggler. Although he had been sidelined by injury for a large part of the previous season O'Rourke had still managed to score ten goals. Now, admittedly weary of the travelling between Fir Park and his home in Edinburgh each day, he no doubt would have welcomed the opportunity to return to the scene of his former glories where his enthusiasm and determination would undoubtedly have been tremendously well received by the fans.

Although it would be of little help to the club at that particular time, after a couple of trial games for the reserves the 18-year-old, 6ft centre-half Craig Paterson, son of the post-war Hibs player John Paterson, had recently been signed from Bonnyrigg Rose although he had yet to make an appearance for the Junior side. Unfortunately, in his first game for the reserves since signing, Paterson had cracked a bone in his leg and would miss most of what was left of the season. Dominant in the air and a good tackler who read the game well, big things had been expected from a youngster who would eventually go on to make well over a hundred first team appearances before a big money move to Rangers in 1982.

Perhaps as a further sign of desperation, in midweek Turnbull had made an unsuccessful attempt to sign the Welsh international striker John Toshack from Liverpool. Not all that long before, the prolific Toshack who had inflicted most of the damage in Hibs' UEFA Cup defeat on Merseyside, had fairly recently lined up against Scotland in the World Cup qualifying game at Anfield when the 2–0 victory had guaranteed the Scots qualification for the forthcoming World Cup finals in Argentina. Currently out of the first team at Anfield, despite the player's Scottish family connections a fee could not be agreed and he would soon be on his way to Swansea. Despite their reputation as a selling club, at that time Hibs still held the Scottish record as buyers after the £120,000 purchase of Joe Harper a few seasons earlier and

SPONSORSHIP AND A BATTLE WITH THE CAMERAS (1977–78)

apparently had now been prepared to put the boat out in the effort to capture the free-scoring Toshack.

A 2–1 home victory over Motherwell on Christmas Eve had been Hibs' third consecutive victory but for Bobby Hutchison it would probably not be a game to remember. His troubles had started when the Dundee to Edinburgh train had been held up at Inverkeithing. Eventually managing to hail a taxi that had just dropped its passengers off at the station, Hutchinson had made it to the ground with just 15 minutes to spare only to be injured midway through the first half and did not reappear after the interval. With the versatile McNamara on top form as sweeper against what had been tough opponents and young Alex McGhee a constant thorn in the side of the Motherwell defence, Hibs had taken a deserved first half lead courtesy of a MacLeod penalty. Hutchison's replacement Willie Paterson too scoring what would turn out to be the winner midway through the second half with his second and last goal for the club. Now showing a spirit and flair that had been missing for much of the earlier part of the season it now seemed that Hibs were on the way back to form and almost as important, the recent slight improvement in attendances had suggested that they still had the backing of the fans.

On the last day of the year a goalless draw against the current leaders Rangers at Ibrox had been enough to keep Hibs in seventh place in the table and incredibly after the events of the previous few months, on track for possible qualification for the following season's UEFA Cup. In what turned out to be a poor game with nothing much to excite the fans on either side, Stewart and McNamara had been at their best in subduing the home forwards. Hibs fully deserving the eventual draw, on their second-half performance alone they might well have collected both points, yet again only the recent habit of failing to capitalise on genuine chances letting them down.

With city rivals Hearts now in the First Division, for some reason the authorities had decided that a Clydebank side then languishing at the foot of the table would be Hibs' New Year's Day visitors, a game that would take place on the second as the first fell on a Sunday. With Alec Edwards making his first appearance of the season, goals by McGhee and MacLeod had secured an easy

2–0 victory against opponents that would be relegated at the end the season and had now lifted Hibs into fifth place in the table.

That same afternoon Edinburgh had lost yet another of its sporting personalities with the breaking news that the former Hearts legend Jimmy Wardhaugh had suffered a fatal heart attack on his way back from covering the East Fife game against Hearts at Bayview for the *Daily Mail*. Although born in the tiny hamlet of Marshall Meadows just outside Berwick and despite the fact that the village lay just inside the English border, to simplify matters an earlier agreement by both the Scottish and English authorities had decided that as far as football was concerned the River Tweed would now be considered the border, a decision allowing Wardhaugh to turn out for Scotland. Capped twice at full level between 1954 and 1956 with a further seven appearances for the inter-league side, Wardhaugh is best remembered as a member of the Hearts 'Terrible Trio' during the late 1940s and 1950s, the talented player widely admired by supporters throughout the country and his untimely passing had been mourned by fans on both sides of the city.

Since the signing of George Stewart at the beginning of the season, the promising Derek Spalding had failed to force himself back into contention. Not content with reserve team football, having only recently married a Chicago girl and with the North American side Chicago Sting showing an interest in the player, Spalding now saw his future in the USA. Although Sting's initial offer of £11,000 had fallen well short of the club's valuation for a player then featuring in the reserves, the clubs would eventually settle for an improved offer of £20,000 and Spalding would be on his way to Chicago. Since breaking into the first team in 1972 Spalding had made just short of a hundred appearances in all games, scoring three goals. However, after a bright start he had never really recaptured his early form and had spent much of the current season in the second team.

With Hearts in the First Division the fans of both sides had missed the drama and excitement of the local derby and had eagerly awaited the final of the East of Scotland Shield that was to have taken place at Easter Road a few days after the turn of the year. However, melting overnight snow had left large pools of water

SPONSORSHIP AND A BATTLE WITH THE CAMERAS (1977–78)

covering almost the entire playing area, the referee left with no other option but to cancel the game and the supporters would now have to wait until the end of the season. The cancellation had also disappointed Eddie Turnbull who had been looking forward to catching up again with his former Famous Five colleague Willie Ormond. Ormond had now replaced John Haggart as manager of Hearts, though it had not gone down too well with a great number of the supporters who were said to have been less than happy at the appointment of a former Hibs player.

Throughout the years Scottish football had been well accustomed to games being called off due to bad weather and with the severe conditions that were then sweeping the country, except for a 4–0 victory over East Fife in the first round of the Scottish Cup, Hibs would not play a home league game since defeating Clydebank at the start of the year until facing Aberdeen in mid-March.

Throughout January the weather had continued to play havoc with the fixture list and now desperate for revenue a tremendous effort had been made to allow the cup game against East Fife at Easter Road to go ahead. In those pre-electric blanket days, an army of volunteers had battled manfully all the previous day spreading a thick covering of straw over the entire pitch and their labours had been rewarded when the game eventually received the go ahead from the local referee Bill Mullan. Any hopes of a cup upset by the Fife side had been quickly dispelled with two goals within the first 15 minutes when MacLeod scored twice inside 60 seconds, and although the visitors had battled manfully throughout, in reality they had been outclassed in every department. In the end the final 4–0 scoreline could well have been even greater.

Except for an away league game against Dundee United when the final 1–1 draw had left Hibs still seeking their first Premier League victory over the Tannadice side, in an effort to keep the players as match fit as possible the club had taken advantage of friendly games against Crystal Palace in London and Dundee at Dens Park.

While not nearly as severe as the big freeze of 1963 when almost no games had taken place throughout the entire country for well over two months, the current shutdown had still been estimated to have cost the club in the region of £50,000 in lost gate receipts alone.

A sudden thaw at the end of February would see Hibs' recent impressive run in taking ten points from a possible 12 come to a sudden end with a 3–0 defeat at Pittodrie. The vast majority of fans inside the ground had been unable to follow the proceedings taking place on the pitch due to a dense blanket of fog that had rolled in from the North Sea, threatening on occasion to bring the game to a premature end although it did eventually manage to finish. However, in no way could the conditions be used as an excuse for Hibs' substandard display that allowed Aberdeen to gain sweet revenge for the earlier defeats at Easter Road. The home side's opening goal had been an absolute tragedy for centre-half George Stewart who could only watch in horror as his intended headed pass-back to goalkeeper McDonald from 20 yards found the custodian off his line as the ball flew over his head and into the net, a defeat that would leave Hibs still struggling in the bottom half of the table.

Just a few days later Hibs' away game against Ayr United would be yet another casualty, but this time nothing to do with the weather. With some Hibs supporters already making their way from Edinburgh the game had somewhat surprisingly been called off just a few hours before kick-off. United had claimed that a flu epidemic had decimated the side effecting at least seven players and that they would be unable to fulfil the fixture. This however cut no ice with Tom Hart who immediately submitted an official letter of complaint to the Scottish League. Not only enquiring as to late timing of the call off, he also reminded the authorities of a similar incident involving Hibs two years earlier when Motherwell had failed in a bid to have their game at Easter Road postponed due to similar circumstances, the outspoken Hibs chairman now demanding clarification of the rules. A statement from United that they had been unable to contact anyone at Easter Road the previous day but had left a message had done nothing to placate the irate Hart who was adamant that the Scottish League should now adopt the SFA regulations that if a team still had 11 fit players available then the game should go ahead as planned. The game would eventually take place near the end of the season but it is not known if any further action was ever taken against United.

In the Scottish Cup Hibs had now been drawn against Partick Thistle in what would turn out to be a drab, goalless and

SPONSORSHIP AND A BATTLE WITH THE CAMERAS (1977–78)

uninspiring home draw. As far as one journalist had been concerned: 'On this performance Partick would easily have won widespread support for the title of the most boring team in the Premier League.' Thistle had clearly come for a draw and had been successful in their aims with a thoroughly negative display from start to finish that had led to many of the fans making their way to the exits well before the end. The replay that was to have taken place at Firhill two days later had been called off after a late inspection by the referee just 45 minutes before the kick-off had declared the pitch unplayable, with a number of fans already inside the ground.

That same morning the sad news had been received that the long-serving Jimmy McColl had passed away in an Edinburgh hospital aged 85. Although born in Glasgow and had scored twice against Hibs in Celtic's 4–1 replayed Scottish Cup victory in the 1914 final, McColl is best remembered for his over 56 years loyal service at Easter Road as a player, trainer and groundsman before eventually ending up as the odd-job man around the ground. Rarely seen without his customary cigar, the popular McColl had still been attending games at Easter Road until just a few weeks before his death and had only stopped travelling to away games with the first team a short time earlier. In a moving tribute chairman Tom Hart declared that in the long history of the club there had probably been no other person that had made such a valuable contribution to Hibs. His funeral later in the week at Mount Vernon would be attended by all the directors, backroom staff, players, supporters and many others from the world of football, all wishing to pay their last respects.

The cup replay against Partick would finally go ahead the following evening. With Thistle leading a 2–1 at half-time both their goals scored by Melrose, who else but Ally MacLeod would pull one back for Hibs, and it was now all to play for. Just minutes after the restart MacLeod had passed up a simple chance to level the score and could only hang his head in disbelief as the ball flashed past the post from only a few yards out with the goalkeeper nowhere to be seen. With 20 minutes remaining substitute Ally Scott who was making his first appearance for several weeks had missed an even better chance when blasting the ball over the bar from just outside the six-yard box when it had appeared far easier to score, and Hibs' long wait to bring the trophy back to Edinburgh was over for at least another year. They again had no one to blame but themselves after failing to take advantage of the several gilt-edged chances that had been created during the 90 minutes.

The third-round draw had been made a few days earlier, but any talk at the time of a potential all-Edinburgh clash in the next round had been firmly put to bed after Hearts had been defeated 1–0 by Dumbarton at Tynecastle, again after a replay.

With the same number of goals scored as conceded, it was obvious that Hibs still remained in desperate need of a proven goal scorer. Only 20 goals had been scored in the 23 league games played so far. Seventeen different players had been tried up front, but with the exception of MacLeod and Duncan none had scored more than once, six not at all. Extremely worrying statistics!

However just four days after the cup exit, a 5–1 home victory over St Mirren would not only turn out to be the most goals scored by Hibs in the same game that season, but would turn out to be the start of a seven-game unbeaten run that included a hard-fought draw at Ibrox. Somewhat unbelievably considering the earlier lack of goals, in the same period 23 had been scored against just eight conceded making Hibs the highest scoring side in the entire country during this time.

Incredibly, this recent tremendous run of form had now seen a rise from third bottom of the table and the threat of relegation just a few months earlier, to third place behind leaders Aberdeen who were then 15 points ahead and second placed Rangers and now well in the running for a European place. So far Bobby Hutchison had been a major disappointment in the goalscoring department but the centre-forward would finally open his long-awaited account for the club by scoring twice in the 5–1 victory against the Paisley side, his first since signing almost four months earlier, the goals as could be expected met with resounding applause from the fans.

During this unbeaten run, after 12 attempts Hibs had finally managed to banish their Premier League hoodoo against Dundee United in style with an extremely satisfying 3–1 home victory, the first time that United had conceded more than two goals in the same game that season. A United defence that had possibly not been at its best had made several elementary mistakes that had been punished by a now extremely confident home side. Once again Ally MacLeod had managed to get his name on the score sheet but the day belonged to Tony Higgins who celebrated his 100th first team appearance in style by scoring twice.

In what would turn out to be yet another hard-fought, stormy encounter against Rangers at Easter Road in midweek, Hibs had been leading at half-time when awarded a disputed penalty after Higgins had been brought down by Forsyth, a tackle that appeared to have been just outside the box. Despite the expected heated appeals by the Rangers players, MacLeod made no mistake from the spot to deprive the now league leaders of both points, but according to the *Evening News* it had been a totally spiteful and forgettable affair, an evil, bad-tempered 90 minutes with the ball at times quite incidental. During the ill-tempered encounter punches had been thrown and boots slung, Rangers' Derek Parlane later ordered off in what in no way had been a pleasing spectacle for the fans although Hibs, not noted for their physical power, had attempted to play the football at all times.

At the beginning of April the first of two games against Celtic that had been postponed earlier in the season took place at Parkhead when a 2–1 defeat brought Hibs' recent impressive run of only one loss from the previous 13 games to an end. Though leading by the almost mandatory penalty by MacLeod just a few minutes after the restart against an admittedly struggling Celtic side, and Hibs looking likely to preserve their recent good run, George McCluskey was to score twice inside the final half hour to give his side the points.

Yet another defeat this time by St Mirren on the Saturday would have done little to inspire confidence before the forthcoming meeting with Celtic at Easter Road in midweek in the second of the games postponed earlier. In what turned out to be a lively and entertaining first half the sides had been level at the interval after Glavin had opened the scoring for Celtic before an equaliser by Higgins. After the excitement of the first 45 minutes however the second half would turn out to be something of an anti-climax with little for the fans of either side to cheer about. Although, Hibs had missed an opportunity to take both points after Duncan and Murray had passed up gilt-edged chances to secure victory when confronted with what looked like easy chances inside the six-yard box. Although the single point in the 1–1 draw still left Hibs in third place, once again they could only blame themselves for missing the opportunity to record a fairly infrequent victory against the Parkhead side.

Just three days later the sides would meet again at Easter Road for the third time in just over a week, but this time Celtic would be swept aside by a confident Hibs side with a quite marvellous performance, particularly in the first half when goals by Duncan and Higgins had given them a half-time lead. Celtic just had no answer to the aggressive raids that had excited the home fans and the eventual 4–1 victory could well have been even greater with more clinical finishing. Thirteen minutes from the end and Hibs leading 2–0, the away fans had shown their displeasure at their team's poor performance. In what appeared to have been nothing more than a cynical attempt to force the game to be abandoned, a number had invaded the pitch resulting in the game being held up for several minutes as the police attempted to restore order. It was only after the appearance of the Celtic manager Jock Stein appealing for calm that the intruders had eventually vacated the pitch. After the restart Hibs scored another twice with goals by Alex McGhee and a second by Higgins before Conroy pulled one back for Celtic, McDonald saving a last-minute penalty from Tommy Burns, the well-deserved victory keeping Hibs well in the running for a place in the following season's UEFA Cup.

It had been widely felt that the pitch invasion by the Celtic supporters had stemmed from an earlier display of weakness by the football authorities. Only a few weeks before during a game at Ibrox between Rangers and Motherwell, the Fir Park side had been leading when a number of Rangers supporters had invaded the field leading to the game being held up for several minutes as the police cleared the troublemakers from the pitch before the game could be restarted. Later enquiries into the incident by the referee's committee had recommended that Rangers, who

SPONSORSHIP AND A BATTLE WITH THE CAMERAS (1977-78)

eventually won the game 5-3, should either forfeit the points or the game be replayed, a decision fully backed to their credit by the Scottish Football Association. Unfortunately, and possibly of no surprise, the Scottish League under whose jurisdiction the game had taken place, completely shirked their responsibility. In what had generally been seen as a victory for the louts, they had merely fined the Ibrox club, the pitch invasion at Easter Road taking place just 24 hours after this weak decision had been announced.

A 2-1 defeat by Partick Thistle in Glasgow a few days later had perhaps been summed up perfectly by one newspaper reporter with the statement that having already taken six points from a possible eight as well as the recent Scottish Cup victory, that Partick Thistle would be well in the running for the championship if they could only play Hibs every week. Hibs had proved over the season that on their day they could beat Aberdeen, Rangers and Celtic, but despite the confidence gained from the recent draw and victory at Parkhead, sadly they had often struggled against sides at the lower end of the table. An Alex McGhee goal, his second of the season and last as a Hibs player, had given his side an early lead before some disastrous defending allowed Thistle back into the game to take both points. Goals that really should have been prevented, the poor defending highlighted yet another of Hibs' problems during much of the season, the defeat now putting any hopes of a European place in some doubt.

Even worse was to come on the Saturday against the already relegated Ayr United at Somerset Park in the penultimate game of the season when a victory had been absolutely vital if Hibs wished to guarantee an automatic European place. However, in what would turn out to be yet another best forgotten occasion for the travelling Hibs fans among what had been considering the circumstances an extremely disappointing attendance of only around 2,500, Ayr had opened the scoring in the first half before making certain of the points against a lacklustre defence eight minutes from time. It was now absolutely imperative that Hibs take something from the final game of the season against Aberdeen if they were to have any hope of European qualification, even then having to rely on results elsewhere.

The final league game of the season at Easter Road was against an Aberdeen side then sitting second in the table and would finally end just two points behind champions Rangers, Hibs desperate for the points that would hopefully secure a guaranteed European place. However, a game that had started well soon turned into yet another nervous 90 minutes for the home support. After a goalless first half Scanlon gave Aberdeen the lead only for Duncan to equalise just three minutes from the end to secure the point that would eventually be enough to secure Hibs a fourth-place finish and qualification for the following season's UEFA Cup, just a solitary point above fifth-placed Celtic.

Just 24 hours later Pat Stanton's testimonial game between Hibs and Celtic would take place at Easter Road, the huge turnout of well over 25,000 including around ten thousand that had made their way from Glasgow on a cold, wet, blustery afternoon testimony to the player's popularity. The word legend is often overused but it is a tribute that sits comfortably on the shoulders of Pat Stanton who had been highly regarded throughout the game by players and fans of all sides alike. A further sign of the high esteem he had also been held in by his former professionals were the number of big-name guest players that had made their way to the city to take part in the game. These included the Partick Thistle and current Scotland goalkeeper Alan Rough; Manchester United's Joe Jordon; Stanton's former Easter Road teammates Jimmy O'Rourke then with Motherwell and Newcastle's John Blackley who turned out for Hibs; Newcastle's Ralph Callaghan and Hearts Eammon Bannon made an appearance for Celtic, as did the now retired Jimmy Johnstone who received a special cheer when taking the field as a late substitute for the Parkhead side. Playing the first half in the colours of Celtic and the second 45 minutes wearing the green and white of his boyhood heroes, Stanton had scored what would prove to be the winner in a 2–1 victory from the penalty spot in the second half, his first attempt from the spot since his miss against Leeds in the Fairs Cup four years earlier. Earlier, Stanton had arranged with the Celtic goalkeeper Latchford that if Hibs were to be awarded the almost obligatory penalty on these occasions that he would let him score. However, by the time the penalty had indeed been awarded, Latchford had

SPONSORSHIP AND A BATTLE WITH THE CAMERAS (1977–78)

been substituted by the former Hibs goalkeeper Roy Baines who had been totally unaware of the earlier arrangement, Stanton still managing to put the ball in the net to the resounding cheers of the fans on both sides. Addressing the supporters after the final whistle, Stanton jokingly stated that when he awoke that morning to the torrential rain he had been convinced that God was a Hearts supporter.

Asked years later why he had let Stanton go, a player that had seemingly still been good enough for Celtic but not for Hibs, Eddie Turnbull admitted that he had possibly been envious of the player's reputation as Mr Hibs. He also confessed that he himself had usually been considered as just the worker in the midfield of the Famous Five forward line, although he was always much more than that, and that he had been envious of the attention the other four received, particularly Gordon Smith.

What had been an unpredictable campaign had finally come to an end with the final of the previous season's East of Scotland Shield against Hearts at Easter Road that had been held back from earlier in the year. Already planning ahead, in midweek Turnbull had travelled to Clydebank to sign the former Southampton and Swindon forward Gerry O'Brian in a £10,000 deal. Because the game was not classed as official, O'Brian had been eligible to turn out against Hearts, the new signing scoring the only goal of the game 13 minutes from the end to put Hibs four ahead in a series that had been running since 1876. The main talking point of the afternoon however had been the sending off of the Hearts player Drew Busby after a couple of quite dreadful tackles, first on Smith and then Duncan. The incidents also appeared to have led to several skirmishes between the opposing fans on the terracing, the Hibs trainer Duncan Lambie having to be physically restrained from confronting Busby as he left the field.

Referee Douglas Ramsey had been in charge of the proceedings, his first ever derby between the city rivals. Several years earlier there had been a minor outcry over a newspaper article highlighting a situation that had been a sore point among the refereeing fraternity on the east coast for some time. The issue centred around an unwritten ruling that prevented referees from Edinburgh and Dundee from taking charge of games involving teams from their respective cities, while still allowing those that lived in Glasgow and the surrounding district to officiate at matches involving local sides, some circumnavigating the issue by claiming to come from Bearsden, Rutherglen or East Kilbride. One who had remained anonymous was said to have regularly controlled games involving west coast sides less than a mile from his Glasgow home. Another based in Wishaw had often officiated at games involving Motherwell. Yet another bone of contention had been the fact that of the 28 grade-one whistlers on the official list at that time, apart from Ramsey only the then newcomer Eddie Thompson had been from Edinburgh while 18 were from Glasgow and the surrounding area. The article also went as far as to suggest that perhaps the same bias that was often thought to have affected the chances of a player from the east coast being selected for the full international side also applied to referees. The issue would quickly die down but the point had been made.

In what had turned out to be yet another inconsistent campaign when only one game more had been won than lost, incredibly Hibs had eventually managed to finish in fourth place, a single point above fifth-placed Celtic to qualify for the UEFA Cup. A quite remarkable turnaround from just a few months earlier when they had been sitting second bottom of the table and at one point staring relegation in the face.

At the end of the season Rangers had been crowned champions for the third time in four years, Aberdeen finishing in second place just two points behind but with a slightly better goal difference. The Pittodrie side however had possibly been denied their first title success since 1955 because of the previously mentioned weakness of the Scottish League Management Committee that had earlier opted out of either ordering a replay or deducting Rangers the points after the pitch invasion by their fans during the game against Motherwell, merely awarding a fine instead. Elsewhere, city rivals Hearts had achieved promotion back into the Premier League at the first time of asking, in second place behind champions Morton on goal difference.

Despite the remarkable turnaround you would not have had to look too far to see just where Hibs' troubles had lain throughout

SPONSORSHIP AND A BATTLE WITH THE CAMERAS (1977–78)

the major part of the season. Apart from regularly dropping points against sides in the bottom half of the table, scoring goals had again been the number one problem. Although 17 different players had featured in the goalscoring charts, only Ally MacLeod had reached double figures with 23 in all games, the nearest Arthur Duncan and Tony Higgins with a measly eight apiece. Bobby Hutchison had not yet been the expected success with a total of just six, although he had missed the final few games of the season injured. Seven others scored no more than three; Stewart and Rae just once.

At the end of the season Ally Scott had been one of only four players handed a free transfer. After a bright start since signing from Rangers in 1976 as part of the exchange deal involving Iain Munro, Scott had since struggled to hold down a regular first team place. Spending the majority of the past season in the reserves while making just seven league appearances for the first team, two from the substitute's bench, he would soon sign for Second Division champions Morton. Also failing to secure a regular first team place had been the at one time highly rated Lindsay Muir who would join St Johnstone in the summer.

Having managed just five starts during the season, the last over four months before, it had been widely anticipated that Alex Edwards would also be amongst those freed and had been something of a surprise inclusion in the list of those retained.

The future Hibs goalkeeper Alan Rough, then with Partick Thistle, would soon be on his way overseas with the Scotland party for what would turn out to be a disastrous World Cup finals in Argentina. Meanwhile at the end of what had been another extremely trying and ultimately frustrating season, new signing Gerry O'Brian had joined his new teammates as they made their own way overseas on a month-long seven-game tour of Canada.

Facing relatively inferior opponents, five of the games would end in victory. The game against a Vancouver Whitecaps side that was then managed by the former Blackpool and England goalkeeper Tony Waiters that included the well-known England players Kevin Hector, Alan Hinton and Phil Parkes ending level. In all, 36 goals had been scored including nine against Vancouver Island Vistas, seven against both Edmonton All Stars and Ottawa

Tigers and six against Manitoba with only four conceded during the entire trip. As could be expected, Ally MacLeod ended as top goalscorer with 16. The tour had also been an ideal opportunity to give the youngsters Craig Paterson, Gordon Rae and Willie Temperley, an end of season signing from Celtic, some much needed game time and all had been introduced at some stage. Although the opposition had at times not been the strongest, victories breed confidence and no doubt the players, particularly the youngsters would already have been looking forward to the start of the new season and European competition.

An International Dispute and Another Cup Final (1978–79)

AFTER A SHORT warm up tour of the Highlands with games against Inverness Thistle, Elgin City and Dundee that had all ended in victory, including an impressive 4–1 defeat of a Dens Park side that had only just failed to gain promotion back into to the Premier League at the end of the previous season, it would now be down to the serious business of competitive football and what promised to be another challenging season.

By this time Hibs had been informed that their opponents for the forthcoming UEFA Cup competition would be the Swedish side Norrköping and immediately on their return from the Highlands, manager Turnbull and coach John Fraser had made their way overseas to run an eye over their future opponents. No sooner had he arrived back in Scotland than Turnbull would be off on his travels again this time accompanied by chairman Tom Hart to meet the directors of Newcastle United in a Carnoustie hotel hoping to conclude a deal to sign the former Hearts player Ralph Callaghan after earlier talks between the sides. Although everything was thought to have been agreed, after another meeting the following morning the move had collapsed after Callaghan who had failed to settle on Tyneside, could not make up his mind about a move to Easter Road and negotiations were now at an end; at least for the moment.

Again, several young players had been signed during the summer, but apart from Colin Campbell, a student at Edinburgh University who had been offered a temporary two month contract, and to a lesser extent Steve Brown, none were to have any great impact during the season ahead. The 22-year-old Benbecula-born Campbell, who had also been attracting the interest of West Bromwich Albion and had already played a trial game for the reserves at the end of the previous season, had made an early breakthrough into the first team from the substitutes' bench when replacing Arthur Duncan against Inverness during the Highlands tour.

Although he had featured in the pre-season team photograph and had replaced Hutchison from the substitutes bench in the pre-season friendly against Dundee, like several others before him the versatile Alex McGhee had struggled to hold down a regular first team place. While he had made around 30 competitive appearances in all games during his two spells at the club, his last as a substitute in the 1–1 draw with Aberdeen in the final game of the previous campaign, he would soon be on his way to Dens Park.

After just a few games for the reserves, his last a 1–0 home defeat by Motherwell at the beginning of October, Alec Edwards would join First Division Arbroath in a £5,000 deal, the departure of the highly talented League Cup winner seemingly not even worth a mention in the official programme at the time. During his five seasons at Easter Road the impressive talents of Edwards had been greatly admired by many others. As well as having been suggested as a makeweight in the earlier exchange deal that had both Scott and Fyfe joining Hibs, Jock Stein was said to have tried on several occasions to take the mercurial player to Celtic only for all the attempts to be rejected out of hand by Turnbull. According to the player there had even been an approach from Hearts, only for Edwards to be told bluntly by the manager: 'You will not make a fool out of me by signing for a club capable of beating us.' Several others had been keen on signing the player only to reject Hibs' possibly inflated asking price for what was then a reserve team player, Edwards himself finding extreme difficulty in understanding why if Turnbull would not play him why he was still looking for a transfer fee. After reluctantly agreeing to speak to the Arbroath manager Albert Henderson at Gayfield, Edwards had rejected the proposed signing terms and arrived back at Easter Road for training the following morning to find Turnbull absolutely furious at him turning down the move. After further signing talks however and now well aware that there was no longer any future for him at Easter Road Edwards had eventually agreed to sign for the Angus side making his debut in a 1–0 defeat by Rangers at Ibrox in the League Cup, the first of only a handful of appearances he would make at Gayfield. Not

AN INTERNATIONAL DISPUTE AND ANOTHER CUP FINAL (1978–79)

overly happy at having to travel from his home in Dunfermline to Arbroath for training and having once been asked to play on after receiving eight stitches in his knee after an on-field injury, after just a few weeks he had had enough and walked out keeping the signing-on fee. He never went back, and at just 32 and potentially still with several years ahead of him, a player who should have received many caps for Scotland would turn his back completely on a game he had graced with his at times breathtaking talents for over 18 seasons.

The new season would open with a game against fellow European challengers Dundee United at Tannadice, always a particularly difficult location for the Easter Road side in recent years. With both Gerry O'Brien and the experienced centre-half Rikki Fleming, a fairly recent signing from Ayr United, starting from the bench, both sides would no doubt have been reasonably happy with the final goalless draw in a game that had been played during a torrential downpour of thunder and lightning, conditions far from conducive for good football.

Signed in an attempt to inject more stability into the defence Turnbull had been a long-time admirer of the experienced 29-year-old Fleming who at one time had been on Rangers' books and had been capped for the Scottish League against the Football League at Maine Road in 1974, a game however that had turned out to be an embarrassing 5–0 defeat. After almost ten seasons at Somerset Park, Fleming, who would now be experiencing full-time football, had replaced George Stewart during the second half at Tannadice doing enough to suggest that he would be yet another decent signing. Unfortunately, it would turn out to be the first of only 18 first team appearances he would make at Easter Road and would join Berwick Rangers at the end of the season.

An earlier newspaper report suggesting that the then Motherwell player Jimmy O'Rourke would be making a return to Easter Road in exchange for John Brownlie had been described by Turnbull as absolute rubbish, but within weeks both would be involved in transfers albeit in entirely different circumstances.

The following Saturday at Easter Road, the home fans would be surprised to see Rab Kilgour, a close season signing from Whitehill Welfare making an early debut at right-back in a game against league champions Rangers. Unfortunately, it would turn out to be the first of only a handful of appearances the youngster was to make for the first team during his two seasons at Easter Road and he would later sign for St Johnstone.

Only that morning Ralph Callaghan who had also been attracting interest from Partick Thistle and Motherwell, the latter rumoured to have offered £40,000 for his services, had finally agreed to join Hibs from Newcastle United. The exchange deal with full-back John Brownlie agreed after the prolonged on-off-on-off negations that had been ongoing for some time had finally been settled. Although Hibs' interest in Callaghan had been well known, an earlier rumour that full-back John Brownlie could possibly be part of an exchange deal had been dismissed out of hand by the manager as ludicrous. But, as Brownlie was making his way to St James Park where he would team up again with his former team mate John Blackley, a hurried dash through to Glasgow had been needed to register the cultured Callaghan in time to make his debut against Rangers that same afternoon. In a fiery encounter with the Ibrox side, again applying their now long accepted strong-arm tactics and Hibs playing the football, the game had eventually ended goalless, both Callaghan and Kilgour however making impressive first starts.

The first local derby of the season at Tynecastle the following week would once again end in a draw, Hibs' third of the season so far but it had been a close run thing. With Callaghan again in fine form against his former colleagues, Donald Park had opened the scoring for Hearts in the first half. The somewhat lethargic looking Easter Road side had to wait until injury time for a goal by MacLeod to preserve their still unbeaten Premier League record, against a side that had already been reduced to nine men after two players had been sent off for different offences. The trouble on the pitch however had once again led to several clashes between rival fans on the terracing with bottles and other missiles thrown indiscriminately into the crowd, events that would eventually result in several dozen arrests and many more ejected from the ground, the incident later described as perhaps the most disgraceful behaviour ever seen in the capital, a stain on the game itself.

AN INTERNATIONAL DISPUTE AND ANOTHER CUP FINAL (1978–79)

Local councillor John Wilson's solution to the problem had been to herd the hooligans into pens until the other decent supporters had gone home, Tom Hart going even further when suggesting that perhaps the dogs should be brought in to control the louts. Many others however had wondered if it was perhaps time for Hearts to take a leaf out of their city rivals' book and install their own anti-hooligan fences at Tynecastle.

Although entirely unrelated to the current hooligan problem, on the morning of the game Hearts had revealed that during the previous season in the First Division the club had made a colossal £81,000 loss, a frightening reminder of the true cost of relegation...

After a bye in the first round of the League Cup, a 3–0 away victory against Second Division Brechin had already made it likely that Hibs would proceed into the next round even with the second leg yet to come, and so it was to prove. Just after the start of the second half McNamara had been sent off after a clash with centre-forward Campbell leaving Hibs to play the remainder of the game with ten men, the event having little effect on the final result after Callaghan had scored his first goal for the club shortly before the end. In the return at Easter Road a few days later Hibs had never been in any danger of an upset against an otherwise spirited Brechin side with a 3–1 victory; Callaghan again managing to find the net, the prolific Ally MacLeod twice.

An announcement a few days later that the popular Jimmy O'Rourke would be returning to Easter Road to coach the youngsters in the evenings as well as having an involvement with the reserve side had been warmly received by the fans. Sometime before, several attempts had been made to entice him back to Easter Road as a player, the clubs failing to come to an agreement. Now back at the scene of his former glories O'Rourke would be a welcome addition to the backroom staff where his enthusiastic and encouraging demeanour would make him instantly popular with the players, particularly the youngsters, his friendly approach in complete contrast to the manager's often abrasive manner. Some years later a former long-serving member of the backroom staff had been asked what it had been like working under Turnbull, his answer with just a hint of sarcasm: 'Like going to the dentists every morning!'

It was also around then that an interesting, but otherwise unimportant article had appeared in the newspapers informing the footballing public that because of the large number of advertising hoardings surrounding the trackside the STV cameras had not covered a game at Ibrox for several months, the piece apparently failing to raise any real concern from Rangers who refused to change their stance regarding the matter.

In the home leg of the UEFA Cup against Swedish side Norrköping, Hibs had taken what was thought to be a comfortable lead early in the game with goals by Higgins and Willie Temperley. Some incredibly lax defending would however allow opponents that had never really looked like scoring, back into the game to draw level. A late goal by Higgins allowed Hibs to take a slender 3–2 lead into the second leg in Sweden, the goal met by what had either been ecstatic or sarcastic cheers from a relieved crowd. At one stage Hibs had been so far on top that they had appeared capable of scoring four or five which would already have guaranteed entry into the next round and Turnbull had been absolutely furious at the final whistle to have surrendered such pathetically cheap goals, particularly as there had seemed little danger throughout the entire 90 minutes.

In the return leg the manager had taken an admittedly calculated risk regarding the fitness of several players by including McNamara, Bremner and Higgins whose experience might well have proved vital particularly on the heavily rain-soaked pitch. Encouraged by a small but vocal group of fans that had made their way from Edinburgh by ferry and train, many forced to spend the night in the nearby railway station due to the lack of accommodation, it had required 90 minutes of sterling effort, courage and organisation to finally subdue an energetic Swedish side that had mainly been confined to long-range efforts from well outside the box. The only real piece of danger during the entire proceedings had resulted in a great save by McDonald near the end, the game eventually ending goalless. The result in Edinburgh was good enough to see them safely through to the next round, the overall victory attributed by the manager to the fantastic team spirit that was then running through the club.

After the fiasco in Argentina the previous summer the Scotland manager and former Hibs player Ally McLeod had now

AN INTERNATIONAL DISPUTE AND ANOTHER CUP FINAL (1978–79)

tendered his resignation. Eddie Turnbull was just one of the names in contention as his replacement, but as far as Tom Hart had been concerned if confirmed it would only be a part-time basis. The then Clyde manager Craig Brown who had led the Shawfield side to promotion at the end of the previous season was yet another name in the hat but in the end the position would be offered to the former Celtic manager Jock Stein who had only recently resigned as manager of Leeds after just 44 turbulent days at Elland Road. Although both Stein and Turnbull were far from personal friends, the astute Stein had been a great admirer of the Hibs manager as far as football was concerned and just days later Turnbull would be appointed his assistant with the added responsibility of also looking after the under-21 side.

A 2–1 home victory against Aberdeen at the end of September now meant that after six games Hibs remained the only unbeaten side in the Premier League. Taking the lead after just eight minutes with a goal by Rae, MacLeod had doubled the advantage from the penalty spot before Jarvie pulled one back for the visitors. In total command throughout against it has to be said a disappointing Aberdeen side that included the inexperienced Jim Leighton and centre-half Alex McLeish, both making one of their very first appearances for the Grampian side, the victory had lifted Hibs into second place in the table just one point behind leaders Celtic. However, according to the Aberdeen manager Alex Ferguson after the game 'Hibs were not a good side but were well organised and hard-working, a view that may well have been acknowledged by Pat Stanton who was now Ferguson's assistant at Aberdeen after his retirement from the playing side at the end of the previous season.

Still unbeaten since the start of the season, a run now stretching to 12 games, 17 counting the Highland tour and UEFA Cup, in mid-October Hibs had come crashing back to earth with a 2–1 defeat by Partick Thistle at Firhill, a ground they had yet to win on since the introduction of the Premier League. Level at half-time after O'Hara had opened the scoring for Thistle and an own goal by McKinnon, overall Hibs performance had been well below that of their previous good form, particularly in the second half when O'Hara's second goal had been enough to give the often unpredictable Thistle both points. Despite the defeat however Hibs were still three points better off than at the same stage the previous season and remained third in the table.

The fact that a previously unbeaten side should only be third in the table although on the same number of points as leaders Celtic and Dundee United with just the single point separating the top four sides in a league when there were no easy games, was perhaps another indication as to the highly competitive nature of the Premier League.

In midweek Eddie Turnbull had been declared runner-up to Rangers' John Greig in the Mackinlay's Scotch Whisky Manager of the Month Award for September, which many found rather confusing as Rangers had won only one of the four games played during the month with two draws and a defeat by Celtic compared to Hibs unbeaten run of three wins and a draw. Perhaps some things will never change!

Now drawn against the French side Strasbourg in the UEFA Cup, in the away leg Hibs had again adopted their familiar habit in European games of attacking straight from the first whistle but for much of the first half had found themselves on the defensive during which time Strasbourg took the lead. In the second half a fighting Hibs side had regained much of its composure particularly in the closing 20 minutes, no one better than Gordon Rae. They had been well on top when a weak referee awarded Strasbourg an extremely soft penalty allowing the home side to double its lead, many in the ground doubting the legitimacy of the award. In his post-match interview however a confident Turnbull had seemingly not been even the slightest dismayed at the 2–0 defeat, convinced that the tie could still be won at Easter Road. He also added that he hoped for a homer in the return leg in Edinburgh, a comment obviously directed towards the Hungarian referee relating to the dubious penalty award.

Despite the manager's optimism, in the return leg at Easter Road Hibs had found themselves up against a wall of blue shirted defenders straight from the start. Their constant offside and time-wasting tactics, a strategy now widely adopted in these two legged affairs, had not only frustrated the players themselves but also the patience of the restless home fans on the terracing. The pace of

AN INTERNATIONAL DISPUTE AND ANOTHER CUP FINAL (1978–79)

the recalled Willie Murray had occasionally created danger in the opposition penalty area while in defence man-of-the-match Brenner had been magnificent in repulsing the rare Strasbourg attacks. But, although desperately attempting to save the game, in the end Hibs could only rely on a second-half penalty by MacLeod, the game eventually ending 3–1 on aggregate to end Hibs' interest in the competition, and allowing them to now concentrate fully on matters nearer home.

Unfortunately, a 1–1 draw at Tannadice in mid-December would lead to a disappointing few months for the club, when after the promising start to the campaign they would manage to draw just four of the following nine league games while losing five. Included in this run had been a 2–1 home defeat by Hearts, the Tynecastle side's first victory at Easter Road for ten years and also the very first against their city rivals in the Premier League. Before the game Hibs had been third in the table but the defeat by Hearts followed by a another in Paisley the following week now meant that in an incredibly competitive league Hibs had now dropped to seventh or fourth from bottom of the table. They would not manage another victory in the league until a 3–0 defeat of Motherwell at Fir Park in mid-February, a sequence however that would again be interrupted by the freak weather that was then affecting the country and cause chaos to the fixture list.

After a shaky start, attendances in the Premier League had now started to rise but not nearly enough for some clubs, including Hibs, to break even. The set-up still had many critics who had been convinced that it encouraged more defensive football, one of them Stewart Brown of the *Evening News* who felt that it had become a platform for desperate football with managers often hesitant to throw in youngsters.

In the League Cup Hibs had earlier been drawn against First Division Morton in the fourth round, the first game at Cappielow. Although facing lower league opposition, considering the side's, at that time, run of poor results, the Hibs players could possibly have been excused for what appeared to have been a planned defensive strategy with little penetration throughout the entire proceedings. They already seemed to be relying on an improved display in the return leg at Easter Road to overcome their lower league opponents.

Trailing by an early goal from the future Easter Road player Bobby Thomson, Hibs had been further handicapped after Jackie McNamara was sent off for the second time that season after a clash with outside right Russell just before the interval. From an attacking perspective the game had been a non-event as far as Hibs had been concerned, and in the end they had perhaps been extremely fortunate to be leaving Greenock at the final whistle trailing by just the single goal.

Meanwhile part of Eddie Turnbull's remit in the Scotland set-up had been to oversee the under-21 side for the European Championship game against the Norwegian under-21s at Easter Road, a game that Scotland would eventually win 5–1 with Hibs' Ally MacLeod one of the over-age players. Although he had ended up on the losing side, the opposition centre-forward Isak Refvik had caught Turnbull's eye with his outstanding, all-round energetic performance. Originally named in the full squad for the following evening's game between the sides at Hampden, almost at the last minute it had been decided that Refvik would play for the under-21 side instead, a decision that was to cause Hibs untold problems in the coming weeks.

At Hampden the following evening countryman Svein Mathisen had also been in brilliant form in helping to set up both the Norwegian goals in Scotland's eventual 3–2 victory, his performance also impressing the watching Hibs manager.

Turnbull however had not been the only one to recognise the potential of both Refvik and Mathisen, but while others dithered Hibs took decisive action. After a trip to London to iron out any potential permit difficulties and now claiming to have clearance for both players, a delegation from Hibs had made their way to Norway with the intention of signing both players in time to play against Hearts at Easter Road on the Saturday. Although Mathisen had been keen to sign immediately, the major stumbling block had been Viking Stavanger's insistence that the Refvic situation could not even be discussed until a full committee meeting later that week, the Hibs delegation reluctantly returning to Scotland empty handed.

Somewhat surprisingly, although they had been left air tickets, just over a week later both Refvik and Mathisen would arrive at Leith by ferry to sign initial three-month amateur contracts that

AN INTERNATIONAL DISPUTE AND ANOTHER CUP FINAL (1978–79)

could be extended if necessary. Both would make their debuts against Morton in the return League Cup tie at Easter Road a few days later when Refvik would become an instant favourite with the fans by scoring both goals in Hibs eventual 2–0 victory, only the third Hibs player to score twice in the same game that season. In the late stages Morton had passed up the opportunity to take the game into extra time when Andy Richie had blasted the ball high over the bar from the penalty spot and Hibs were now through to the semi-finals. Although both had played well, Refvik in particular had been magnificent, his speed, shooting ability and determination finally bringing to the forward line something that had been missing for some time.

In the money-spinning League Cup semi-final at Dens Park Hibs would come up against an Aberdeen side then sitting second in the table and had already defeated the Easter Road side 4–1 at Pittodrie not all that long before, two of the goals scored by former player Joe Harper.

By this time Hibs had been notified that as Refvik was not a full international he was to be refused a work permit. Although Hibs had the backing of the SFA, the Scottish League and the Players' Union, the local MP Alex Fletcher, a well-known Hibs fan would go even further by raising the matter in the House of Commons. When informed that an applicant should have the obvious ability to make a difference in his field, Fletcher had raised a laugh from his fellow MPs when suggesting that perhaps the Prime Minister Jim Callaghan should make the trip to Pittodrie on the Saturday so he could judge for himself.

Although Refvik had been included in the line up against Alex Ferguson's Aberdeen in the semi-final there would be no place for Mathisen in what would turn out to be an exciting encounter with several near things at either end and plenty to excite the fans. Despite numerous missed chances by both sides the game still remained goalless after 90 minutes and it was now onto extra time. In the 107th minute a rare moment of misjudgement by goalkeeper Mike McDonald had cost his side a place in the final when he had allowed a seemingly aimless cross from well out on the touchline by full-back Stuart Kennedy to soar over his head and into the far corner of the net for what would turn out to be the only goal of the game. Ironically Hibs only had McDonald to thank for even managing to reach extra time after a string of tremendous saves, one in particular from Harper late in the game from point blank range. In a game when there had been numerous exciting incidents and no shortage of thrills it had appeared that neither side had been capable of breaking the deadlock until the goalkeeper's tragic error. Over the piece however Aberdeen had possibly been the better side, particularly in the later stages and had probably deserved go through to face Rangers in the final where they would eventually lose 2–1. Although McDonald would feature in the next couple of games, after 170 consecutive appearances his mistake at Dens would ultimately cost him his place in the first team at Easter Road and a return for Jim McArthur after an absence of almost three years. The following season McDonald would make only a handful of appearances for the first team before eventually signing for Berwick Rangers in the summer of 1980.

By this time the Department of Employment had now entered the work permit debate by agreeing to investigate the matter but that in the meanwhile Refvik and Mathisen could still play on a visitor's permit until the matter had either been resolved or until their short-term contract had expired, and both players returned to Norway for Christmas intending to return. Before leaving Mathisen had been presented with the Norwegian Player of the Year trophy in a ceremony in the Easter Road boardroom.

Around the turn of the year the country had been in the grip of Artic weather that was to decimate the fixture list. As a result 2–1 defeat by Dundee United at Tannadice two days before Christmas would turn out to be Hibs' last competitive game until the middle of January, the severe frost bursting the pipes in both Easter Road dressing rooms and leaving the entire area badly flooded.

To the great disappointment of both sets of fans, particularly those of the maroon persuasion, after the confidence gained from the fairly recent victory at Easter Road, the always eagerly awaited New Year's Day derby, this time a potential relegation battle at Tynecastle between the now seventh placed Hibs and second bottom Hearts, had become an early casualty of the extreme weather.

AN INTERNATIONAL DISPUTE AND ANOTHER CUP FINAL (1978–79)

After a heavy overnight fall of snow had melted leaving pools of water all over the pitch, the game had been called off and it would now not take place until the end of March.

Instead, Hibs would take the opportunity to exchange the miserable Scottish weather for a few days in the sunshine with a trip to Israel and a hastily arranged game against a local Tel Aviv XI, the recently returned Isak Refvik scoring what would turn out to be his last goal for the club in the 1–1 draw, countryman Mathisen making an appearance from the substitute's bench in the second half.

Just days before the turn of the year Bobby Smith had joined Leicester City for a fee said to have been in the region of £80,000, the deal also including home and away games between the sides to be arranged sometime in the near future. Around that time the former Dundee and St Johnstone player Duncan Lambie, brother of the Hibs coach John, had joined the club from the German Second Division side Furth, a move apparently that had been on the cards for some time. Although not nearly as bad as the terrible winter of 1963 when most clubs had not managed a single competitive game from boxing day until around the middle of March, the recent bad weather would eventually result in Hibs missing five games. Lambie would have to wait until the end of January to make his first official start against Aberdeen and McArthur his return to the first team after an absence of almost three years.

Perhaps predictably the poor weather had again raised talk of a winter shutdown, Tom Hart however mirroring the view of the then Hibs chairman Harry Swan when the issue had been raised as far back as 1963 that the unpredictability of the Scottish weather would make the idea of a fixed shutdown totally impractical.

Lambie would finally make his Hibs debut in a 1–1 draw with Aberdeen at Easter Road at the end of January, another point dropped at home, but even a point had seemed highly unlikely after Harper had opened the scoring in the first half when his side had been well on top. A Duncan goal just a few minutes after the restart however had sparked new life into the side but once again the lack of penetration had been all too evident, the final result now leaving Hibs eighth in the table, or third bottom.

In the Scottish Cup Hibs had been drawn against Second Division Dunfermline at East End Park. The players of both sides had slithered and slid throughout the entire 90 minutes on a surface that although heavily sanded had still resembled a skating rink and quite clearly unplayable, making good football all but impossible. It had been evident to almost everyone in the ground at the start that the referee had made the wrong decision in allowing the game to go ahead, and considering the terrible conditions the eventual 1–1 draw would probably have satisfied both sides. Both goals had been scored in the second half, Higgins with a drive from only a few feet, Leonard equalising for the Fife side with 20 minutes remaining as the heavy snow had again started to fall. Although, any thoughts of the game being abandoned at that stage after what had gone on during the previous 70 minutes would have been laughable, Ally MacLeod later declaring the surface to have been the worse he had ever encountered.

With the country still in the grip of the severe weather the replay at Easter Road on the Monday had only been possible due to the tremendous efforts of the ground staff with the added assistance of several volunteers and the old fashioned remedy of braziers who had laboured all day to ensure that the game could go still go ahead. On a cold February evening that was said to have been reminiscent of Siberia, just over 5,000 hardy, or possibly foolish, souls had braved the elements to witness Hibs' eventual 2–0 victory. Again, both goals had been scored in the second half, the first from a MacLeod drive, Callaghan making sure of a victory that had never been in any real doubt when scoring a second just a few minutes from time to set up an all-Edinburgh affair against Meadowbank Thistle in the next round.

Originally to have taken place at Meadowbank, in the interests of crowd safety it had always been highly unlikely that the game would have been allowed to go ahead at the stadium and it had now been switched to Easter Road. Twice postponed due to the atrocious conditions at the time, it would eventually go ahead a few weeks later when in showing commendable aggression against their full-time opponents Thistle had worked hard in the early part of the game. But, as could be expected, it had been

AN INTERNATIONAL DISPUTE AND ANOTHER CUP FINAL (1978–79)

too easy for Hibs in the end as the part-timers tired, the eventual 6–0 victory Hibs' best since defeating Queen of the South 9–2 four years earlier.

Never a fan of the highly competitive nature of the Premier League, in his programme notes before the home game against Dundee United, Eddie Turnbull made his feelings clear on the matter. He stated that as far as he was aware, in no other league could a side be just five points from the top of the table yet only four points clear of relegation, the side at the very foot at that time having scored just four goals less than the then leaders Celtic. Any fears of the drop however had been eased slightly, even if only temporarily, when a late goal by Bremner, his fourth in the last five games, would give Hibs their first home win for almost six months. The 1–0 victory only the club's sixth of the season after 22 games, although ten had been drawn, the points dropped were attributed by the manager to either poor finishing or preventable defensive mistakes.

By this time the Refvic/Mathisen saga had taken yet another twist. Just when both players had seemed on the verge of being granted a work permit the club had now been informed that the home office, apparently concerned at the number of foreign players then plying their trade in the country – particularly in England – had now decided that from now on each club would only be allowed one overseas player on their books. With their initial three-month contracts now at an end both Refvik and Mathisen would return to Norway. Permanently as it would turn out, Refvik to re-sign for Viking Stavanger. Mathisen who had also been attracting the attention of the Dutch club Van Haag returning to his previous club IK Start with whom he would go on to twice win the championship. Their premature departure had left many at Easter Road contemplating as to just how the immediate future might have turned out if things had been different, particularly Refvic whose all-round enthusiastic style of play had already made him extremely popular with the fans. As far as the club and the majority of the general public had been concerned however both players had been treated outrageously in their quest for a work permit and that the authorities concerned should be ashamed of how they had handled the matter.

THE RISE AND EVENTUAL FALL OF TURNBULL'S TORNADOES

Around that time a letter had appeared in the local press from a disgruntled supporter pulling no punches in wondering just how the manager and the board could sit snugly in the directors' box week after week and watch a once famous and proud club collapse around them. According to the writer the supporters had shown that they had had enough by staying away in numbers, and a crowd of less than 5,000 the previous Saturday had been an embarrassment. To his mind too many ordinary players had been bought needlessly, the signing of Lambie a perfect example when there had already been a number of players with the same ability at the club. The Norwegian farce when two international class players, one playing out of position on the wing and the other struggling to get a game was yet another example, before going on to say that although it is always easy to blame a manager, in this case it would appear that Turnbull had completely lost the plot and wondered if it would only take relegation to bring a solution. Extremely harsh words but an opinion no doubt shared by a great many others at the time, the poor crowd an obvious reference to the 4,991 that had attended the recent 1–1 draw against an Aberdeen side that had left Hibs struggling in the relegation zone just one point above Edinburgh rivals Hearts and just six from the bottom side Motherwell.

Both Edinburgh rivals would meet each other twice at Easter Road inside a few days, the first in a Scottish Cup tie before a league game between the pair the following Saturday. In the cup a bad-tempered, foul-packed encounter, goals by Stewart and Rae had been enough for Hibs to qualify for the semi-finals for the first time in seven seasons and a meeting with Aberdeen. In what had turned out to be just the latest tough, and at times overcompetitive, encounter between the sides, trouble had again broken out in the traditional away end at the south end of the ground. Due to what appeared to have been Hearts supporters fighting among themselves after Hibs had taken a two-goal lead in the second half, the police had once again been called into action to bring the situation under control. With the game appearing to be all but won and Hibs possibly becoming somewhat complacent, centre-forward O'Connor pulled one back for Hearts in the

AN INTERNATIONAL DISPUTE AND ANOTHER CUP FINAL (1978–79)

late stages to give his side a chance but there was to be no more scoring.

After a 1–0 defeat at Ibrox in midweek, a result that left Hibs even deeper in relegation trouble, the recent habit of drawing league games in front of their own fans had continued with a 1–1 draw against their city rivals at Easter Road in front of a disappointing crowd of just 13,297, over 9,000 fewer than had attended the cup tie the previous Saturday. In a game that had been badly affected by the high winds and flurries of snow, conditions that made it extremely difficult for the players on both sides, Colin Campbell scored his first goal for the club early in the first half with a lob over the head of the former Hibs goalkeeper Thomson Allan, a recent signing from Dundee. A Gibson equaliser from the spot after just 25 minutes ended the scoring and while both sides were still struggling in the relegation zone, second bottom Hearts would undoubtedly have taken slightly more positives from the final result.

After a 2–1 away victory over St Mirren the previous Saturday Hibs and Hearts met again for a third time in just over two weeks, this time at Tynecastle in the game rescheduled from New Year's Day. Once again the heavy snow had put the game in some doubt but after a late pitch inspection was allowed to go ahead. Hibs' eventual 2–1 victory however would be won far easier than the final scoreline would perhaps suggest, producing more skilful football during the entire game than their opponents, whose desperation at times had resulted in several reckless tackles. With the scores then level at one each, just a minute before half-time an intended cross by Callaghan had completely deceived goalkeeper Allan to drop behind him into the net for the winner. A freak goal, but nevertheless one that had remarkably now lifted Hibs into fourth place, leaving Hearts still struggling in all kinds of difficulty near foot of the table, a result that had also maintained Hibs' unbeaten run in all five games between the sides during the season.

Stevie Brown, a promising left-sided player who had joined the club as an S-form signing aged 15 straight from school had already made several appearances for both the Scotland under-15 and under-18 sides. He would finally make his full debut in a 2–1 home victory against Celtic a few days later, the first of ten appearances he would make for the first team that season. Unfortunately, his early promise would not be sustained and although he would make rare appearances during the following few seasons he would return to non-league football with Whitehill Welfare in 1980.

In a goalless draw against future cup opponents Aberdeen at Pittodrie four days before the semi-final, Hibs had again started much the better against an admittedly under-strength home defence. Although, they would yet again pass up several good chances to win the game after what could only be described as woeful finishing and could well have suffered the consequences as Aberdeen came more into the game in the later stages, McArthur coming to his side's rescue with a number of decent saves.

The teams were to meet again in the semi-final at Hampden in midweek, but because of the travelling involved, particularly for the Aberdeen fans, the supporters of both sides had been strongly opposed to the game taking place in Glasgow. This perhaps had been reflected when just 9,837 had turned up on the night, the low attendance however somewhat excusable on a cold, wet and miserable evening miles from home.

Third in the table, Aberdeen had perhaps rightly been considered favourites to reach the cup final where the winners would eventually play either Rangers or Celtic. But Hibs had other ideas and the players presented manager Eddie Turnbull with an early birthday present after a 2–1 victory over his former side. In front of the ghostly, almost empty terraces in a stadium capable of holding almost 150,000 that had done little to create an exciting atmosphere, Hibs had initially been frustrated by their opponent's constant use of the offside-trap. Eventually they started to take control of the midfield to deny in particular the gifted Gordon Strachan from influencing the proceedings while again failing to take several decent chances to take the lead. Midway through the first half Archibald had opened the scoring for Aberdeen well against the run of play to stun both the Hibs players and the fans. Hibs were still the better side however and it was no great surprise when shortly before the break Gordon Rae had levelled the scores. Just a few minutes later Ally MacLeod had scored the

AN INTERNATIONAL DISPUTE AND ANOTHER CUP FINAL (1978–79)

winner from the penalty spot after he had been brought down inside the box by Rougvie.

In the second half, except for an incredible miss by Harper just a few feet from goal, Hibs had never really been in any trouble, MacLeod's goal enough to send Hibs into their tenth Scottish Cup final since the war. The final whistle was greeted by ecstatic acclaim from the fans who would now have been cautiously optimistic of their favourites finally bringing to an end the 77 year wait to see the coveted trophy back at Easter Road.

In what had possibly been a last desperate attempt to remedy the lack of goals, Turnbull had approached Derby County in an effort to sign the former Dundee and Spurs striker John Duncan on loan until the end of the season. Any potential move however came to a quick end when it was discovered that the then County manager Tommy Docherty was not interested in a loan deal but had been looking for around £100,000 for the prolific goal scorer's signature, a figure at that particular time well beyond Hibs' reach.

Still desperate for points, in back to back games against Morton, after a 2–2 draw at Cappielow, Ralph Callaghan scored his first double for the club, Bobby Thomson scoring one of the Morton goals. The game at Easter Road four days later would end in a surprise but thoroughly deserved 3–0 victory for the visitors, the first time that season that Hibs had conceded more than two goals in the same game. Interviewed later Turnbull had seemingly found it unbelievable that a side could have so much of a game and still fail to score even one goal, sadly not an entirely new experience. Now with just two points from the last four games Hibs once again found themselves seventh in the table, or third bottom, and with just seven games remaining, they were once again in desperate trouble.

The first of a double header against Partick Thistle inside three days that had been postponed from the turn of the year would turn out to be a humiliating and totally unexpected 6–1 defeat at Firhill by a side then sitting second bottom of the table. Although they had been forced to field an under-strength side due to injury, it had probably been by far the worst performance by any Hibs side for several years. Partick, the second lowest scorers in the league had opened the scoring after just 15 seconds and had been four ahead at half-time, their sixth scored with 20 minutes remaining, and it could have been more. The Hibs players may well have had their minds on the forthcoming cup final but in no way could this be used as an excuse for what had been a totally woeful and inept display. Near the end Callaghan pulled one back to take his tally into double figures since his move from Newcastle, but this would have meant little to the travelling fans that made their way through to Glasgow for the game and who had been entitled to have been absolutely furious at what had been a totally substandard performance.

Referee Eddie Ramsey however had made his own piece of football history by becoming the first official from Edinburgh to take charge of a league game involving a side from the capital outside of a derby game after the archaic rules regarding hometown referees had at last been relaxed. Ironically the Edinburgh referee Eddie Pringle had earlier officiated at a Hibs game, curiously also against Partick Thistle, but although residing in the capital at the time of the game had been living in Aberdeen at the time of the appointment.

A few days later Hibs would gain a modicum of satisfaction with a 1–0 victory over the Firhill side at Easter Road, a result that would mean little to the majority of the now clearly frustrated fans. With just two league games remaining, both against the Old Firm, a 3–1 defeat at Parkhead had hardly been an ideal preparation for the forthcoming Scottish Cup final against Rangers.

On Saturday 12 May the sides took the field at Hampden for the 1979 Scottish Cup final that had been televised live on both channels, few outside Edinburgh giving Hibs a chance. Once again cup fever had gripped the city and well over a hundred buses, two special trains and a fleet of private cars had made their way from Edinburgh for a game that had widely been expected to have been a thrilling end to end encounter with plenty of excitement in both penalty areas. Sadly it would turn out to be anything but, and would soon turn into a dour defensive battle with neither side giving anything away appearing much more concerned at stopping the other rather than creating anything productive themselves. Both

AN INTERNATIONAL DISPUTE AND ANOTHER CUP FINAL (1978–79)

MacLeod and Callaghan, probably caught up in the dreary midfield battle had failed throughout to make any real impression on the proceedings and although statistically Rangers probably had most of the pressure, at no stage did Hibs appear inferior. If anything, encouraged by man-of-the-match McNamara and ably assisted by the as usual highly competitive Bremner, in the final 20 minutes with the game still goalless Hibs had created several good chances to claim victory. In the closing minutes and immediately after the Rangers goalkeeper McCloy had made the save of the match and a replay looming, Hibs had been denied a blatant penalty after Campbell was fouled inside the box by goalkeeper McCloy. Clean through, the Hibs player was desperately attempting to stay on his feet only to shoot wide of the post, the furious appeals by the Easter Road players waved aside by referee Brian McGinley, the decision stunning almost everyone inside the ground, TV evidence later that evening seemingly confirming that the challenge on Campbell had been illegal. After the game numerous running battles had broken out in the surrounding streets between rival supporters, a great number of the Hibs supporters returning to their coaches parked in nearby Prospecthill Road only to find dozens with their windows smashed, events that would later be described as possibly the worst experienced at a football match in the city for some time. Regardless, it was now on to the replay in midweek.

Taking confidence from their display on the Saturday, in the replay Hibs had been that much sharper and could well have scored twice inside the opening 20 minutes, Rangers only real threat during this time a long-range effort from Cooper that struck the bar before being cleared to safety. The 90 minutes however would again end without a goal and it was now on to extra time. During the extended 30 minutes the best chance of the game fell to Gordon Rae when, finding himself totally unmarked inside the opposition penalty area, had failed to control the ball and with the goal gaping had blasted the ball wide of the post. This meant that it would now require a then unprecedented second replay to separate the sides.

After a break of just over a week, on Monday 28 May the second replay would again take place at the national stadium, when after 228 goalless minutes the deadlock was finally broken when Higgins put Hibs ahead after clever lead up play by Campbell,

Rae and Duncan, only for two goals by Johnston to give Rangers a 2–1 interval lead. The score would remain the same until with just over ten minutes left, MacLeod had equalised from the penalty spot after Hutchison had been brought down inside the box and once again it would be on to extra time. In a game where both sides had been evenly matched and just when it appeared as if it was going to require an unprecedented fourth game to separate the sides, minutes from the end the issue was finally settled. After a desperate attempt to intercept a Cooper cross from reaching several Rangers players inside the Hibs box, left-back Arthur Duncan had sent an unstoppable header past the helpless McArthur to give the Ibrox side the cup for the third time inside four years while absolutely stunning the watching Hibs fans who could only watch in disbelief. Over the piece every man had played his part – McArthur even saving a penalty taken by the future Hibs manager Alex Miller – in their magnificent although ultimately doomed efforts to bring the trophy back to Easter Road. Somewhat ironically if Rangers had also won the championship instead of Celtic to qualify for the following season's European Cup then Hibs as runners-up would automatically have qualified for the Cup Winners' Cup.

Hibs: McArthur, Brazil and Duncan, Bremner, Stewart and McNamara, Hutchison, MacLeod, Campbell, Callaghan, and Higgins. With the exception of Hutchison who had been replaced by Rae for the first replay, the same players had contested all three games.
Rangers: McCloy, Jardine and Dawson, Johnstone, Jackson and McDonald, McLean, Russell, Parlane, Smith and Cooper. The same side playing in the first two games, Watson replacing McDonald at left half who himself would take Smiths place in the forward line for the second replay.
Referee: B McGinley (Glasgow) for the first two games; I Foote (Glasgow) for the second replay.

Although it had certainly been anything but a laughing matter at the time, in an otherwise amusing end to the affair that is possibly apocryphal, it is said that a number of Hibs-supporting soldiers from the BAOR (British Army on the Rhine) stationed in Germany

AN INTERNATIONAL DISPUTE AND ANOTHER CUP FINAL (1978–79)

had attended the first game, but had been unable to stay for the replay. All that is except one individual who had apparently disobeyed orders and remained behind for the replay in midweek. Unable to stay for the third game and possibly then confined to barracks, in those pre-mobile phone days he is said to have enquired as to the result at Hampden that evening only to receive the reply that one side had won 3–2 although the person didn't know which one, all they knew was that someone called Duncan had scored the winning goal. One can only begin to imagine his feelings when discovering the truth the following morning!

The curtain would finally fall on what had been another extremely disappointing season with yet another game against Rangers at Easter Road just a few days after the final when goals by Ally Brazil and Gordon Rae would give the home side a 2–1 win, the winner coming just eight minutes from time, a somewhat hollow victory after the result at Hampden a few days earlier. Watched by a poor crowd of just 3,242, the vast majority the now completely dispirited Hibs fans, many probably not even staying until the final whistle.

After long periods of the season struggling in the relegation zone, the victory had been enough to finally lift Hibs into fifth place. Yet again however far too many games had been drawn, 13 as opposed to just the 12 wins with 11 defeats, the extremely poor number of goals scored again perhaps telling its own story, only the bottom three in the table having scored less than Hibs' 44.

At the other end of the city things were even worse when second bottom Hearts had been relegated for the second time in three seasons, six points above bottom-placed Motherwell.

At the end of the season, just three players, O'Brian, Temperley and the unused Aitchison had been released with 23 retained. The fact that Hibs had reached the semi-final of the League Cup and the final of the Scottish, combined with the eventual recovery from a disastrous spell in the middle of the season would perhaps have given the supporters some reason to believe that things could only get better the following season, a confidence however that would soon be found to be badly misplaced. The earlier transfer of John Brownlie to Newcastle now left only Arthur Duncan from the League Cup winning side of just a few seasons before, conclusive evidence if any was still needed that a golden period in the club's rich history was now well and truly over.

Just a few months earlier representatives from all ten Premier clubs had met secretly to discuss a possible reorganisation of the leagues. For some time the general consensus had been that the present arrangements had been far too tight often leading to more negative play and a drop in the number of goals scored. All were now in agreement that the way forward should be three leagues of 12, 12 and 14, an arrangement that would eventually be agreed by the authorities but not for another 20 years. Since the advent of the Premier League the points gap between the top and bottom sides had been decreasing each year, the at times defensive football also leading to an average drop in the number of supporters attending the games. Also on the agenda had once again been the thorny issue of fees regarding the games covered by the TV cameras that for some time had been considered derisory and yet again the clubs would be demanding an increase, perhaps even double.

As part of his Scotland duties, in June Eddie Turnbull had been in charge of the Scottish under-21 side against the Norwegian under-21s, Hibs' Ally McLeod again one of the over-age players. He had also been in charge of the full side's 4–0 European Championship victory in Oslo the following evening when he had taken the opportunity to catch up again with Svein Mathisen who had featured in midfield. During his short time at Easter Road Mathisen had made just five appearances for the first team, failing to score. Refvik who had made nine appearances while scoring three would eventually go on to make seven appearances for the full Norwegian side. Sadly, Mathisen who would eventually gain 25 full caps passed away in 2011 aged just 56.

George Best, the End of the Road for Eddie Turnbull and Relegation (1979–80)

WHAT WOULD TURN out to be one of the most traumatic episodes in the long history of the club had kicked-off with a game against St Mirren in the Anglo Scottish Cup competition at Love Street. A 3–3 draw had been followed in midweek by a 1–0 defeat at Easter Road, bringing an early end to Hibs interest in a competition that Tom Hart had earlier described as a tournament for losers after he had threatened to withdraw the club from the tournament after the pathetic and unsporting display by some of the Bristol City players in 1977. The early exit however, possibly an early sign of what was to come.

The novelty of a pre-season four team round-robin tournament had now been introduced to the Edinburgh public for the first time when Hibs, Hearts, Manchester City and Coventry City had all been invited to compete for the Skol Festival Trophy sponsored by the brewing giants Ind Coope. Played in a mini league format over five days at both Easter Road and Tynecastle with all four sides taking part in a double header on the same ground on the same day, the fans were able to take advantage of both games for the same admission price. In the opening game at Easter Road, Hibs 2–1 victory over Hearts had been followed almost immediately by Coventry defeating a Manchester City side that included its new £750,000 striker Mick Robison 3–1. On the following Monday at Tynecastle the game between Hibs and Manchester City had ended in a 1–1 draw, but the major talking point of the afternoon had been the horrendous collision between City's giant goalkeeper Joe Corrigan and the Hibs centre-forward Colin Campbell. With both players chasing a high ball into the City penalty area, Campbell had taken the full force of what many felt to have been a reckless challenge by the England goalkeeper. Only the quick reactions of both trainers had prevented a more serious outcome when it was discovered that Campbell had swallowed his tongue, the centre-forward required to spend a few days in the Royal Infirmary. With the game between Hearts and Coventry City later that evening also ending all square, the winners of the tournament would now be decided between Hibs and Coventry at Easter Road on the Wednesday evening. A City side that included the Scottish internationals Tommy Hutchison, Jim Holton, Ian Wallace and goalkeeper Jim Blyth had taken the field resplendent in an all chocolate coloured strip, the then unusual innovation taking the eye of the fans. However in what turned out to be a largely unexciting game in front of an extremely poor crowd, the no-score draw against an injury weakened Hibs side had ultimately been enough for Coventry to be declared the inaugural winners of the competition. What had initially been proposed as an annual competition would never be played for again.

The former Hearts captain Jim Brown who had received a free transfer at the end of the season had joined Hibs during the summer on a part-time basis. He would soon be joined by centre-forward David Reid and midfielder David Whyte, who had both been signed from Leeds United in what was said to have been a £30,000 double deal. Neither Reid nor Whyte would make any impact on the side, the former managing just one competitive appearance as an unused substitute in a 1–1 draw with Morton at the beginning of October, Whyte failing to make a single appearance. The unsettled Willie Murray, yet another of the talented youngsters that were then experiencing great difficulty in establishing a place in the first team on a regular basis had now been placed on the 'open to transfer' list at his own request with the promise that he would be notified of any interest.

In the league Hibs had been handed a difficult start with games against the previous season's runners-up Rangers at home before facing fourth-placed Aberdeen at Pittodrie, both particularly troublesome opponents at the best of times.

Before the game against Rangers the fans had been surprised to see the 20-year-old Jim Farmer making his first start at right-back in place of Brazil and a young Craig Paterson making his competitive debut at left-half in place of McNamara. Although Paterson would go on to make well over a hundred appearances for the club, unfortunately it would turn out to be the first of only two appearances the young farmer was to make for the first team and he would join Stirling Albion at the end of the season.

In what would otherwise turn out to be a fairly even first half Rangers had scored twice inside three minutes to take a two-goal lead into the interval, the second a quite spectacular solo goal by Davie Cooper that drew the applause from many of the fair-minded supporters in the ground. In the second half and now determined to take something from the game, just after the restart Rae had reduced the deficit only for a late Russell goal to seal the points for the visitors. Although both McNamara and Brazil had missed the game because of suspension there had been no lack of spirit or confidence during the entire 90 minutes, particularly in defence. Although the forwards appeared at times to have lacked the desire of the Rangers front men, in the end the eventual 3–1 victory had probably been fully deserved.

A 3–0 defeat at Pittodrie the following week had resulted in Hibs dropping to the foot of the table, a position unfortunately that they were to occupy for the majority of the season. Although showing plenty of promise, particularly in the early stages when efforts from both Callaghan and Campbell had come crashing back off the woodwork, an Archibald goal on the stroke of half-time had put his side ahead, McMaster scoring twice more in the second half to put the final result beyond doubt. Although his decisions had not affected the final outcome, according to one watching reporter, referee Delaney had frequently baffled not only the players themselves but also the watching fans with some of his strange decisions. According to the critic he would have been far from satisfied at his overall performance if he had watched the highlights of the game on TV later that evening.

Still on the subject of the TV cameras, the seemingly never-ending saga between the football authorities and both the BBC and ITV regarding payment for the rights to broadcast highlights of games had once again ended in stalemate. The new offer by the TV companies was felt to be derisory and falling several thousand short of the valuation of both the SFA and Scottish League. Both broadcasters had immediately countered regarding their own concerns at what they felt to be the excessive amount of trackside advertising at some games, but still unable to reach an agreement a TV blackout had once again come into operation, a decision however that would lead to a furious Celtic chairman Desmond White claiming that such a blackout would have a serious effect on his club's finances. White's statement had clearly infuriated the outspoken Tom Hart who had immediately accused White of nothing more than self-interest, reminding the Celtic chairman that the ongoing negotiations had been on behalf of all 38 Scottish clubs, not just the Parkhead side. A temporary compromise would eventually be reached when the broadcasters had agreed to pay £2,000 for each game covered by the cameras, both the participating clubs on the day to receive £750 each, the remainder going into a common fund. However, on later discovering that each of the clubs involved were now to receive just £500, Hart had again declared his own blackout by banning both the BBC and STV cameras from Easter Road.

After two defeats from the opening couple of games and memories of the dark days of the previous season still fresh in the mind, Hibs were now desperately in need of a victory to kick-start their season. The extremely concerning situation would be only slightly improved after a 5–2 defeat of Dundee Easter Road the following week when the highlight of the afternoon had been a fantastic solo goal by Ralph Callaghan that was said to have been as good as any seen at Easter Road for many years. After collecting the ball 30 yards from goal Callaghan had proceeded to take on one Dundee defender after another before dribbling around the goalkeeper to finally tap the ball into the net, the goal bringing the house down and the ecstatic congratulations of his teammates. The impressive victory was to bring just temporary relief when none of the following 11 league games would end in victory, results that now left the side firmly rooted at the foot of the table six points below fellow strugglers Dundee.

For the first time the League Cup was now to be sponsored, the distilling giants Bell's Whisky investing around £270,000 in the competition, a more than welcome financial boost for the game at a time when many clubs including Hibs had been struggling to survive on gate receipts alone. In the opening round they had been drawn against Second Division Montrose for the third time in five years, the recollections of the embarrassing night at Links

Park not all that long before still vivid in the memory. This time however there was to be no such problems although it would be tight. In the first leg at home a late goal had been needed to give the Easter Road side a 2–1 victory against determined opponents, the unsettled home fans leaving the players in absolutely no doubt as to their feelings as they left the field at the end of what had been a careless and casual performance against far more determined lower league opponents. In the return leg at Links Park Montrose had been leading 1–0 at the end of 90 minutes against it has to be said a lethargic Hibs side, and with the aggregate scores now level it was once again on to extra time when a Higgins goal in the 95th minute had finally secured Hibs' place in the next round. Possibly in a humorous attempt to placate the frustrated travelling fans, although not many would have been laughing, Jackie McNamara had later declared, 'Well at least we did better than the last time.'

After the game Tom Hart had released a press statement condemning what he called the actions of the bigots among a section of the Hibs support at Montrose, finding the IRA chants and other obscene slogans disgusting. Now, with the support of the police, he was determined to silence the small but vocal group, even at the risk of smaller gates. On several occasions already that season the Eire flag had been seen on the terracing and he had instructed the police that they were to be removed. He stated that this is a non-sectarian club with no religious or political connections and it is a long time since they have been affiliated with either, ending by reinforcing his view that most Hibs fans are well behaved and that his message applied only to a very small number.

Hibs' interest in the League Cup would also be short lived after 2–1 home and away defeats by Kilmarnock in the second round, results that now allowed the side to concentrate fully on the potential dangers that lay ahead.

Just a few weeks earlier 20-year-old Derek Rodier who had only joined the club from Edinburgh University during the summer made an unexpected early debut in a 1–0 defeat by Kilmarnock at Rugby Park. While failing to find the net himself, Rodier's energetic performance had impressed the watching Turnbull. Although suggesting that Hibs could possibly have found of the answer to their goalscoring problems, this would have been asking a lot of an inexperienced youngster at that time particularly in a side struggling at the foot of the table. Managing just three appearances for the first team during the season, like others before him Rodier would eventually find first team appearances difficult to come by, and although he would remain at Easter Road for the next few years he would manage only the occasional appearance, often as substitute, before joining Dunfermline in 1982. Yet another defeat, this time by top of the table Celtic at home now meant that including the five against Dundee, Hibs had scored just seven goals in opening first five league games as opposed to the 14 conceded, and even this early had been extremely concerning statistics.

So far that season centre-half Fleming had failed to make even a single appearance for the first team even as a substitute. Yet another of whom big things had been expected, particularly as he had been experiencing full-time football for the first time, after just 18 appearances in all games and now not figuring in the managers long-term plans he would join Berwick Rangers during the season.

Although Turnbull had earlier announced that he would not be spending money just for the sake of it, even this early the alarm bells had started ringing loud and clear. In yet another attempt to solve the ongoing goalscoring problem, an approach had been made to Airdrie with what was said to have been a five figure sum for striker Sandy Clark, the offer firmly rejected. Around this time Hibs would be involved in the transfer market themselves but this time as the selling club when the energetic and versatile Scottish international Des Bremner had been allowed to join Aston Villa in a move said to have been worth £275,000. The former Clyde player Joe Ward would move to Easter Road as a £80,000 makeweight as part of the deal, Aston Villa gaining by far the better of the transaction. As expected the move had been condemned by the vast majority of the support, but at that time Hibs had been trying to attract new faces to Easter Road and had been in desperate need of the money.

At Villa Park Bremner would soon go on to win not only a League Championship medal the following season but also the European Cup in 1982 although perhaps surprisingly failing to add to his solitary Scotland cap. Yet another who had been keen try his luck in England for some time, Bremner had already requested a transfer the previous season but had agreed to remain at Easter Road in the meantime after a promise that any offer would be listened to. Now regardless of a proposed new long-term contract at Easter Road including a testimonial he had been delighted to join Villa, just missing out on the opportunity to line up alongside his former Easter Road colleague Alex Cropley who had now moved to Newcastle on a short-term contact before eventually deciding to further his career with Toronto Blizzards in the North American league.

A regular goal scorer with Clyde before his move to Aston Villa, on his Hibs debut against St Mirren, a 2–0 home defeat, Ward almost scored with his first kick of the ball before the danger was cleared, but possibly as another sign of what was to come he would fail to find the net in just 11 competitive appearances before joining Dundee United at the end of the season. A few weeks earlier Pat Carroll, yet another promising youngster who had struggled to break into the first team on a regular basis with just 20 appearances in all games during his five seasons at Easter Road had joined Raith Rovers.

With the club still struggling at the foot of the table, just before the forthcoming game against Rangers at Ibrox the entire squad had spent a few days at Turnberry away from the pressures of football taking part in games of golf, snooker and other relaxing pastimes. In an attempt to take the players' minds off the current situation, the break appeared to have done little to help after a 2–0 defeat on the Saturday in Glasgow. Just before half-time and the game still goalless Jackie McNamara had been sent off for the third time in just over a year after a fairly innocuous tackle on the Rangers shrinking violet Alex McDonald, a tackle that according to most neutral observers, had warranted at best no more than a booking. The highly controversial decision was to prove costly for a Hibs side that had been playing well at the time, Smith opening the scoring against ten-man Hibs just before half-time, Alex Miller adding a second from the penalty spot midway through the second half to put the final result beyond doubt and give manager Turnbull a restless night. Most of the sports writers the following morning had also been surprised at McNamara's red card. *The Sunday Express*: 'If the referee had treated everyone on the pitch the same as McNamara then we would have finished the game with only seven players on each side.' *The News of the World*: 'The game was finished as a contest in the 35th minute after just the latest of the questionable ordering off decisions that has affected Scottish football this season.' However, few of the Hibs fans inside Ibrox would have been overly surprised after only another of the poor decisions that regularly appeared to go against visiting sides in Glasgow.

While still only the start of November, in what was already turning out to be an absolutely disastrous season Hibs had failed to win any of the previous nine games, a 2–1 defeat by Dundee at Dens Park leaving them facing an uphill battle to achieve safety, and manager Turnbull shaking his head in frustration. The current concerning situation had been highlighted in the official programme before the home game against Kilmarnock, stating the patently obvious: with five points separating bottom-placed Hibs from second bottom Dundee it would now be extremely difficult although not impossible to secure safety before the end of the season. Probably not lost on the majority of the Hibs support who would have been well aware of the fact for some weeks, the eventual 1–1 draw now extending the gap at the foot of the table to seven points.

Despite numerous attempts to address the lack of goals that had so far all proved fruitless, a possible solution to the problem would come from an unlikely source when the highly respected *Evening News* sports journalist Stewart Brown had suggested in his column that Hibs could do worse than attempting to sign George Best who at that time was unsettled at Fulham. In what had initially been seen as merely a publicity stunt, and apparently against the wishes of manager Turnbull, Tom Hart had travelled to London for talks with the Fulham chairman who had agreed to allow Hart to talk to the player and after initial discussions with the player Best had made his way to Edinburgh for signing talks. Later, both he and his model wife Angie would be seen in the director's box for the game against Kilmarnock, Angie perhaps understandably receiving far more attention from the male fans than her husband. After agreeing Fulham's £50,000 transfer demand, Best had agreed to join Hibs on an initial one year's pay-as-you-play deal on a reputed £2,000 per game, an astronomical figure at that time that was said to have been paid personally by the Hibs chairman although this is now thought not to have been the case. He would then make his way back to England to take part in a testimonial game for the then Ipswich manager Bobby Robson against an England select at Portman Road.

Released by Manchester United in 1974 Best had since become something of a football nomad with appearances for numerous lower or non-league sides and also in North America. Eventually agreeing to join Second Division Fulham they had given him permission to turn out for Fort Lauderdale Strikers during the close season. As could be expected his signing for Hibs had made front page headlines throughout the country. Although it had initially been hoped that the mercurial Irishman would be in the side to face Celtic at Parkhead on the Saturday, a knee injury received in the Robson testimonial had ruled him out of contention, the eventual 3–0 defeat seeing Hibs sink even deeper into the relegation mire.

However, in front of a much bigger crowd than normal Best would finally make his long-awaited debut against St Mirren at Love Street on Saturday 24 November 1979, the heavy rain-soaked pitch doing little to prevent the Irishman from displaying his mesmeric skills and captivate the watching supporters. Although the game had ended in yet another 2–1 defeat, Best himself had scored Hibs' solitary goal in the final few minutes to raise the expectations of the watching Hibs fans that he could possibly be their salvation and save the club from the lower division.

He made his home debut the following Saturday against Partick Thistle in front of a huge, highly excited 20,622 crowd, more than four times what normally could have been expected for the fixture, a tribute to the player's still tremendous drawing power. Two goals ahead at the interval after an own goal by Whittaker and what else but an Ally MacLeod penalty, Thistle came storming back in the second half with a goal from O'Hara. Goalkeeper MacArthur then rescued a valuable point with a tremendous save from the penalty spot late in the game to secure Hibs' first victory in the league for over three months. Just before half-time a typical piece of Best magic had enthralled the crowd when his free kick from all of 40 yards had struck the inside of the post leaving the Partick goalkeeper Rough stranded before being cleared to safety. As some perspective as to the interest created in the city at Best's arrival, that same afternoon at Hampden the attendance for the League Cup semi-final between Aberdeen and Morton had been attended by just 12,000.

In the week leading up to the Partick game the players had been changing in the dressing room after training when goalkeeper McArthur had questioned why Best was being paid such a large amount compared to the other players wages. With his teammates desperately attempting to draw his attention he had looked up to see chairman Hart standing outside the changing room door listening to his every word before quietly walking away. As the players were preparing for the game against Thistle on the Saturday, McArthur had been called outside by Tom Hart who asked what he could see outside from one of the small windows. McArthur's answer, 'a big crowd, Mr Hart' bringing the immediate response from the chairman: 'That my son is why Best is being paid so much', before walking away.

As mentioned earlier Bobby Smith's move to Leicester City had also included home and away games between the sides. The first taking place at Easter Road at the beginning of December against a City side that as well as Smith had also included the former Hibs loan signing Martin Henderson and a very young Gary Lineker, ending in a 3–2 victory for Hibs, the unsettled Ally MacLeod at that time playing without a contract of any kind, scoring a hat-trick. The then Hajduk Split goalkeeper Milo Nizetic had earlier been invited to Easter Road for trials, and after a friendly against Kilmarnock at Rugby Park two days before, the goalkeeper had been selected for the game against Leicester only to break a bone in his hand while making a save. He would soon return to Yugoslavia without any signing talks having taken place. Instead, after a move to sign the former Ayr United goalkeeper Jim Stewart from Leeds United had fallen through, Turnbull had now turned his attention towards the veteran St Johnstone goalkeeper Derek Robertson. Robertson however would fail to impress during his short time at the club and would be freed at the end of the season after just a handful of games for the reserves.

Yet more vital points had been dropped after a 2–0 away defeat by a Morton side at that time perhaps surprisingly sharing the top of the table with Celtic. To the great dismay of the Hibs fans making their way through to Greenock it had been announced that Best would not be playing that afternoon as he had received permission from Tom Hart to return to London for further treatment to the knee injury received a couple of weeks earlier during the Robson testimonial.

Despite his superstar status, Best was said to have been anything but a prima donna in the dressing room and extremely popular with his teammates both on and off the field. His presence was regularly said to have opened doors at various function rooms throughout the city for himself and his teammates, on one occasion also resulting in free suits at one of the top tailors in the city. Jim McArthur also recalled the time he had been receiving some serious abuse from a spectator in the crowd behind his goals during the pre-match warm up. Spotting what was going on Best had then proceeded to demonstrate his amazing dead ball accuracy by deliberately striking the abuser on the head with the ball.

Fortunately, he had recovered sufficiently to face third-placed Rangers at Easter Road seven days later, a game that sadly had once again been marred by needless violence on the terraces. With bottles and other missiles being thrown randomly into the crowd, the police had once again been kept busy dealing with the troublemakers, many, though not all, Rangers fans that had invaded the traditional home end of the ground. Although still firmly entrenched at the foot of the table Hibs' eventual hard-fought 2–1 victory had been a tremendous boost to any slim hopes of avoiding relegation at the end of the season. A victory that had only been achieved by an energetic workmanlike performance and an ability on the day to use the ball better on the heavily frosted surface than their opponents, Best had once again captivated the home crowd with his exquisite talents.

Despite the extremely impressive display it seemed at one time that a first half goal by Tommy McLean might well have been enough to give Rangers both points, only for goals by Campbell and Higgins to secure an extremely welcome victory and provide manager Eddie Turnbull with an early Christmas present.

With Hearts now in the Second Division, Dundee were to have been Hibs' New Year's Day visitors at Easter Road. A game that had been changed to the following day to avoid the exorbitant police charges on the first, only for the fixture to be cancelled almost at the last minute due to the severe weather that was affecting parts of the country.

In a week of surprises, the following morning Pat Stanton had announced that he would be leaving Aberdeen to pursue a career in management in his own right. The breaking news followed just a few days later with an announcement that Willie Ormond had been sensationally sacked as manager of Hearts, the news immediately leading to Tom Hart offering the former Hibs player the position of assistant manager under Eddie Turnbull at Easter Road. However, because of the pending legal action for wrongful dismissal, Ormond had been unable to accept Hart's offer, at least in the meantime.

For perhaps obvious reasons Ormond had never really been accepted by a great number of the Hearts supporters. Although the Tynecastle side were then sitting at the top of the table and still with a game in hand, after a 3–3 home draw with Clydebank on the Saturday Ormond had been ordered to attend a meeting in the boardroom in midweek only to be informed that he was to be out of Tynecastle by the Saturday. The decision, made by what Ormond would later describe as the worst by far of any board of directors he had ever served under, was now in the hands of an industrial tribunal.

On the Saturday Best opened his home account with a quite brilliant goal in the eventual 1–1 draw with Celtic. Having again missed several chances to take the lead, including a miss from the penalty spot by MacLeod, in a quite magnificent overall performance by the Irishman that had frustrated the visitors and enthralled the home support, Best had set Easter Road alight when, after collecting a pass from Campbell out wide on the left, he cut inside before unleashing a tremendous unstoppable right-foot volley past the despairing dive of goalkeeper Latchford and high into the net. In an overall display of fabulous football Best had quite simply been head and shoulders above everyone on the park with a performance that could well have graced any ground in Britain. The only slight downside was that Hibs were left to reflect on yet another miss from the penalty spot and the loss of a precious point.

In a break from the anxiety of the league, the Scottish Cup draw had yet again thrown up an all-Edinburgh tie when for the second consecutive season Hibs had come out of the hat alongside Meadowbank Thistle, once again away from home. Because of safety concerns and also in the hope of drawing a much bigger gate, the previous season the authorities had allowed the game to be switched from Meadowbank to Easter Road. Now, despite both sides having no objections to the game again taking place at Easter Road, in what had generally been considered a ridiculous and quite unnecessary decision, the game had been changed to neutral Tynecastle instead. The move would ultimately lead to understandable criticism from the Hibs fans, partly because of the segregation arrangements that had the expected large Hibs turnout having the use of just eight turnstiles at the Gorgie Road end of the ground, two reserved exclusively for juveniles, while the anticipated few hundred Meadowbank fans would have the use of 14 turnstiles in the Wheatfield stand if necessary. Yet another example of what was felt to have been the then customary ineptitude of the football authorities.

The game itself however would ultimately prove a great disappointment for any Hibs fan that had turned up expecting an easy game with plenty of goals similar to the previous meeting between the sides. After a scoreless first half, Hibs had been leading by a solitary Callaghan goal when just minutes from the end the Thistle substitute McGauran had missed a tremendous chance to equalise only to blast the ball high over the bar from close range when it seemed easier to score. Apart from Best, Hibs had no one on the field that remotely took the eye, the Hibs players leaving the field at the end of what had been another poor performance once again in no doubt whatsoever as to the fans frustrations. According to one newspaper article the following morning: 'Hibs may have won the game but part-time Meadowbank all the plaudits'.

Before the home game against Morton a few weeks later it was reported that George Best had been suspended by chairman Tom Hart after failing to turn up for training in midweek as per his contract that stipulated that he must arrive in Edinburgh on the Wednesday for training on a Thursday and Friday. Best's excuse that he had remained back in London as his wife Angie had been ill with a heavy cold cutting absolutely no ice with the no non-sense Hart. Best's absence however had given Willie Murray the opportunity to score his first goal of the season and his first for almost two years in the eventual 3–2 victory. In a tremendous first half display considered by many to have been the best seen at Easter Road for some time, the 3–1 interval score had flattered their opponents. However, after failing to capitalise on their first half dominance, midway through the second half the future Hibs player Bobby Thomson had reduced the gap before passing up several other decent chances to equalise as Hibs were left desperately hanging on until the final whistle.

In midweek the George Best saga took yet another twist when after flying up to Edinburgh to apologise personally to Tom Hart, the player had surprisingly been forgiven by a usually unbending Hibs chairman. Reintroduced into the squad for the forthcoming Scottish Cup tie against Ayr United, it was only the second time that Hibs had played a game on a Sunday. But, at the players' usual pre-match lunch and team talk there had been no sign of Best. After waiting as long as possible for the player to arrive, eventually coach John Fraser had been despatched to his hotel to see if anything was wrong only to find the player obviously still well under the influence of alcohol and in no fit state to play. It later turned out that the Irishman had spent a large part of the previous evening and well into the early hours drinking with the French rugby team that had played against Scotland at Murrayfield that afternoon. The incident immediately led to yet another suspension, only this time it appeared that there would be no going back.

Despite an early goal by recent signing Duncan Lambie, his first for the club, Hibs had found themselves up against formidable lower league opponents and would have to wait until midway through the second half to secure a place in the next round after an Ally MacLeod goal finally put the end result beyond doubt. United's spirited display throughout the entire 90 minutes however had not only been a tremendous advert for the First Division but would also have provided the Hibs players with some idea of the kind of opposition that they would most likely be facing the following season.

After just the latest non-appearance, as expected Best had once again been suspended, placed on the transfer list and banned from playing for any other club. It appeared that there was now definitely to be no way back for the wayward genius at Easter Road, only to be surprisingly offered one last chance to get his act together by a usually stubborn and unwavering chairman. With the player again back in the fold, only now did Hart admit that he had already covered up for Best on several occasions including his non-appearance against Morton earlier in the season when although he had turned up at the ground in time he had been in no fit state to play, Hart only discovering later that he had actually attended a function in Manchester into the early hours of the morning. It now came out that the chairman had been in regular contact with the player's wife and family in an attempt to keep Best from coming completely off the rails, and while pleading with the media to lay off the troubled player had insisted that this definitely had to be his last chance at Easter Road.

After an absence of almost five weeks Best had been recalled to the side in time for the home game against Rangers at the beginning of March that unfortunately for the now thoroughly dejected supporters would turn out to be another defeat, the Irishman to everyone's surprise substituted midway through the second half. It would later be claimed that Best had taken a knock, but having missed several weeks training while living it up in London it was far more likely that he had been unfit and had found the going tough. Rangers had been the better side throughout the opening 45 minutes when they had taken the lead, but a much improved second half performance by Hibs had resulted in them managing to stretch their opponents defence on numerous occasions only for the familiar problem of failing to take their chances to ultimately defeat them. Once again it had been the same old story and probably the main reason why they remained firmly anchored at the foot of the table, now 11 points below second bottom Dundee, and although they still had three games in hand, for a side that had won only four of their last 23 league games there now seemed no possible chance of escaping relegation.

After ten highly successful seasons in England with Nottingham Forest, Liverpool and latterly Bristol City, the former Hibs favourite Peter Cormack was said to have rejected a five figure approach from the American side Tulsa Royals to sign a two year contract at Easter Road. He would make his debut second time around in a Scottish Cup tie against Berwick Rangers at Shielfield that would eventually turn out to be just the latest drab no-score draw. Despite the inclusion of the experienced Cormack, Berwick had been the better side against their Premier League opponents, creating far more chances over the entire 90 minutes. Although Hibs had again improved in the second half they could perhaps have considered themselves somewhat fortunate to have a second chance back in Edinburgh in midweek. At the end of what had otherwise been another drab and unexciting encounter almost totally lacking in skill, the players, but now in particular the manager, had once again been left in absolutely no doubt as to the dissatisfaction felt by the small band of travelling Hibs fans at the final whistle.

In the replay at Easter Road a solitary Ally MacLeod goal 13 minutes from time would be enough for Hibs to reach, or according to one member of the press, stumble, into the semi-finals where they would now face league leaders Celtic.

The recent run of poor results had also led to a far from happy Tom Hart lashing out publicly at certain players for what he considered to have been a lack of effort, and although it was not his style to interfere in team matters he now found it impossible to just sit back and accept the recent poor performances.

In a last, but ultimately futile attempt to secure safety, just before the transfer deadline Hibs had added the former St Mirren player Bobby Torrance to the squad along with Lawrence Tierney from Hearts. At the same time, allowing the talented Willie Paterson who had made just six appearances for the first team, four as substitute during his three seasons at the club, to join Falkirk for a small fee. There was to be even more movement in the market when Tony Higgins who had been a first team regular for the majority of the season had perhaps surprisingly, considering the current situation, been allowed to join his former teammate Bertie Auld who was now manager of Partick Thistle just before the transfer deadline for around £25,000. Auld had tried to sign Higgins earlier in the season as part of a player exchange deal that had been rejected at the time by Turnbull but he had now joined the Maryhill side in a straight cash transaction.

Only one of the following five games would end in victory including the cup rehearsal against Celtic in Glasgow. Despite Hibs holding their own for the first 45 minutes, Celtic scored three goals in a seven minute second-half spell against an Easter Road side now appearing totally lacking in conviction, the final 4–0 result hardly inspiring confidence for the forthcoming semi-final at Hampden just over two weeks later. Throughout almost the entire second half the Easter Road players had been met by almost relentless jeers and cat-calls from the now thoroughly dispirited Hibs fans that had made the journey through from Edinburgh. Although it was still mathematically possible to beat the drop it now appeared highly improbable and those behind the scenes would now have absolutely no illusions at just how serious the situation had become. The *Evening News* reporter Stewart Brown was even more forthright in his column the following morning in claiming that the club was now in desperate need of a complete clear-out.

To the dismay of the now clearly frustrated fans, most of them having long accepted that Hibs would probably be playing their football in the lower division the following season, a 2–0 home defeat by fellow strugglers Dundee United had also meant the side losing – or perhaps surrendering might be a better word – a six month unbeaten home record, both goals scored in the second half once again due to slack defending. It had also turned out to be a vitally important victory for United as it had allowed them to move that bit closer to safety, two points clear of city rivals Dundee who now looked almost certain to be joining Hibs in the Second Division the following season.

A few weeks earlier almost the entire league programme including Hibs' game against Kilmarnock had again fallen victim to the weather. As a result, Tom Hart took the opportunity to reveal that his son Alan just only recently travelled down to England to meet representatives from a firm that specialised in underground heating systems with a view to having a similar system installed at Easter Road in time for the start of the following season.

A 2-0 defeat by St Mirren in Paisley at the beginning of April now made relegation a mathematical certainty leaving only the Scottish Cup if anything was to be salvaged from an otherwise truly horrendous season.

On Saturday 12 April both Hibs and Celtic took the field at Hampden in front of 33,445 fans, again a somewhat disappointing turnout for a national cup semi-final. In a Hibs side much changed from previous weeks, perhaps surprisingly there had been no place for top scorer Ally MacLeod, with Callaghan replacing the vastly experienced Cormack in midfield and the now fully recovered McNamara replacing Tierney at inside left. The changes however were to have absolutely no effect on the final outcome as Celtic strolled to a 5-0 victory. Already one behind at half-time, Hibs had completely folded just three minutes after the break when Provan put his side two ahead, and although there was still 42 minutes to play it was already more than obvious that there was now no way back for the Easter Road side. With Celtic scoring another three goals before the end, the final whistle brought a welcome relief both for the players and the few Hibs fans that had remained until the very end. Although Best had put up a determined display, using the ball intelligently in an effort to bring his teammates more into the game he had received little support. One of the very few to come out with any real credit was centre-half George Stewart who like Best had battled manfully although vainly throughout the entire 90 minutes.

Just two days later it would perhaps have come as no great surprise to learn that after a 30 minute meeting with Tom Hart, Eddie Turnbull, then the longest serving manager in the Premier League had been sacked, or as it is usually diplomatically put it on these occasions: 'resigned by mutual consent'. Just a few weeks after rejoining the club Willie Ormond had now been made his replacement, the former Scotland manager reported as having tremendous sympathy for his friend and former Famous Five team colleague.

One of the new manager's first tasks had been to completely revamp the scouting system that meant the appointment of the former player Archie Buchanan as chief scout. Another change that would be warmly welcomed by the players had been the return of the highly regarded physiotherapist Tom McNiven, a position that had remained unfilled since his sudden departure three years earlier. His return was probably even more evidence that his relationship with the previous manager had been far from ideal.

Of the eight games still to play only one would end in victory with two drawn, Ormond's first game in charge a 1–1 draw with Aberdeen at Pittodrie. Incredibly, although it was now the end of April, yet another 1–1 draw this time at Cappielow would be only Hibs' second away point of the season, which perhaps says it all.

What would undoubtedly have made the pain of relegation even more unbearable for the long-suffering Hibs fans however had been the 5–0 defeat by Alex Ferguson's Aberdeen at Easter Road on the penultimate Saturday of the season, the Grampian sides first victory at Easter Road for five years. The victory would also give Aberdeen the league title for the first time in 25 years, and also the first Winners of the Premier League title outside of either Rangers or Celtic since its inception in 1975. During the earlier part of the decade both Hibs and Aberdeen had regularly been tipped as the most likely challengers to the dominance of the 'Old Firm'. Now, with bitter irony, as Aberdeen were at the very beginning of what would soon turn out to be the most successful period in the club's history, Hibs would be facing a new challenge in a lower division.

Although not overly important compared to the events of the previous Saturday, in midweek Tom Hart had been highly critical of the police after an East of Scotland cup tie against Hearts at Easter Road had been cancelled; a lack of security due to a planned protest march at Torness Nuclear Power Station causing the cancellation. Hart was reportedly angry, stating that it was a sad state of affairs that a football match would not be able to go ahead in the circumstances: 'We pay dearly for the police presence at games whereas the taxpayer has to fork out for protests and demonstrations.' His proposal to play without the presence of the police or even switch the game to Tynecastle rejected by the authorities.

What had been a truly disastrous season would finally come to an end with a totally lethargic Hibs side defeated 1–0 at home by Partick Thistle. It was game that had been watched by just 1,191, Hibs' lowest home attendance by far, not only during the past season but for many years, with few even remaining until the final whistle. Yet again the inability to score goals had cost them dear and at that particular time had looked ill prepared to make a quick return to the Premier League, the signing of a proven goal scorer remaining a top priority.

As had been a foregone conclusion for some months, Hibs had finally ended the season rock bottom of the table, eight points below fellow strugglers Dundee who would join them in the lower division the following season. During the campaign only six of the 36 league games had ended in victory with six drawn, 24 ending in defeat, the goals column perhaps again telling its own story with a miserly 29 for, the lowest in the entire three divisions, against the 67 conceded. Once again Ally MacLeod had ended the season as top league goal scorer this time with a miserly eight, the next best Rae with just four and it was clear that Ormond would have his work cut out for him if promotion was to be achieved at the first time of asking. His experience in the First Division with Hearts however would possibly prove invaluable in a season that promised to be just as challenging as the one just passed.

After such a calamitous campaign it was more than obvious that a major clear-out had been needed and 12 players including Hutchison, Lambie, Campbell, goalkeeper McDonald, youngsters Farmer and Kilgour and both the pre-season signings from Leeds United Whyte and Reid had all been released with 23 retained.

The attendances at home games, with exception of those against Rangers and Celtic and to a lesser extent Aberdeen, had fallen steadily as the season progressed, rarely exceeding 7,000. The season's average just over 9,000, well below that of the previous few years and was now almost guaranteed to be even lower in the lower division.

Meanwhile George Best had been allowed to spend the close season playing in America with San Jose Earthquakes although the club still retained his registration, but it would not be the last we were to see of the wayward genius at Easter Road.

The previous ten years had been a remarkable parallel to the 1920s. Hibs had started the decade brightly with what had been regarded as a celebrated side that reached consecutive Scottish Cup finals in 1923 and 1924 although unfortunately losing both, before a gradual decline leading to relegation for the first time in the club's history in 1931.

The three tier system that had been in operation since the birth of the Premier League in 1975 had not been overly popular either with some of the players or supporters, particularly the sides in the top division. Given that it was highly unlikely that Rangers or Celtic would ever finish in the bottom two of a ten team league this had left a quarter of the remaining sides guaranteed to be relegated at the end of each season. Perhaps understandably the set-up had also encouraged defensive play, managers often unwilling to promote talented but inexperienced youngsters into the first team. The fans were also not slow in demonstrating their dissatisfaction at the at times negative play by staying away in numbers.

Perhaps the last word should be left to the chairman of the Hibernian Supporters Association George Telfer:

> The demise of the club had come as no great surprise to me. I have been one of their most loyal supporters, travelling everywhere both home and away and Europe but I said four years ago that a change of policy was needed and I still stand by that. Earlier many of my friends, like myself, had been keen to invest in the club by purchasing shares but had received no encouragement whatsoever.

The Aftermath (1980–81)

THE NEW DECADE would bring perhaps the biggest changes in the Scottish game since the creation of the league in 1890. In the mid-1950s the game in Scotland had been watched annually by around six and a half million but by 1980 attendances had fallen to almost half that number and clearly something had to be done. During the following few years several changes would take place in an attempt to address the situation although none would initially prove successful. The once popular League Cup competition was now tired and although several different formats had been tried none had ultimately proved successful in drawing back the missing fans. One change however that was particularly popular with the bigger clubs, and one that the Hibs chairman Tom Hart had attempted to address several years earlier when he had called a meeting of the so-called 'top six' clubs to discuss the matter, was the removal of the visiting team's guarantee. This would now allow the home side to keep its entire gate money and also set its own admission prices.

TV would continue to have an even greater part to play in the game, but in its constant battle for viewing figures there would be regular complaints from the lower league sides that they were being ignored, rarely, if ever featuring on camera and also largely ignored by the national press. In England attendances had also been falling steadily and a new system of awarding three points for a win instead of two had recently been introduced in an attempt to encourage more entertaining and attacking football. The innovation however would not be widely adopted by others until the 1994 World Cup finals in the USA, Scotland implementing the system shortly after.

Trouble between rioting fans at the end of the 1980 Scottish Cup final between Rangers and Celtic that had required the intervention of mounted police to disperse the battling supporters on the pitch had led to the passing of the Criminal Justice Act

THE AFTERMATH (1980–81)

(Scotland) 1980. The new act had now made it an offence to be in an intoxicated state or in the possession of alcohol either on a football coach or in the vicinity of the stadium. While it would also lead to a marked decrease in the hooliganism that had been a major blight on the game during the 1960s and '70s it would fail to totally eradicate the problem. Later, the tragedies at Heysel, Bradford and Hillsborough would lead to other major changes to the game as we knew it. Other sweeping powers relating to fans invading the pitch in an attempt to influence the result, a rare but increasing problem, had also been introduced. Now, if circumstances warranted, matches could be replayed at a venue of the authorities choosing, the result either allowed to stand or in a points deduction.

The start of the 1980–81 season however would now see Hibs preparing for life in the First Division. Relegated for only the second time in its 105-year history at the end of the previous campaign, statistically it had been the club's worst for 43 years. With only six of the 36 league games won, not since 1937 had Hibs fared so badly. Long gone were the days of the Turnbull's Tornadoes side of the early 1970s that had thrilled the fans wherever they played with a quality of football that had not been seen at Easter Road for many years. Since then there had been a steady but sure decline that had eventually led to manager Eddie Turnbull's resignation and relegation. Almost from the very start of the season the club had found itself firmly entrenched at the foot of the table rarely looking capable of escaping the drop. Even the signing of the legendary George Best midway through the campaign did little to stem the tide, the 5–0 defeat by Alex Ferguson's Aberdeen at Easter Road perhaps the final straw for many of the supporters.

Now managed by the former Famous Five legend Willie Ormond who had rejoined Hibs as Eddie Turnbull's assistant the previous season, the new manager had taken a circuitous route back to Easter Road. After 15 seasons wearing the famous green and white jersey, during which time he had won three League Championship medals and six full caps for Scotland, in 1961 he had been handed a free transfer as a reward for his loyal service to the club. Joining hometown side Falkirk where he would eventually take over as assistant trainer, he had perhaps been a surprise appointment as manager of St Johnstone in 1967 leading the Perth side to its first ever national cup final in 1969 and also into Europe for the very first time two years later. His time at Muirton had not gone unnoticed by the selectors and he had been the popular choice to replace the Scotland manager Tommy Docherty in time for the 1974 World Cup finals in Munich where Scotland would exit the tournament at the first-round stage only on goal difference, the country's best ever performance in a World Cup finals. His time as manager however had not got off to the best of starts with a 5–0 defeat by England in a friendly at Hampden to commemorate the centenary of the Scottish Football Association, but his eventual record of 18 victories and just 12 defeats from 38 games still stands comparable to most.

Later missing the day-to-day involvement in the game, in May 1977 he had resigned from Scotland to take over the already relegated Hearts from John Haggart. Tasked with taking the Tynecastle side back into the top tier, at the first time of asking he had led them back to the Premier Division in his first season. Probably for obvious reasons he had never been universally popular with many of the Hearts fans and in January 1980 he had been sacked before making a return to Easter Road a short while later as assistant manager under his former teammate Turnbull.

As Tom Hart had promised earlier, that summer Hibs became the very first Scottish side to install under-soil heating, the system costing in the region of £60,000, a not inconsiderable sum at that time, plus around £5,000 per annum in running costs. Consisting of around 18 miles of hot water pipes situated nine inches below the surface just 12 inches apart, it had required around 3,000 gallons of water during its operation. The ambitious venture that was said to have a life expectancy of 50 years and would now prevent games being cancelled due to adverse weather conditions had started to pay for itself just a few months later when Hibs' home game against Falkirk had been one of only two senior games in the country to escape the ravages of the winter weather. In 1958 Everton had been the first club in the entire country to install its own underground blanket and would soon be followed by several others including Manchester City and Oldham, while in Scotland envious eyes had often been cast in the direction of Murrayfield that had installed its own underground blanket in 1959. Today it is a prerequisite that all topflight clubs have their own system and it is now extremely rare for a major game to be cancelled due to the weather.

In other news, around that time it had been announced that with Hibs now in a lower division, and with the expected reduction in the number of supporters coming through the gates in the season ahead, a large expanse of the main terracing was to be completely closed as a cost cutting measure, a move designed to considerably reduce the expense of hiring police, stewards and turnstile operators. A barrier situated near the halfway line would now extend from the touchline to the top of the huge main terracing. The entire south end of the ground and the extended terracing now completely closed, it was a decision that would ultimately lead to many of the games taking place in front of a somewhat surreal backdrop, the half-empty spaces helping to create a distinct lack of atmosphere. During the coming season, games in a stadium capable of holding over 70,000 would often now take place in front of crowds numbering around 4,000, the lowest an extremely disappointing 2,825 that had paid to watch Hibs defeat East Stirling 2–0. But, popular or not it had probably made sense to reduce the terracing to around its pre-war size. In what was to be a new experience for the club, the 12-team First Division would now mean each side playing the others only three times a season, twice at home and once away or vice versa, not an entirely fair system. Even worse, Hibs had now been drawn to play only once at home against all of what had been expected to be their main challengers for the title, Motherwell, Dundee, Ayr United and Dumbarton.

Now wearing kit by the sports manufacturers Umbro, Hibs would no longer be featuring a sponsor's name on their jerseys. In England, at that particular time several clubs had been involved in their own dispute with the TV companies regarding the displaying of a sponsor's logo on their shirts if a game was to be televised. A somewhat ironic situation according to Tom Hart as none at any time had offered Hibs any support when they were encountering their own problems regarding the matter just a couple of seasons earlier.

After yet another short three-game tour of the Scottish Highlands and an uninspiring 1–1 draw in a friendly against Swansea City at Easter Road, the season had kicked-off in earnest with a home game against Raith Rovers. Although Raith had somehow managed to survive some tremendous early pressure, the visitors had silenced the disappointingly poor Hibs support when Ballantyne scored the only goal of the game in the very last minute. If the Hibs players or the fans for that matter thought differently then they now knew that it was going to be yet another extremely difficult season with promotion far from a formality.

It was around then that the funeral of the club's former owner and chairman William Harrower took place at Warriston Crematorium. Then aged 80, the well-known bookmaker who owned over 50 betting shops and numerous other properties in the area had purchased the club from Harry Swan in 1963 and had been chairman for seven years until handing over to Tom Hart in 1970. Originally accepting the role of President, he had not been a regular visitor at Easter Road for several years.

Meanwhile, attempts to improve the squad had again been disappointing. Although several promising youngsters had joined the club during the summer, except for occasional appearances by goalkeeper Colin Kelly, Hugh Hamill and Ian Black who had been signed on a short-term contract from Hearts, only the former Whitburn Amateurs player Brian Rice was to make any real impact on the first team.

The disappointment of the opening day defeat by Raith Rovers however would be quickly forgotten when goals by Peter Cormack and Gordon Rae put Hibs back on track with a 2–0 victory over Stirling Albion at Annfield. With the former Hearts player Ian Black making his debut, Albion had never at any time been more than stuffy opponents, rarely troubling the Hibs defence. The victory was incredibly Hibs' first away from home in the league for more than 17 months, Cormack's goal his first since rejoining the club during the previous season.

With Hearts now back in the Premier League and Hibs in the lower division, the East of Scotland cup tie between the sides at Tynecastle had been the first meeting of the sides for 18 months, a game always eagerly awaited by the fans of both sides. With just ten minutes remaining in what, as expected, had been another fiercely contested encounter, Hearts had been leading 2–0 when Brian Rice scored his first goal for the club with a 25-yard drive that gave goalkeeper Westwater no chance. Gordon Rae levelled the score with a tremendous header just before the end to take the game into penalties, Hibs eventually retaining the Shield five by penalties to four. A surprise inclusion in the side had been left half Ross McGinn. Formerly with Manchester City he had been recommended to the club by former player Bobby Johnstone. Unfortunately, it would be the first of only two appearances the youngster would make for Hibs before a return to England.

Just a few weeks after the start of the new season the former St Johnstone, Everton and Birmingham City forward John Connolly had become Hibs' latest acquisition when he was signed from Newcastle United in time to make his debut against Clyde in the League Cup. The gifted Connolly had been a member of the St Johnstone side then managed by Willie Ormond that had earlier reached the League Cup final and the later stages of the UEFA Cup. Winning his only cap in Scotland's 1–0 defeat by Switzerland in Berne in 1973, at 29 the experienced Connolly would have a prominent part to play in the club's attempt to return to the Premier League at the end of the season.

Meanwhile, with the North American season now at an end George Best had arrived back in Britain to be contacted by Tom Hart who suggested that he could perhaps play in the forthcoming game against Dundee. Still a registered Hibs player Best could not move elsewhere without the permission of the club. However, it had been made clear that he would be allowed to leave if a suitable offer was forthcoming, and he made his return to the Hibs side a few days later in a 2–1 victory at Dens Park. Outplayed in almost every department for the greater part of the game, a Gordon Rae goal near the end would give the visitors an entirely undeserved victory against a spirited Dundee side. One newspaper report the following morning described the Hibs performance as 'frankly deplorable' and the victory as, 'The biggest smash and grab since the Great Train Robbery.'

Only now did Best admit to his long-standing problem with alcohol that in the past had led to him regularly failing to turn up, not just for training but also games even during his time at Manchester United. As a Hibs player he had even occasionally caught a flight to Edinburgh only to change his mind before even leaving the airport to catch the next available flight back to London.

Despite the opening day defeat by Raith Rovers, a 3–1 victory over Ayr United at Somerset Park now meant that after just six games Hibs topped the table, a lead that they would hold until the end of the season.

At the end of the month Terry Wilson had been signed from Arbroath in one of the very first cases involving the independent transfer tribunal that had recently been set up by the Scottish League to come into operation if both clubs failed to agree a fee. Wilson had eventually cost Hibs in the region of £35,000, more than double the club's original valuation of the former Aston Villa and Cowdenbeath player but much less than Arbroath had been asking. Unfortunately, after only a few starts and several others as substitute, after his one and only goal against Ayr United in the League Cup Wilson would soon be on his way to Dunfermline.

On Saturday 11 October George Best had made his 25th and final appearance in a Hibs jersey in the home game against Falkirk before his return to San Jose Earthquakes. Captain for the day, Best had once again delighted the home fans with another marvellous display of sparkling football. The goals in Hibs' 2–0 victory had been scored by Connolly and Jamieson but it was the master showman Best that had inspired the side to victory. After the game Best had been interviewed in the Radio Forth kiosk at the ground surrounded by hordes of adoring admirers and would later mingle with the fans in the supporters' clubrooms. Many years later Tom Hart would be surprised to receive a signed copy of Best's latest autobiography including a handwritten apology for his at times unforgivable behaviour during his time at Easter Road.

Yet another signing had been Jas Brown who joined the club at the beginning of November on a short-term contract from Aston Villa. Signed in time to make his debut in an extremely disappointing and dour 1–1 draw with East Stirling at Fir Park, he would be joined at Easter Road a few weeks later by the Morton defender

Billy McLaren and Gary Murray from Montrose, both players costing the club around £60,000.

Only seven months after rejoining the club, in mid-November, manager Willie Ormond had retired on medical grounds. Unwell for some time and now finding it almost impossible to continue, he had been left with no other option but to offer his resignation. Probably already aware of the manager's impending decision, Tom Hart had wasted no time in offering the position to the former Celtic and Hibs player Bertie Auld, then manager of Partick Thistle and he would be joined at Easter Road by another former Hibs player Pat Quinn in the role of assistant manager. After 25 years at Easter Road both as a player and coach the long-serving John Fraser had now felt it the right time to seek pastures new, his place as first team trainer taken by John Lambie with Jimmy O'Rourke continuing as reserve team coach.

With Hearts now back in the Premier League, for a second consecutive season there would be no traditional New Year's derby against their city rivals. Instead, the Easter Road side had made its way to Berwick to take on the 'wee Rangers' at Shielfield. Goals by MacLeod and Duncan inside a 15-minute spell in the first half gave Hibs a comfortable victory and reinforced their place at the top of the table while even this early possibly condemning bottom-placed Berwick to the Second Division.

At this time both Hibs and Raith Rovers had been neck and neck at the top of the table and due to face each other at Stark's Park. Although the Easter Road side still held a point advantage Raith had two games in hand and something had to give. Such was the demand for the game that at one stage huge queues had stretched well over 200 yards from the ground, leading to the kick-off being delayed for several minutes. With Alan Sneddon, a recent £60,000 signing from Celtic making his debut at right-back, the atmosphere inside the ground had been electric as Raith raced into a two-goal lead early in the second half thanks mainly to mistakes by Duncan and debutant Sneddon, the score remaining the same until the end. Despite the defeat however, the new signing had done more than enough to suggest he would be a sound acquisition and ironically at the end of the season he would have made enough appearances for both Celtic and Hibs to qualify for championship medals with both clubs.

The following week Hibs' investment in the under-soil blanket had started to pay for itself when the home game against Falkirk became one of only two senior games in the entire country to escape the severe winter weather, the game also attracting a host of interested onlookers from other clubs all keen to see the blanket in operation for themselves. In a stuffy encounter, on second half pressure alone Hibs had probably deserved the victory. They would however have to wait until the very last minute of the game when a header from Craig Paterson, only his second goal of the season, had eventually secured the points. It would turn out to be only the start of a tremendous 13-game run interrupted only by a solitary defeat by St Johnstone, and set the Easter Road side well on the way to the title.

At the end of the month Ian Hendry, a recent signing from Cambridge United had made his first start for the club against Berwick Rangers at Shielfield. Unfortunately, in what must surely have been one of the shortest ever debuts on record, Hendry had been carried from the field with a broken leg after just 20 seconds. Rushed to a hospital in Berwick before being transferred to Edinburgh Royal Infirmary it would turn out to be one of only three appearances he would make for the club. The others, as a substitute against both St Mirren and Celtic in the League Cup at the start of the following season before returning to play in England with non-league side Nuneaton Borough. Midway through the second half of the eventual goalless draw, the Berwick inside left Tait also had the misfortune to be carried from the field with suspected broken ribs.

In a season that had seen an exit from both the League Cup after defeat by Ayr United and the Scottish Cup after a fourth round defeat by Rangers at Ibrox, the championship would finally be secured with a convincing 3–0 victory over Clydebank at Easter Road with two games still to play. The players received a tremendous and deserved ovation from the fans among what considering the circumstances had been an otherwise disappointing attendance of just 3,691. In what had turned out to be goalkeeper

THE AFTERMATH (1980–81)

McArthur's 20th shut-out of the season, goals by Rae and Paterson had been more than enough to assure the Easter Road side of a place in the Premier League where they would now be joined by second top Dundee. During the season just ended 24 of the 39 league games had been won with just six lost and 67 goals scored against just 24 conceded, the lowest in all three leagues; Hibs eventually finishing five points clear of their nearest challengers Dundee and St Johnstone. Once again Ally MacLeod had ended the season as top marksman with 18 in all games closely followed by Gordon Rae with 16, but perhaps the find of the season had been the young Willie Jamieson. Eddie Turnbull's last signing for the club, he had managed 12 in the league in his first full season and another two in the League Cup. While goal scorers generally get most of the acclaim, major praise should also go to the defence for their sterling efforts throughout the entire season, particularly goalkeeper Jim McArthur who had earlier received a giant bottle of Mackinlay's Scotch Whisky as runner-up in the whisky firm's Personality of the Month Award for February and was to soon receive further deserved recognition when voted the Hibs Supporters Association's Player of the Year.

A major concern however, even if expected, would no doubt have been the drop in the number of supporters attending home games during the season. With the exception of the 8,071 that had watched the recent game against Raith Rovers, none of the others had managed to attract over 7,000, including the extremely disappointing turnout when Hibs finally secured the title with a 3–0 win against Clydebank in the penultimate game of the campaign. The season's average attendance just 4,460, more than 5,000 down on the previous season.

As a reward for his tremendous service since signing for the club in 1969, the extremely popular Arthur Duncan had now been awarded a testimonial. The game between a Hibs XI and an International Select at the end of the season had seen the return, albeit briefly, of the former Hibs players John Brownlie then with Newcastle United; Alex Cropley of Aston Villa; Tony Higgins from Partick Thistle; and Bobby Smith who was then with Leicester

City, all absolutely delighted to provide their services for such a tremendously popular player. Only a fixture in the USA preventing George Best from making his way to Scotland for the game, to the great disappointment of the fans it had also been rumoured that despite the offer of a five figure sum, only a previous appointment had prevented the legendary Pelé from making an appearance at Easter Road.

However, it was now back to life in the top division!

Eddie Turnbull

ALTHOUGH THE END of the road for the manager had probably been coming for some time it had nevertheless been an extremely sad end for a man who had given the club and Scottish football so much for over 25 years, first as a player, coach and finally manager.

The scorer of the first ever goal by a British player in the inaugural European Cup competition against Rot Weiss Essen in 1955, the winner of three League Championship medals as a member of the illustrious Famous Five and capped nine times for Scotland, for him personally things had never been quite the same after the defeat by Hajduk Split in the Cup Winners' Cup in 1973. Along with almost every other Hibs supporter in the land he had been convinced that the club would go all the way to the final, perhaps even win the competition itself.

However, he would have been only too well aware of the later steady decline of a once great side that had earned its place in Scottish football folklore particularly in the early years of the decade. Apart from the furious reaction to the sale of the fan favourites Jimmy O'Rourke and Alan Gordon, the subsequent signing of Joe Harper had been felt by many of the supporters to have been the catalyst for the start of the slow decline. He had also been heavily criticised at the time for allowing Cropley, Brownlie, Blackley and latterly Bremner to leave the club, moves however that had probably been necessary at the time due to the club's desperate lack of finance. None of this had done the manager any favours but had nevertheless been contributing factors that would eventually lead to relegation at the end of the decade.

There had been many other reasons for the eventual collapse, including poor signings and often having to rely on gifted but relatively inexperienced home-grown talent. Many of which had failed to realise their full potential and failing to have a decent run in team when called upon were still expected to replace established stars. And although the situation had often been forced on him there had also been far too many, sometimes odd, changes to the line up as he attempted to find a settled side, particularly in the later seasons.

The situation however had not always been helped by his often gruff and abrasive manner. Several of the younger players would later admit that they had been literally terrified of his legendary ill temper and stubbornness that had only grown worse over the years; actions rarely helpful in developing a good team spirit. Probably a victim of his own abrasive personality, on occasion both the players and backroom staff would be in the dressing room after a game celebrating a particularly pleasing victory when the manager would simply enter the room collect whatever he was after and leave without even a smile or a well done. At times he would also appear to go out of his way to create a regime ruled by fear, often finding it too easy to fall out with anyone, even on the slightest whim. This behaviour also far from helping to create a bond with the players who had needed to be tough mentally, actions he himself would admit in later years that he would not have got away with at that time.

To give him his due though, no one can ever take away the tremendous sides he had assembled at both Aberdeen and Hibs, particularly during the earlier years of the decade at Easter Road. Extremely well-respected and widely admired throughout the game he had often been compared to the Celtic manager Jock Stein; although generally considered to be far superior tactically, he had lacked Stein's man management skills. Even in his early days at Dunfermline Stein would often mix with the players both young and old, challenging the younger ones to the occasional game of pool after training. Sometimes even inviting some to travel to the away games on the team coach on match days, he was always prepared to offer words of advice or a comforting arm around the shoulder when needed. For some reason however Turnbull had found this approach extremely difficult, treating the youngsters the same as the more experienced players with rarely a word of encouragement, some of the younger players even describing him rather unkindly as a 'terrorist in a track suit'.

Although his man management skills had often left a lot to be desired, he could occasionally, though rarely, let his guard down usually during trips abroad when he would regale the players with his exploits with the Famous Five or his time in the navy during the war. As a coach he had been second to none, far ahead of his time, his often innovative training sessions always varied and interesting and everything recorded in a dossier by John Fraser for future reference. Fraser himself, as mentioned earlier, later admitting that he would often just stand watching in awe at what was taking place on the training ground in front of him.

Now turning his back completely on the game to become a publican in Easter Road – the watering hole always a popular destination for supporters on match days while keeping him close to the scene of his former glories – the final separation had been so painful that he would not step inside the stadium again for many years. Until, much later in life he would be a regular visitor to the boardroom until his death in 2011.

Perhaps the greatest tragedy however had been the enormous wealth of experience and tactical know-how being completely lost to the game.

A return to the Premier League had now been achieved at the first time of asking and although there would still be challenges ahead, no one can ever take away Eddie Turnbull's legacy. Not only as a member of perhaps the finest forward line in the country during the immediate post-war years, but as the man behind the creation of one of Scottish football's greatest ever sides. A side that anyone privileged to have seen at their very best left with sublime and unforgettable magical memories.

Luath Press Limited

committed to publishing well written books worth reading

LUATH PRESS takes its name from Robert Burns, whose little collie Luath (*Gael.*, swift or nimble) tripped up Jean Armour at a wedding and gave him the chance to speak to the woman who was to be his wife and the abiding love of his life. Burns called one of the 'Twa Dogs' Luath after Cuchullin's hunting dog in Ossian's *Fingal*. Luath Press was established in 1981 in the heart of Burns country, and is now based a few steps up the road from Burns' first lodgings on Edinburgh's Royal Mile. Luath offers you distinctive writing with a hint of unexpected pleasures.

Most bookshops in the UK, the US, Canada, Australia, New Zealand and parts of Europe, either carry our books in stock or can order them for you. To order direct from us, please send a £sterling cheque, postal order, international money order or your credit card details (number, address of cardholder and expiry date) to us at the address below. Please add post and packing as follows: UK – £1.00 per delivery address; overseas surface mail – £2.50 per delivery address; overseas airmail – £3.50 for the first book to each delivery address, plus £1.00 for each additional book by airmail to the same address. If your order is a gift, we will happily enclose your card or message at no extra charge.

Luath Press Limited
543/2 Castlehill
The Royal Mile
Edinburgh EH1 2ND
Scotland
Telephone: +44 (0)131 225 4326 (24 hours)
email: sales@luath. co.uk
Website: www. luath.co.uk